מסורה

ArtScroll Mesorah Series®

Expositions on Jewish liturgy and thought

Rabbis Nosson Scherman / Meir Zlotowitz
General Editors

BRIS MILAH

BRIS MILAH

CIRCUMCISION — THE COVENANT OF ABRAHAM / A COMPENDIUM OF LAWS, RITUALS, AND CUSTOMS FROM BIRTH TO BRIS, ANTHOLOGIZED FROM TALMUDIC, AND TRADITIONAL SOURCES.

Published by

Mesorah Publications, ltd

By
Rabbi Paysach J. Krohn

Overview by
Rabbi Nosson Scherman

FIRST EDITION
First Impression . . . March 1985

SECOND EDITION
Twelve Impressions . . . April 1986 — September 2009

Published and Distributed by
MESORAH PUBLICATIONS, Ltd.
4401 Second Avenue
Brooklyn, New York 11232

Distributed in Europe by
LEHMANNS
Unit E, Viking Business Park
Rolling Mill Road
Jarrow, Tyne & Wear NE32 3DP
England

Distributed in Australia & New Zealand by
GOLDS WORLD OF JUDAICA
3-13 William Street
Balaclava, Melbourne 3183
Victoria Australia

Distributed in Israel by
SIFRIATI / A. GITLER — BOOKS
6 Hayarkon Street
Bnei Brak 51127

Distributed in South Africa by
KOLLEL BOOKSHOP
Ivy Common 105 William Road
Norwood 2192, Johannesburg, South Africa

ISBN 10: 0-89906-197-4 / ISBN 13: 978-0-89906-197-9 (hard cover)
ISBN 10: 0-89906-198-2 / ISBN 13: 978-0-89906-198-6 (paperback)

Typography by Compuscribe at ArtScroll Studios, Ltd.
4401 Second Avenue / Brooklyn, N.Y. 11232 / (718) 921-9000

Printed in the United States of America by Moriah Offset
Bound by Sefercraft Quality Bookbinders, Ltd., Brooklyn, N.Y.

Table of Contents

יעקב קאמענצקי

מאנסי, נוא יארק

RABBI J. KAMENTZKY

38 SADDLE RIVER RD.

MONSEY, NEW YORK 10952

בכבוד ידידי הרב נסן יוסף קראהן נ"י שלו' וברכת כל טוב.

זה זאת נענתי עצתי והצעתי לו שבנק עסק להכין סדר לרבים
על הלכות מילה.

חכמינו ז"ל אמרו (ערכין ט"ו ע"ב) לעולם אל ישנה אדם
מאגרתו לאזונות אפותי', וזה יפה נאמרת עתיק בעניין
אגרות ולהכרס כשהאזונות היא בדבר מצות מילה, כי תמצינו
ז"ל טינו את הטוב לדף אלאא (שבת קל"ב ע"ב) נהרי אתה
הדבר התהיו' של וטבלות ביששהכתב החולה, זק נאה ולק
יאה להיות נאה דברי כמו שבנק נאה אקיים.

אגרת שהבק קרא פי הנקר ידיד אגרבת על פי אפק
הרב אברהס צליג ל"ו עם זה יוצא מן בעיני. הכרת את אביך
הטוב, וב' אבוק פי ובהשלמת מאב. אך לזה תחרות על
אתר עדן שליטא) בי אי הוצרות שלאו הן וסל טוב בעיני
אלקיס ואדק.

גרפת נקרב לי שימלו עיינותיך חולה ותתלהלה לעורר
לרות אחינו פני ישראל תתחקק בטובק מילה. נעירת ידיב
שמחתק ולביבק הסתב לישועה יצ..

הרב שלום מרדכי הכהן שבדרן

שערי חסד, ירושלים

בס"ד, אור ליום ה' ו' סבת תמוז תשע"ב לפ"ק, פה עיה"ק ירושלים

לידידי היקר מערכין אשר נפש חפץ לקנין של...

ואתי שמח כי ...

RABBI
ISRAEL GROSSMAN
BATEI WARSHA
JERUSALEM
Tel. 287056

ישראל גרוסמן
רב ור"מ ודומ"ץ
פעיה"ק ירושלם תובב"א
מח"ס : שיעורי בבא קמא שיעורי כתובות
ושו"ת חליכות ישראל -
בתי ורשה ירושלים
עי. Tel. 287056

בעזה"י כ"ח אייר ל"ג לעשאומרניית תשמ"ג

בקרבת הימים בשמחתו של התחבר הנעלה בתוך מצות עולה
שתיבר יקירי ותהביבי הגאונלם התלוי. רב הפלים בכיר הגאון
הרב פסח קדמון שליט"א

כן הרבת הנועם לשת לון ה... האמפורים באשי הצדקה והולכס
אולבר ולברותיה שליג ל'

לכבה לאדל ... אתמחת ידו דבר מתקן. דבר לשה ואצמקאל.
ליקום תשוב אמולץ אמל ה אמשאיית הקשורית לצדוה ...
ולל ה ... הקסושית אשר ...קשש ...
שתרי תנוסי ומותבי תירה. ואמולה אלף שלתתה את הנ...ים
אמדו לבל ... שהקבמבת מצוה זו נצב לשתה אלת נמי קהי

... שעויית, ושה שעות ... ל... הצקוית תת...
שאלוא היטב
...
... ...ל קיניון שלכתל

ואלה ... ...

מכתבי ברכה [x]

ביהמ"ד גבול יעבץ
ברוקלין, נוא יארק

דוד קאהן

"אמרו לו הקב"ה (דוד) אם כל ישראל את אינשאן
ולא אריך קטיף אלא על כל קטן וקטן מעבירים את
שמך ואומרים שירים משלך מאחר שיר חניכת הבית לדוד
(אמר רבה ק"ח)
כי קדש דוד ריב"ה שליונך קדש או כלאא על
אריך דתפלאא קדש ל"ב (תהלים כ,ד,א)

סב"ג

כבוד יקירי מחמדי רחימאי דנפשאי
הרב ר' יהושע יוסף קראהן
נ"י יאיר ויזרח

מאמרי חז"ל הכתובים למעלה מתאמים את רצות לבי שנתפארתי לבנך אסיף
לחבר ספר על ענ"ו מילה, וקראמין "ב"ה אברהב" על שם אריק החנות הרב אברהם
טליש ל"ב. הלא המה סברית לי אוגות עניותן ולשיכתן הקלנו ותכונת ופתו,
שהיה ח"ים מצין ולא מים שאובים ושהיה קול מתלב והיה מצפה לע יתן על
הבית לי שאלא המה סברית הענין מילה והיה בצאת למאר חיבר על
הלבת מילה.

דוד המלך פסק כל יאין לרבכן חומר צפוה בנין בית המקדש אמ"
שלא נצרית האקום שלא זכה את יבנך את הבית אלא שלאשה בנו הוא יבנך אבל
אתרעים מכוון שלוא נאמרתו פרעות והקדש כמו לאמכן בכה שאין ואל ולא
מרית המקדש לקולף. והלא הדן ורוא האהב לצבה אריק שבקר יירא על
שאו אלו ש"מ כ"ש שאינו עלו ואין השמום פלא יהרו.

אריק צבית לביות ברא האצבה לאבא, שצאת לשאה פלאן הלהדרה
אץ דרו חיר ספר ועש"י פלאמן שדעקר יהיה תקולות הרבים.
הכו"ה בידי"י אהבה ויביבות
דוד קאהן
עד חנוכה תק"ם

ⴄ Preface

It is with gratitude and a sense of honor that I present this work to the reading public: Gratitude to *Hashem* that He granted me the opportunity to complete a book in my field of *milah;* and honor that I was chosen to write this book as part of the ArtScroll Mesorah series.

The widespread proliferation of the ArtScroll Series, both here and abroad, and the standards of excellence that readers have come to expect routinely from this series added to the challenge and responsibility of writing this work. I pray that the thousands of man-hours that have gone into this project have met this noble challenge.

❀ ❀ ❀

'There are three partners in man: *Hashem,* one's father and one's mother' (*Kiddushin* 30b).

Parents are role models for their children. Their varied interests, their likes and dislikes, often shape and mold the lives of their offspring. As individuals we blaze our own trails, but their guideposts are ever present.

My father, Harav Avrohom Zelig ל״ז, known for his *chesed, ahavas Yisrael* and for the fulfillment and joy he found in Torah life, made a lifestudy of the field of *milah.* Amassing a collection of *milah seforim,* articles and instruments unsurpassed in the world, he reveled in the time he could spend in the practice and research of all aspects of *milah.*

My mother, Hindy, שתחי׳, the personification of a woman's commitment to Judaism, though not a person of many spoken words, is recognized for her magical ability with the written word. Her capacity for the elegant phrase or the exquisite expression is nothing short of artistic. The long endless hours we shared together working on this project, debating, scrutinizing, and rewriting, were precious moments that we will always cherish.

This book, a blend of both *milah* and writing, is dedicated to

them. It was my good fortune that *Hashem* chose my parents as His partners in my creation. As my parents reared and guided me, I acquired a love for the fields of their endeavor and expertise. With gratitude I say, "That which is mine is theirs."

❧ ❧ ❧

Milah, the act of ritual circumcision, is a *mitzvah* that has been celebrated with great joy ever since its inception. Our first Patriarch, Abraham, accompanied the performance of his son Isaac's *bris* with a festive meal (*Tosafos, Shabbos* 130a). This is unusual, for with no other *mitzvah* do we find our forefathers or anyone else in the Torah tendering a festive meal.

It has been suggested that the inherent joy in a *bris* is because it is everlasting. The imprint of a *bris* placed on a child remains with him forever, stamps him as a partner in the covenant, and identifies him with his Jewish brethren throughout the world (*Zichron Bris LaRishonim*). *Rambam* writes: 'There is an empathy of mutual love and assistance among people who are united by a sign they consider the symbol of a covenant (*Moreh Nevuchim* Chap. 3:49).' Furthermore, it is the delight of a parent's first commitment to the child that he will be reared in a way of life prescribed by *Hashem*.

How fortunate then is the *mohel* who is able consistently to participate in this great moment in the lives of parents and their newborn infant. To be a silent partner with those who understand the significance of the *bris*, to teach those who do not comprehend, and to guide those who wish to know more — these intrinsically bring satisfaction to the *mohel*. A *mohel* is not only the father's proxy in performing the *bris*, but he is also *Hashem*'s emissary to secure the bond that the new child will have with his Creator. One is humbled by the task and grateful for the privilege to participate.

❧ ❧ ❧

Every *mohel* has his fascinating incidents and anecdotes that go along with the myriad of people and situations that he comes across. I have felt the awe of performing a *bris* with Harav Moshe Feinstein, שליט"א, as *sandak*, the thrill of performing my own sons' *bris*, and the delight of my first *bris* in Jerusalem. I have sensed the drama of performing a *bris* at West Point, the excitement of traveling to Bermuda for a *bris*, the amazement at the commitment of a Russian teen-ager undergoing a *bris*, and the heartbreak of a *bris* on an infant whose mother died in childbirth. I have known the ecstasy of

performing the *bris* on a child born to a couple after seventeen years of marriage, when nine months earlier I had performed the *bris* on their adopted son.

Yet one *bris* in particular stands out in my memory and bears telling and retelling for its lesson and inspiration.

At a *bris* in Merrick, Long Island, I noticed a woman standing to a side and crying to herself. Realizing that her tears were not tears of joy, I approached her and asked if I could be of assistance.

Trying to compose herself, she explained that she had no children after numerous miscarriages and that the *bris* of her friend's child had awakened her to the sad plight of her life. 'It's not that I'm jealous,' she said, 'but why can't I have my own child?'

As I listened to her predicament, a Talmudic teaching came to mind, for our Sages discussed similar situations. I suggested, 'Try and find someone who has the very same problem that you have, and then pray for them to be helped, for the Talmud instructs that if one has a problem and prays for another who has the identical problem, he who has prayed will be answered first (*Bava Kama* 92a).' I encouraged her to do so for it was not my own personal advice but that of our Sages. I assured her that prayers would be said in her behalf and took down her name and that of her mother.

I placed her name among a list of people for whom prayers are recited almost daily at one of the local *yeshivos*, and forgot about the incident.

One evening about a year later I received a call. The woman identified herself but I had no recollection of her name. She then reminded me of our meeting and of the Talmudic advice. Suddenly I recalled every detail and waited with anxious anticipation. Then she said, 'I have prayed every day since then, and today I had a boy!' I could not contain my exuberance, and after an excited *Mazel Tov* I exclaimed, 'You've made my day', to which she replied the words that will stay with me forever, 'You've made my life.'

That *bris* was special.

To participate, to guide, to teach; may *Hashem* grant me the merit and the privilege to continue.

❦   ❦   ❦

Writing this book on *milah* is a major milestone in my life. Much has preceded this event and I would be remiss if I did not acknowledge, at least in part, some of the many people who made it their personal concern to help me.

As a fifth generation *mohel*, I had the opportunity to learn from the experience and expertise of some of those who came before me. My grandfather, the gentle Harav Chanoch Henoch Krohn, ז״ל, who practiced *milah* primarily in the Scranton and McKeesport, Pennsylvania areas, spent many hours with me discussing all aspects of *milah*. His silken character manifested itself in the gentle manner with which he treated every child with whom he came in contact.

My father, Harav Avrohom Zelig, ז״ל, my primary teacher, a *mohel* in the New York metropolitan area, served as an example of total dedication to the discipline of one's endeavor. His research and diligence were an inspiration to all who knew him. In his honor I have named the Laws and Ritual sections *Yedid Avrohom*, for in his lifetime he exemplified the characteristics of Avrohom Avinu in *bris milah* and *hachnasas orchim*.

Very little could have prepared me for his untimely passing in 1966. My sudden thrust into *milah* at age 21 made this responsibility awesome.

Starting with men like Harav Label Chait, who gave me the strength to face life and its vicissitudes; Dr. Henry Lowey, who afforded me opportunities when I needed them most; and Mr. Chaim Israel, who made my struggles his personal concern, there have been many rabbanim, doctors and laypeople who have been very helpful. To mention them all would require a book by itself. May *Hashem*, the Source of all blessing, repay every one of them with His utmost kindness.

❧ ❧ ❧

New York today is blessed and honored with a group of *mohalim* who are a credit to their profession. Among this emiment group are four men from whom I have gained immeasurably.

Rabbi Ephraim Rubin and Rabbi Irving Grossman, my father's closest associates, have been mentors, advisors and instructors to me from the moment I was 'on my own'. Over the past eighteen years I have consulted with them regularly and they have treated me with unusual generosity. They are always 'there' when I need them and I am honored that today they consider me a colleague.

Rabbi Moshe Bunim Pirutinsky, author of the classic *Sefer HaBris*, and Rabbi Mordechai Zimmerman have always made themselves available to answer my questions in all aspects of *milah*. I am fortunate and privileged that I have these *mohalim* with whom

to consult.

The standards of dignity and excellence of these four in our generation is noteworthy for emulation for future generations. Each may be called, 'the *mohel's mohel'*.

❧ ❧ ❧

It is difficult to put into words the feelings of love and admiration that I have for Harav David Cohen. Readers of ArtScroll material are familiar with his broad-ranging gems of insight, comment, and explanation.

But to me, personally, Harav David has carried the Talmudic dictum 'Your students are your children' to its fullest extent. For the past thirteen years he has been a rebbi, a confidant and a *moreh derech*. Most of the ideas in this *sefer*, whether in essays or commentaries, and specifically every *halachah*, have been filtered through his brilliant mind. His vast Torah knowledge has flavored this *sefer* far beyond the few times that he is specifically quoted.

My sentiments to him are those of the weary traveler (*Taanis* 5b) who said in gratitude to the beautiful tree that had given him comfort and sustenance, 'I pray that your fruits shall be just like you.'

❧ ❧ ❧

Two people took countless hours of their limited time to read the entire manuscript. The first, Rabbi Sholom Spitz, a distinguished *talmid chacham*, and prominent member of the Yeshiva Shaar Hatorah Kollel in Kew Gardens, checked sources and diligently considered every aspect of the work. His broad Torah knowledge and *sechel hayashar* were invaluable.

The second, Mrs. Helene Lederer, a woman involved in a multitude of communal affairs in Kew Garden Hills, read the manuscript from the layman's point of view and added her interesting perspective. The reader will be greatly aided by her insight and comments.

Faigie (Zylberminc) Weiss and Myron M. Weinstein were exceptionally helpful with supplying rare material from the Library of Congress. Many individuals were kind enough to lend me *seforim* and texts that were required for this work. A special thanks is due the Kleinkaufman family for the many volumes they provided. I am grateful to Rabbi Edwin Katzenstein for his helpful information regarding the customs of the German Jewish

community, to Rabbi Avraham Ben Haim for his assistance in recording the Sephardic ritual and customs, and to Dr. Norman Klein and Dr. Leonard Sacharow for their counsel on the medical matters in this book.

The staff at ArtScroll is a unique blend of individuals whose talents mesh to inspire Jews throughout the world. I was fortunate to benefit from Rabbi Hirsch Goldwurm's analytical review of the *Halachos*, Rabbi Avie Gold's meticulous attention to detail and clarity, Rabbi Shimon and Mrs. Tova Finkelman's painstaking editing and observations, Miss Sima Gluck and Miss Malka Glatzer's phototypesetting, Mr. Stephen Blitz's marketing finesse, Reb Daniel Fleischmann's layout talents, Reb Shea Brander's outstanding graphic design, and Mrs. Faygie Weinbaum's proofreading; and the other members of the Mesorah staff: Leah Freier, Mrs. Esther Feierstein, Mrs. Shonnie Friedman, Yosef Timinsky, Moshe Schaum and Michael Zivitz.

Most of all though, the encouragement, counsel and direction that I received from Rabbi Nosson Scherman and Rabbi Meir Zlotowitz, the architects and wellsprings of the ArtScroll Mesorah series, inspired me far beyond the parameters of this book. They are paragons in their commitment to excellence. As a cohesive unit they have set the standard for the presentation and teaching of Torah through the written English word in our generation. May *Hashem* give them strength to continue.

King Solomon said that every Jew should honor *Hashem* with whatever talents he possesses (*Proverbs* 3:9). I hope that the writing of this volume has to some extent, fulfilled this teaching.

I pray that this *sefer* be a source of merit to my wife, Miriam, תחי׳, and our children, שיחיו. Their total devotion and encouragement were a constant inspiration. This project could not have come to fruition without them, for they understood my commitment, and with pride and selfless dedication they gave their gracious support.

May we share together in our family's תורה חופה ומעשים טובים.

יהיו לרצון אמרי פ״י והגיון לבי לפניך ה׳ צורי וגואלי

Paysach J. Krohn
Kew Gardens, N.Y.
Feb. 6, 1985

פסח יוסף קראהן
חמשה עשר בשבט תשמ״ה

ᴥᔤ Preface to Second Edition

I am deeply grateful to HASHEM for the wonderful response that the public has given this sefer. It is gratifying to know that the volume has filled a certain need, and that it is now being printed for a second edition.

In the thirteen months since the first edition appeared I have had the joy of performing for the first time *brisim* on a set of triplets, and participating in the phenomena of doing a *bris* on a boy in the Samuels family whose father's *bris* was done by my father, and whose grandfather's *bris* was done by my grandfather in Scranton, Pa.

ברוך אלקים אשר לא הסיר תפלתי וחסדו מאתי

פסח יוסף קראהן
ז' אדר ב' תשמ"ו

Paysach J. Krohn
March 18, 1986

The publishers are grateful to
Aaron L. Helmowitz
*for his kind efforts in helping make this
volume available to the Jewish public*

⋙An Overview

Milah — Body and Heart

An Overview/
Milah — Body and Heart

מַעֲשֶׂה שֶׁשָּׁאַל טוּרְנוּסְרוּפוֹס הָרָשָׁע אֶת ר׳ עֲקִיבָא
אֵיזוֹ מַעֲשִׂים נָאִים, שֶׁל הַקָּדוֹשׁ בָּרוּךְ הוּא אוֹ שֶׁל
בָּשָׂר וָדָם. אָמַר לוֹ ר׳ עֲקִיבָא שֶׁל בָּשָׂר וָדָם נָאִים ...
הֵבִיא לוֹ ר׳ עֲקִיבָא שִׁבֳּלִים וּגְלֻסְקָאוֹת ... אֵין אֵלּוּ
נָאִים יוֹתֵר מִן הַשִּׁבֳּלִים? אָמַר לוֹ טוּרְנוּסְרוּפוֹס, אִם
הוּא חָפֵץ בַּמִּילָה, לָמָּה אֵינוֹ יוֹצֵא הַוָּלָד מָהוּל מִמְּעֵי
אִמּוֹ? אָמַר לוֹ ר׳ עֲקִיבָא ... לְפִי שֶׁלֹּא נָתַן הקב״ה
אֶת הַמִּצְוֹת לְיִשְׂרָאֵל אֶלָּא לְצָרֵף אוֹתָם בָּהֶם.
It happened that the wicked Turnus Rufus
asked R' Akiva, "Whose deeds are more
beautiful, God's or man's?"

R' Akiva said to him, "Man's are more
beautiful" ... R' Akiva brought him ears of
grain and baked rolls ... "are not these
[rolls] nicer than these [grains]?"

Turnus Rufus said to him, "If He
desires the circumcision, why doesn't an
infant emerge from his mother's womb
already circumcised?"

R' Akiva told him, "... God gave the
commandments to Israel only to purify
[Israel] through them" (Tanchuma, Tazria
5).

I. The Roman's Question

Turnus Rufus was the ruthless Roman governor
who ruled *Eretz Yisrael* about sixty years after the
destruction of the Second Temple and who
attempted to put down the Bar Kochba rebellion
(132C.E.). When the Jewish uprising had been

bloodily smashed, Turnus Rufus turned his attention to vengeance and to the imposition of decrees that would break the Jewish spirit. Rome had come to realize that Israel's strength lay not in independent statehood, but in Torah study and the observance of commandments that stamped it as God's nation rather than Rome's vassal. Turnus Rufus made it a capital offense to teach the Torah in public and he sought to prevent the performance of *bris milah* [circumcision]. Eventually, R' Akiva, the leading sage and teacher of Israel, was publicly tortured to death by Turnus Rufus for courageously teaching the Torah in defiance of the Romans.

Like many oppressors throughout history, Turnus Rufus fancied himself a thinker, and he sought to convince his victims — the more helpless, the better — that his beliefs were superior to theirs. The Talmudic and Midrashic literature record several debates between Turnus Rufus and R' Akiva. The patronizing, arrogant, abrasive Roman would attempt to show the illogic of the Torah, and the saintly sage would toy with him and demonstrate the superficiality of his arguments.

So it was that Turnus Rufus argued against circumcision by claiming that if it were truly a mark of human perfection, why wasn't man created that way? Was man's handiwork superior to God's? And R' Akiva replied by showing his antagonist raw grain and baked goods, and speaking of man's mission to perfect not only the universe given him by a generous Creator, but also to transform himself from a human animal into a human being.

Or HaChaim (Leviticus 12:3) explains that R' Akiva's answer must be understood on two levels. Superficially it was a clever retort to the haughty Turnus Rufus, who saw the world in terms of grain and rolls; raw materials and processed comforts. But R' Akiva's response was also meant to be a lamp in the hand of those who seek to find a way into the deeper recesses of life and of God's purpose. Otherwise, his response would not have been a

satisfactory answer. In effect, the Roman's question was: If God wants man to be circumcised, why did He create him with a foreskin? The fact that *man* prefers dainty rolls to coarse kernels is his *personal* choice, not God's. In the same way that man can make rolls, cake, or crackers, as he prefers, God should have created man already circumcised, if that is *His* preference. Clearly, R' Akiva meant something far more meaningful than appeared on the surface. What, then, does circumcision represent?

God should have created man already circumcised, if that is His preference.

II. Barriers to Holiness

אָדָם הָרִאשׁוֹן יָצָא מָהוּל שֶׁנֶּאֱמַר וַיִּבְרָא אֱלֹהִים אֶת הָאָדָם בְּצַלְמוֹ.

Adam, the first man, was created circumcised, as it is said (Genesis 1:27), So God created man in His image (Avos d'R' Nassan 2:5).

ר' יִצְחָק אָמַר מוֹשֵׁךְ בְּעָרְלָתוֹ הָיָה.

R' Yitzchak said, [Adam] caused his foreskin to be extended [and cover his circumcision] (Sanhedrin 38b).

In the Way

The physical act of circumcision consists of removing the עָרְלָה [orlah], foreskin. This small bit of surplus flesh is called *orlah*, a name that gives us an indication of what it represents. Wherever the term *orlah* is used in Scripture, it refers to a barrier standing in the way of a beneficial result. The first three years of a tree's produce are called *orlah*, because the decree of the Torah bars people from enjoying it in any way (*Leviticus* 19:23). A person's resistance to repentance is called עָרְלַת הַלֵּב, *the orlah of the heart*. The "heart," if left to its sincerest, purest impulses, should long for the ideal state of closeness to God and His will; it should yearn for the soul to be reunited with the holiness it enjoyed before coming into contact with the animal drives and corroding greed that characterize much of life on earth. Why, then, doesn't the heart propel man to

Wherever the term orlah is used in Scripture, it refers to a barrier standing in the way of a beneficial result.

repent? Because people tend to become habituated in sin or luxury or unethical practices or the gradually solidifying conviction that life cannot escape the grip of "business as usual." Once that happens, there is an emotional, intellectual barrier that stifles the heart's inner cry for repentance. That barrier is the *orlah* of the heart.

Every one of us often experiences something akin to this resistance. When we have been deeply committed to a course of action that turned out to be erroneous, it is excruciatingly difficult to say, "I was wrong." After a fierce, emotional argument, it is impossible for most people to say, "I'm sorry, I made a fool of myself. I was wrong." Why is this so? Because the *orlah* of the heart stands in the way of honesty. Families have been destroyed and nations gone to war because of it. Should it surprise us that repentance, too, is one of the casualties?

Families have been destroyed and nations gone to war because of it. Should it surprise us that repentance, too, is one of the casualties?

Changing Nature

The foreskin, too, symbolizes a barrier to holiness. Adam was born without it because he was as close as a physical being can possibly be to God. So great was Adam at the time of his creation, that the angels thought he was a divine being before whom they should sing praises. No aspect of creation was incomprehensible to him and his body was as brilliant as the sun. Adam's closeness to God found physical expression in the fact that he was born circumcised; that is, that there was no *orlah* intervening between him and God. Even the organ that represents man's worst animal-like urge was totally harnessed to God's service. Nothing stood between Adam and God.[1]

When he sinned, he caused his nature to change. Before then, Godliness had been natural to him and sin had been repulsive, bizarre, foreign. Once he disobeyed God he fell into the traps of illicit desire and self-justification. Temptation became natural to him and God became distant; and when God

Temptation became natural to him and God became distant; and when God reproached him for having disobeyed, Adam hastened to defend himself rather than repent.

1. Adam's greatness, the meaning of his sin, and its aftermath are discussed at length in the Overviews to ArtScroll *Bereishis/Genesis*, pp. 13-26; and 376-379.

reproached him for having disobeyed, Adam hastened to defend himself rather than repent. After his fall, the angels had no trouble recognizing his human vulnerability.

Adam was created circumcised for he was a superior being, but by succumbing to sin, he fell prey to the natural forces that should have been his servants. Having set his sights downward toward earth, he could no longer look to the heavens as he was created to do. His personal failure created a barrier against the spirit, a barrier that was mirrored in his body, when the symbol of his closeness to God, his circumcision, was covered by a growth of flesh.

Because Adam's sin was the failure of mankind, the foreskin symbolizing it became part of the human body.

Because Adam's sin was the failure of mankind, the foreskin symbolizing it became a permanent part of the human body. For the twenty generations from Adam to Abraham, mankind failed to raise itself from those depths. There were righteous exceptions, like Enosh, Methuselah, and Noah, but they were individual stars in a dismal horizon. Even God cannot guarantee that man's mind and heart will choose truth over evil, light over darkness, spirit over flesh, love of God over love of pleasure, recognition that the Master is God and not whatever inexorable force happens to find favor in the eyes of any current generation of non-believers. Humanity had fallen, and it awaited someone great enough to raise not only himself but the race (*Maharal, Chiddushei Aggados*).

Abraham removes the Barrier

Until Abraham's time, the world had spun in a downward spiral of apathy and sin; creation had lost meaning and failed to serve its intended purpose. Then Abraham revealed new vistas of recognition that Hashem was everywhere and controlled everything. He earned the privilege of being designated the father of a nation that would carry on his mission of standing up to skeptics and enemies, until the day when all nations would acknowledge Israel's Godly message.

Abraham saw God everywhere. Obstructions to holiness withered away. The human race still was encumbered with the spiritual and physical foreskin of Adam, but Abraham had demonstrated that man could surmount it. God recognized this change in his spiritual essence by giving him the commandment of circumcision.

Perhaps it was in recognition of this overriding symbolism that Abraham refrained from circumcising himself before being specifically commanded to do so, unlike other commandments which he fulfilled voluntarily (see *Eretz Yisrael* — *The Supremacy of the Land, Bereishis*/Genesis, vol. II, pp. 400-417). Because circumcision represented

God's acknowledgment that the barrier caused by Adam's sin had been removed, Abraham could not perform it without a specific command. Only God could testify that Abraham had become worthy of the deed in all its meaning, that he had become father of the nation that would fulfill the failed hope of Adam. Circumcision without the inner portents of the deed would have no more value than removing some flesh from the elbow or shoulder, therefore, Abraham would not perform it without a specific command.

It was this new dimension of service to God based on all-embracing recognition that made Abraham the successor to Adam as the father of God's nation. The sequence of *Genesis* 17 makes it clear that the gift of offspring and the final pledge of the Land — the nation and its home — were dependent upon circumcision. From the words of the Sages regarding Adam, we see that circumcision was a critical indication of a loyalty to God that transcended the limitations of the flesh — and even the strictures of

natural law.

Like a sheath holding a sword, the body is a vessel containing the soul. Just as the contours of a sheath tell much about the contours of the sword within, so the body can reveal much about the condition of the soul. Good judges of character study eyes and

gestures. The lines of age treat people differently and often reveal the personality of the person they furrow. Similarly, the soul of the first human being retained its intimacy with the One Who blew it into Adam's nostrils. The human body mirrored this phenomenon. When the soul had no spiritual impediment, the body had no *orlah;* but when Adam's sin caused a barrier between him and God, the *orlah* became the natural condition of his posterity.

Rabbi Akiva's Answer One result of Adam's sin was that he and his mate were banished from the Garden of Eden and the earth's produce would become accursed. No longer would tempting, nourishing food grow directly as it had in Eden. From then on, man would be forced to labor long and hard to grow and process his food, until the coming of the Messiah, when — as the *Zohar* and the Sages teach — mankind would return to its original state of bliss and its food would again grow from the ground without need for the sweat of man's brow.

This was the import of R' Akiva's allegory to Turnus Rufus. The wise sage showed the arrogant butcher two products, one as it grew from the ground after Adam's sin, and a second as it grew before the sin — and will grow once again, when the catastrophic results of that error are erased by man's repentance and God's merciful acceptance of it. Which is better, R' Akiva asked, God's handiwork, raw grain, as it has been blighted by human sin, or a tempting roll, the tasty result of man's effort to elevate himself to what he once was and can become again? Turnus Rufus may have been amused by the clever repartee of the powerless rabbi who would one day become his victim. But those who understood R' Akiva must have felt a simultaneous twinge of remorse and surge of challenging pride. By his sin, man had transformed a delectable roll into tasteless kernel — the metaphor for his loss of the sublime proximity to God that should have remained his —

By his sin, man had transformed a delectable roll into a tasteless kernel, but he can yet regain his former state of spiritual greatness.

but he can yet regain his former state of spiritual growth. Israel is reminded of this every time it joyously initiates its newborn sons into the covenant of Abraham, the covenant whereby God signified the self-perfection of Abraham, who had made himself worthy of the role once held by Adam.

III. Orlah of the Heart

Will and Body It is apparent from this discussion that the relatively simple, mechanical task of removing the physical foreskin is parallel to the much more difficult and ultimately more meaningful duty to remove the עָרְלַת הַלֵּב, *orlah of the heart*, that bars mankind from achieving its noblest goal. Commentators through the centuries have noted that bodily circumcision is *Circumcision is performed on the organ that responds to man's most powerful, instinct, and that represents man's most sublime gift.* performed on the organ that responds to man's most powerful, hardest-to-control instinct, and that represents his most sublime gift: the ability to produce new life and guarantee his own continuity. In the moral and intellectual spheres, the heart represents these same aspects. The heart desires and instigates passions. It can ignite lusts that drag people down through filth and perversion, and it can fire passions that make people soar to intellectual brilliance and spiritual peaks. Judaism believes that man's essential nature is pure, and that he can overcome his animal instincts. If he succeeds, then both his body and soul are both servants of God, without conflict. Indeed, if that happens, the body can be like a lens that intensifies the luminescence of the soul, because man's accomplishment in consecrating his animal body to God's service is greater than that of an angel, a completely spiritual entity that serves God without any impediment. A human being is pulled in many directions while an angel has no temptations whatever — so the man who masters his urges is greater than the angels.

Man Begins, God Completes

The *Tanya (Iggeres HaKodesh,* ch. 4) notes that the Torah speaks twice of the "circumcision of the *orlah* of the heart" and that there is an apparent contradiction between the two verses:

וּמַלְתֶּם אֵת עָרְלַת לְבַבְכֶם.

You are to circumcise the 'orlah' of your heart (Deuteronomy 10:16).

וּמָל ה' אֱלֹהֶיךָ אֶת לְבָבְךָ וְאֶת לְבַב זַרְעֶךָ.

And HASHEM, *your God, will circumcise your heart and the heart of your offspring (ibid. 30:6).*

The first verse presents it as a commandment; the second verse gives a pledge that God will do it for us.

The first verse presents it as a commandment that we must remove from our hearts the impediments to goodness. The second verse gives a pledge that God will do it for us.

The circumcision of the heart involves two steps, one more difficult than the other.

The *Tanya* explains that, like the circumcision of the foreskin, the circumcision of the heart involves two steps, one more difficult than the other. In physical circumcision, first comes the removal of the prepuce, a loose fold of skin, a relatively simple task. Then comes a much more delicate and difficult procedure: the folding back of a thin membrane to prevent the foreskin from growing and covering the organ again. These two acts symbolize the two steps of repentance. Man is charged with the duty to rid himself of, or at least control, his base passions.

People can perfect themselves to an enormous degree; there are many who do so and it is axiomatic that God would not demand it unless it were possible. Nevertheless, the fact of our humanity prevents us from totally removing all barriers from the heart. The effects of Adam's fall and man's resultant new nature still, at least to some extent, prevent our attainment of ultimate spiritual heights.

This 'thin membrane' over the human heart will be removed only when God brings the final redemption.

This 'thin membrane' over the human heart will be removed only when God brings the final redemption. Then He will complete the circumcision of all hearts and return mankind to the state of creation.

Limitation and Hope

Sfas Emes points out that when God assured Abraham that he would achieve perfection through

circumcision, He introduced Himself as Shaddai, the Name that denotes limitation (*Genesis* 17:1). As *Rashi* explains frequently throughout the Torah, the Name Shaddai comes from the word דַי, *enough*. God set limitations upon the growth of the earth, upon man's capacity, upon the amount of suffering he must endure, and so on. God commanded Abraham to be perfect — but by using that Name, He also suggested to him that there were limits to how far he could go. Abraham longed to bring himself and mankind back to Adam's original level of greatness, but God intimated that this was more than he could do. Circumcision can bring one to profound heights — witness Abraham and his posterity — but there is a degree of circumcision that, as *Tanya* declares, must await the coming of the Messiah and the ultimate perfection.

God commanded Abraham to be perfect — but there were limits to how far he could go.

Circumcision is an affirmation of Abraham's ancient and still vibrant covenant and an expression of confident hope in a redemption that will return man to the pedestal on which Adam once stood. Perhaps this is why Jews have always rejoiced in the privilege of bringing their offspring into the covenant, why even people who have grown estranged from many other aspects of Judaism rejoice in the *bris milah* of their children.

Our Sages said:

רשב״ג אוֹמֵר כָּל מִצְוָה שֶׁקִּבְּלוּ עֲלֵיהֶם בְּשִׂמְחָה

... עֲדַיִן עוֹשִׂין אוֹתָהּ בְּשִׂמְחָה

It was learned, Rabban Shimon ben Gamliel said; every mitzvah that they accepted upon themselves with joy ... They still perform with joy (Shabbos 130a).

There is something in the soul and psyche of the Jewish people that embraced the mitzvah of bris milah.

There is something in the soul and psyche of the Jewish people that embraced the *mitzvah* of *milah*. Great scholars knew why, ordinary people didn't. But all sensed — if they did not understand — that a circumcision was an event to be marked with pride and joy. There were times when danger hovered over

the celebrants, but this did not deter them. King Antiochus, the Syrian-Greek tyrant of the time of Chanukah, made *bris milah* a capital offense. In times of later persecutions, too, circumcision was forbidden. Nevertheless, Jews brought their children into the covenant of Abraham. In Nazi concentration camps, mothers circumcised their newborn sons. In the Nazi ghettoes, there were doctors who would hide the mark of circumcision for Jews who wished to pass as gentiles — but there were few takers. A Jew keeps his identity, and does it with joy.

In his classic work *Kuzari* (3:7:8), *R' Yehudah Halevi* has the Jewish sage explain *bris milah* to the king of the Khazar kingdom.

The king replies:

> Indeed, you have duly accepted this law and you perform it with great zeal, with a public ceremony to praise it and to bring out its basic concept. Hence it brings blessings. Other peoples desired to imitate you, but they had only the pain, without the joy, which can be felt only by him who remembers the cause for which he bears the pain.

We remember the cause. We long for the future. We are confident it will come.

Rabbi Nosson Scherman
27 Teves, 5745

Other peoples had only the pain, without the joy, which can only be felt by him who remembers the cause for which he bears the pain.

❧ Background Essays

Names:
Their Choice and Significance

A Tapestry of Eights

The Sandak's Role:
A Study in Contrasts

Names:
Their Choice and Significance

IN CONJUNCTION with the inauguration of the *mitzvah* of *bris milah*, God told Abram that his name would be changed to Abraham forever. From the day that Abraham achieved perfection of his physical being through the act of circumcision, his new name and its implication would reflect his broadened mission.

PREVIOUSLY, HE HAD been destined to be the spiritual father of his native land Aram, a destiny indicated by his Hebrew name: אַבְרָם, **A Bris —** which may be interpreted as אַב (אֲ)רָם, *father of* **Hence a** *Aram.* Now, however, his scope would be global. **New Name** by *your name Abram, but your name shall be Abraham, for I have made you* אַב הֲמוֹן גּוֹיִם, *father of a multitude of nations'* (Genesis 17:5). The Hebrew letter ה was added to his name, making it אַבְרָהָם, *Abraham*, an allusion to אַב הֲמוֹן, *father of a multitude [of nations]*. At first you were only a father of Aram, your native land, but now you are a father for all the world (*Berachos* 13a). Following the precedent of God who gave Abraham a new name at his circumcision, we traditionally name a boy at his *bris* (*Zichron Bris LaRishonim*).

At this juncture Abraham was instructed that his wife Sarai's name would also be changed. God said to Abraham, *'As for Sarai, your wife, do not call her by the name* שָׂרַי, *Sarai, for* שָׂרָה, *Sarah, is her name'* (Genesis 17:16). At first she was a princess to her own nation (i.e., Aram), but later she became a princess to all the world (*Berachos* 3a). [Sarai literally means *'my princess'*; Sarah means *'princess,'* i.e., universally without limitation.]

Once again a name assumed a global scope, a universal purpose, this time represented by our first Matriarch, and here too reflected by the unassuming letter ה.

The change in both names consisted of the addition of the letter ה, a letter for which no guttural sound or mouth formation is required. One need only breathe out to pronounce the letter *hei*. The addition of this simple-sounding letter to Abraham and Sarah's names signified their elevated roles from that of local dignitaries to that of Patriarch and Matriarch.

THE MIDRASH (*Bereishis Rabbah* 12:2) notes that it was a simple task for God to create the world. Bringing into being the profound phenomena of the universe and its galaxies

The Letter ה — God's World Plan required no toil on His part; it was as effortless as pronouncing the letter *hei*. This is homiletically referred to in *Genesis* (2:4): אֵלֶּה תוֹלְדוֹת הַשָּׁמַיִם וְהָאָרֶץ בְּהִבָּרְאָם, *These are the products of the heaven and earth when they were created*. The word בְּהִבָּרְאָם is written in the Torah Scroll with a diminutive ה, to point out that it may be read as two words: בְּה בְרָאָם *He created them with a* ה (*Menachos* 29b).

The Talmud explains further that the shape of this letter symbolizes mankind's relationship with God. The bottomless ה represents the open chasm through which one will fall if he voluntarily strays from the path of the righteous and chooses the life of a sinner. However, God leaves a door open even for a sinner (note the opening on the left side of the ה). Man can elevate himself from the depths by repentance and be welcomed through the open door at the 'top'. The ה is thus the microcosm of God's plan for the world.

This, then, was the message to Abraham and Sarah. From today, with this act of *milah*, you are paragons for all the world to emulate. The world and its inhabitants that have been created with the letter ה are now yours to teach, guide, and correct. The penitents of the world will be inspired by your behavior — for, as the Midrash notes (*Bereishis Rabbah* 30:8), Abraham was destined to lead the entire world to repentance.

The Midrash comments further that the word בְּהִבָּרְאָם, *when they were created*, has the same letters as בְּאַבְרָהָם, *for the sake of Abraham*, thus alluding further to his new purpose defined by his new name.

If an individual letter added to an already existing name can signify a world of difference, then, a complete name, bestowed by parents upon a child at the threshold of life, should certainly be chosen with cognizance of its inherent significance.

Names: Their Choice and Significance [36]

Naming A Child

IN JUDAISM, a name is not merely a conglomeration of letters put together as a convenient way to refer to someone. Ideally, it is a **A Name** definition of the individual — a description of his **Defines** personality and an interpretation of his traits. It may even be a portent of the person's future , or perhaps a **the Man** prayer that the person bearing this particular name shall live up to the potential expressed in the name.

The Torah (*Genesis* 5:29) relates that Noah was given his name with the prayer, זֶה יְנַחֲמֵנוּ מִמַּעֲשֵׂנוּ וּמֵעִצְּבוֹן יָדֵינוּ, '*This one will bring us rest from our work and the toil of our hands*' (נֹחַ from the word יְנַחֲמֵנוּ). The intent was that Noah would lighten the burden of his family's toil by introducing agricultural tools (*Radak*).

Arizal writes that the nature and behavior of a person, whether good or bad, can be found by analyzing his name. Even the numerical value of the name's letters is an indication of the individual's character and personality.

The Talmud (*Yoma* 83b) describes the incident of R' Meir and his colleagues R' Yose and R' Yehudah who sought lodging at an inn for the Sabbath. R' Meir was known to pay close attention to a person's name. Upon learning that the innkeeper's name was כִּידוֹר, *Kidor*, he refused to entrust his purse to him, for the name Kidor brought to mind the phrase: כִּי דוֹר [Kidor] תַּהְפֻּכֹת הֵמָּה, *for they are a generation full of changes, children in whom there is no trust* (*Deuteronomy* 32:20; see also *Berachos* 7b, שְׁמָא גָּרֵים).

Nevertheless, R' Yehudah and R' Yose, who did not pay heed to names, entrusted their money to the innkeeper. Subsequently, the innkeeper denied taking their money from them for safekeeping, and it was lost. R' Meir's money, however, was spared.

THE TALMUD (*Sanhedrin* 98b) tells of a debate regarding the exact name of the Messiah. Four of the suggestions are מְנַחֵם, Menachem; **From** שִׁילֹה, Shiloh; יִנּוֹן, Yinon; and חֲנִינָה, Chaninah. **Abraham to** The *Vilna Gaon* notes that the combination of the first letters of these four names spells the **the Messiah** word מָשִׁיחַ; Messiah, in Hebrew. Extending this thought, *R' Avigdor Miller* explains that the debate was not solely regarding the actual name of the Messiah, but included a discussion regarding the outstanding characteristics of our future redeemer.

Menachem (מְנַחֵם) means comforter. The solace and comfort that

the Jewish nation will experience after thousands of years of anticipation will be reflected in their sentiments towards the Messiah. He will indeed console the Jewish people for their agony throughout the lengthy exile.

Shiloh (שילה) is the term used by Jacob (*Genesis* 49:10) in his final blessing to his son Judah, the tribe from which the Messiah will descend: עַד כִּי יָבֹא שִׁילֹה, *until Shiloh will come*. Regarding this name, *R' S.R. Hirsch* comments that the root of the word Shiloh (שילה) is שׁוּל, meaning the lower *hem* of a garment, and *Sforno* notes that the first two letters of the word שָׁלוֹם, *peace*, are also present in Shiloh. Taken together, the term Shiloh signifies that at the *end* of the exile the Messiah will bring *peace* to the world. Additionally, the word Shiloh (שילה) consists of the letters שֶׁל יָה, *belonging to God*, indicating the Messiah's role as the messenger of God.

Yinon (ינון) stems from the word נִין, *a generation of children* (*R' Hirsch*; *Psalms* 72:17), and is related to the word מָנוֹן, *kingdom*. It thus reflects the thought that the Messiah's message and teaching will withstand the test of time. The peace and prosperity that he will bring will endure for generations afterward. This name is based on the verse: יְהִי שְׁמוֹ לְעוֹלָם לִפְנֵי שֶׁמֶשׁ יִנּוֹן שְׁמוֹ, *May his name endure forever, and may his descendants (ינון) endure as long as the sun* (ibid.).

Chaninah (חֲנִינָה), denoting grace and charm, teaches that the Messiah's deeds will be beautiful and pleasant in the eyes of the watchful world. The favor that he will find will be universal.

Consolation, the end of an epoch, everlasting leadership, grace and charm - all traits of the Messiah, all expressed by his name. From the inception of Jewish history with Abraham, to its culmination with the Messiah, names have served to define our purpose and our potential.

Eternal Evaluations

רַבָּן שִׁמְעוֹן בֶּן גַּמְלִיאֵל אוֹמֵר: הָרִאשׁוֹנִים עַל יְדֵי שֶׁהָיוּ מִשְׁתַּמְּשִׁין בְּרוּחַ הַקּוֹדֶשׁ, הָיוּ מוֹצִיאִין לְשֵׁם הַמְּאוֹרָע — אֲבָל אָנוּ שֶׁאֵין אָנוּ מִשְׁתַּמְּשִׁין בְּרוּחַ הַקּוֹדֶשׁ, מוֹצִיאִין לְשֵׁם אֲבוֹתֵינוּ.

Rabban Shimon ben Gamliel said: The previous generations who availed themselves of the Holy Spirit would bestow names according to events. However, we, who cannot avail ourselves of the Holy Spirit, bestow names after our ancestors (Bereishis Rabbah 37:7).

TO LABEL SOMETHING properly is to define its nature. What one may see as a rusty old spoon, another will see as antique silverware;

Adam's Wisdom in Naming what one may consider random scribbling, another will consider abstract art; and what one observes as a heap of scrap in a city square, another will call modern sculpture befitting a large metropolis.

Rabbeinu Bachya (Bereishis 2:19) comments that Adam revealed his great wisdom when he named all species of creation. With his superior intellect, every name that he chose, together with the combination of its letters, defined the nature and characteristic of that creature.

He named the lion אַרְיֵה. The letters י־ה — which are part of the name of God the King of kings and Ruler of the universe — represent the lion's role as king of the jungle. Adam named the ordinary weak-minded donkey חֲמוֹר, a word that is cognate with חוֹמֶר, *simple elementary matter.* חוֹמֶר is also a measure of volume — as in the verse חוֹמֶר שְׂעוֹרִים, *a measure of barley (Hoshea* 3:2) — signifying the load which the donkey forever carries on its back.

At the outset of mankind, to name meant to define.

It was just this kind of definition that Moses sought when he asked God at the burning bush, *(Exodus* 3:13) *"When I come to the children of Israel and say to them, 'The God of your fathers has sent me to you,' and they will then say to me, 'What is His Name?' what shall I answer?"* Ramban comments that it could not have been merely a literal name that Moses sought, for if Israel were to question the existence of God, it would be inconsequential for Moses to reveal a name to them. Rather, Moses requested a Divine Name that would signify the existence of His supervision and benevolent nature, for that would assure the Jews of their redemption. 'What is His Name?' meant, 'What is His main characteristic?'

THE SAME IDEA WAS expressed to Jacob by the guardian angel of his brother Esau. After Esau's angel had struggled with Jacob until

No Name — No Purpose the early hours of the morning, and informed Jacob that God would confer upon him the new name of Israel, Jacob, in turn, asked the angel, *'Tell me, please, what is your name?' (Genesis* 32:30). The angel replied, *'What purpose is there in asking my name?' Rashi* explains that the angel told Jacob, 'Our names have no permanence, for our names change according to the mission on which God sends us.' A

lack of a permanent name implies a lack of a permanent purpose.

A HISTORIC EVENT needs both hindsight and foresight to be interpreted properly. Even after weighing every nuance and

Names as Commemoratives

balancing the significant against the insignificant occurrences, man still struggles with the interpretation of long-term implications. Many events in contemporary Jewish history have been judged differently by Jews with different perspectives. Only with *ruach hakodesh*, the Holy Spirit, i.e., Divinely inspired wisdom, can one make a precise evaluation.

Because we lack such capabilities, R' Shimon Ben Gamliel tells us that we do not bestow original names on our children. Commentators note, however, that it is proper to use names that commemorate events, provided one uses names that had been utilized previously. For example, a war has ended and one wishes to name his son *Shalom* (peace); a person witnesses the helping hand of God and chooses the name *Eliezer* (my God aided me); or a refugee fleeing from country to country finally finds an area where he can settle and build his future selects the name *Noach* (rest) — all these are acceptable (*Bris Avos* 8:37).

It is indeed customary to name a child in relation to a Jewish holiday or commemorative event that coincides with the child's birth. For a boy born on Purim, one might use *Mordechai*; on Chanukah, *Mattisyahu* or *Yehudah*; on Pesach, *Moshe*; on Yom Kippur, *Rachamim* (mercy); on Tishah B'Av, *Menachem* (comforter) or *Nechemiah* (God comforts); on Succos, the name of the special guest (*ushpizin*) corresponding to that individual day (first day, *Avraham*, second day *Yitzchak*, etc.). Some name a child with a name found in the weekly portion of the Torah reading that corresponds to the child's birth or *bris*.

The name given to a newborn child is eternal; it behooves one to evaluate the choice carefully.

Looking Back ... to the Road Ahead

לְעוֹלָם יִבְדּוֹק אָדָם בְּשֵׁמוֹת לִקְרוֹא לִבְנוֹ הָרָאוּי לִהְיוֹת צַדִּיק כִּי לִפְעָמִים
הַשֵּׁם גּוֹרֵם טוֹב אוֹ גּוֹרֵם רָע.

One should always be careful to choose for his child a name
that denotes righteousness, for at times the name itself can be

an influence for good or an influence for bad (Tanchuma, Ha'azinu 7).

THERE IS A SPIRITUAL connection between the name of an individual and his נְשָׁמָה, *soul.* The word נְשָׁמָה stems from the word

**A Name —
The Soul's
Essence**

נְשִׁימָה, *breath,* for it is the 'breath' of God that gives life to man (*Genesis* 2:7). A soul's essence is Divine, and a person's name defines this essence.

It is interesting to note that the central letters of the word נְשָׁמָה are שֵׁם, *name.* Indeed some have written that the higher soul comes to the child when he is given his name (*Sefer Me'or Gadol,* cited by *Taamei HaMinhagim* 929, in *Kuntros Achron*). Perhaps the first and last letters, נ and ה, allude to נֵר ה', *the light of* HASHEM, a term used to refer to the soul, as it says: נֵר ה' נִשְׁמַת אָדָם, *the light of* HASHEM *is the soul of man* (*Proverbs* 20:27).

Noam Elimelech (Bamidbar) advises naming a child after a deceased *tzaddik* (righteous person). When a child is named after the deceased, the latter's soul, which dwells in the World of Truth, is aroused. A spiritual affinity is thus created between this soul and that of the newborn child which has profound effect on the child. Additionally the departed soul is itself exalted when the name it bore on this world is again used.

Given the above, the term זֵכֶר צַדִּיק לִבְרָכָה, *the memory of the righteous is for a blessing* (*Proverbs* 10:7), can be interpreted in a novel fashion. When one names a child after a deceased *tzaddik,* thus perpetuating that *tzaddik's* memory, the result will be a twofold blessing, for both the child and the deceased will benefit by virtue of the child bearing this name. The verse concludes, וְשֵׁם רְשָׁעִים יִרְקָב, *but the name of the wicked shall decay,* which can be understood to mean that the names of evil people shall decay and wither because they will not be used (see *Yoma* 38b).

WHEN CHANNAH WAS granted her wish and finally bore a son, she was faced with a dilemma regarding his name. For ten years she had

**A Mother's
Dilemma**

suffered the pangs of childlessness. She had poured out her heart in prayer and promised that if she bore a child, he would be consecrated to the service of God. When the child was born her expression of gratitude was כִּי מֵה' שְׁאִלְתִּיו, *I have borrowed him from God* (*I Samuel* 1:20). By right, then, the child should have been called שָׁאוּל, *Saul,* meaning borrowed. However, says the *Chasam Sofer,* Channah knew that

there had been an Edomite king named Saul (see *Genesis* 36:37). She was also aware that Zimri, the rebellious Jew who was killed by the zealous Phineas (*Numbers* 25:14), had been known by the name Saul (*Sanhedrin* 82b).

'For these reasons, I am positive,' states the *Chasam Sofer*, 'Channah saw fit to abide by the verse וְשֵׁם רְשָׁעִים יִרְקָב, *the name of the wicked shall decay*. So after choosing to use the name שָׁאוּל, *Saul*, she altered it by adding the letter מ [and reversing the letters א and ו], thus making שְׁמוּאֵל, *Samuel*' (*Responsa, Even HaEzer* II §22).

She chose the letter מ, *mem*, so that the letters comprising the name שְׁמוּאֵל would contain the phrase שָׁאוּל מֵאֵל, *borrowed from God*, the expression of her gratitude (*R' David Cohen*).

Channah's son Samuel grew up to become a great prophet. God instructed him to anoint Saul, from the tribe of Benjamin, as the first Jewish king. *This* Saul was truly righteous, as it says: *And there was none among the Jews who was finer than he* (*I Samuel* 9:2). We know that the name Saul is used today. Why, then, is Channah's dilemma not our dilemma? A similar question can be raised regarding the name מְנַשֶּׁה, *Menashe*, which was the name both of the righteous son of Joseph (*Genesis* 41:51) and the evil son of Hezekiah (see *II Kings* 21). The question can also be asked about the name יִשְׁמָעֵאל, *Ishmael*. Ishmael, the son of Abraham, was known for his wickedness (see *Genesis* 21:9), yet one of the *Tannaim* bore that name.

Sefer Haflaah (*Kesubos* 104b) writes that names that were shared by both righteous and evil people may be used today if the intention is to give the name of the righteous individual who bore it. As for Ishmael, *Tosefos Yeshanim* (*Yoma* 38b) infers that he repented at the end of his days. Thus, his name may be used.

IN CERTAIN SEPHARDIC communities, it is considered auspicious (a *segulah*) for long life for a father to name a child after himself.

The Sephardic Custom Some in those communities extend the custom to name their newborn sons and daughters after a living grandfather or grandmother, so that older people, too, have the good fortune and blessing of continued long life (*Bris Avos*).

The Talmud (*Chullin* 47b) tells of a distraught mother who was concerned about having her son circumcised because there had been a history of illness in the family. The *bris* was delayed until R' Nassan HaBavli said it was safe to circumcise the child. In gratitude

the child was named after him.

It was common practice in the family of R' Yehudah HaNassi (the Prince) to name children after living forebears. Talmudic commentaries note, however, that it was only due to the great merit of the Torah and good deeds of these *Tannaim* and *Amoraim* (teachers of the *Mishnah* and *Gemara* respectively) that they could practice this custom without fear of harm (See *Teshuvos Chelkas Yaakov, Responsa* 120).

There is a classic letter written by *Ramban* (Nachmanides — R' Moshe ben Nachman; a thirteenth-century Sephardic Torah giant) to his son R' Shlomo and daughter-in-law upon the birth of their son. R' Shlomo's wife was the daughter of Rabbeinu Yonah, who had passed away before his daughter gave birth. The *Ramban* wrote in part, 'Although I know that it is proper for you to name the child after me, with the name of Moshe, since I am the child's father's father, I defer this honor to the child's other grandfather and I advise that you name him Yonah, with the hope and prayer that the verse, וְזָרַח הַשֶּׁמֶשׁ וּבָא הַשָּׁמֶשׁ, *And the sun rises and the sun sets* (*Ecclesiastes* 1:5), be fulfilled. The rising and setting of the sun homiletically symbolizes the proximity of the birth of a future leader of Jewry close to the passing of another Jewish leader (see *Midrash Koheles*).

Finally, R' Yosef Karo, author of the *Shulchan Aruch* (Code of Jewish Law) and a Sephardi, was named after his grandfather who later became his primary teacher.

IT IS THE GENERALLY accepted Ashkenazic custom, however, not to name children after living people. This is based on *Sefer Chassidim* (§460) which states: 'Although gentile parents name their children after themselves and no harm befalls them, Jews are very careful to refrain from this practice.'

The Ashkenazic Custom

It is hard to ascertain the exact reason for the Ashkenazic custom of naming only after the deceased. The following reasons have been suggested:

If a father were to name his son after himself, his other children would no doubt at times address their brother by name in the presence of their father, who had the same name. This would be disrespectful and a transgression of the commandment to honor one's father and mother, for not only is it forbidden to address one's parents by their first names, it is not even permitted to address a

friend who has the same name as one's parent by name, in the presence of that parent (see *Yoreh Deah* 240:2; *Bris Avos*).

Another rationale for this custom is that it arose as an effort to avoid harsh feelings on the part of the one whose name is being used. There were, indeed, some who considered it a bad omen to have a baby named for them while they were still alive. To them the practice indicated that people were waiting for them to die (*Zocher HaBris* 24:14). [This fear may have been generated by the very custom of naming a child after the deceased.]

At times, the Ashkenazic custom of naming only after a deceased person may lead to a problem. For example, would it be permissible to name a child after a deceased grandfather, if the second grandfather, who is still alive, carries the same name? Numerous rabbinic authorities have ruled on this delicate question. Most are of the opinion that a child should not bear the same name as his living father or grandfather. However, some have ruled that if a child is given an additional name, it is permissible. For example, if the deceased grandfather was named Yaakov, the infant may be named Yaakov Yoseph.

A person's name, like a fire, carries within it enormous potential. If it is a symbol of the glowing righteousness of generations past, it can illuminate its bearer's future; if it is meant to recall the wicked, it can symbolize flames of destruction. By reflecting back, we can help our future be bright.

The Fortune of Names

HIDDEN IN THE NAME OF an individual is the portent of his future and a description of his life. The fortunes and misfortunes of man

**A New Name —
a New Mazal**

are concealed in the secrets of the letters, vowels and meaning of the Hebraic name that he carries. If a person is seriously ill, often a name like *Chaim* ('life') or *Refael* ('God heals'; the name of God's healing angel) is added to his existing name, with the hope and prayer that the new name will signify a new *mazal*, or fortune, for the one who is ill (*Yoreh Deah* 335:10). The new name usually precedes the old one as in Chaim Zechariah, Refael Aharon, etc.

Because a man's name is so definitive, there has been a hesitancy to use the name of a person who died at a young age, or suffered an unnatural death. The reluctance stems from the fear that the

misfortune may, in a spiritual manner, be carried over to the new bearer of the name.

Although dying young is a relative term, *HaGaon R' Moshe Feinstein* in his *Igros Moshe (Yoreh Deah* 122, 5733/1973 edition) offers some guidelines. If a person died a natural death and left children, this is not considered רִיעַ מַזְלֵיהּ, *bad fortune*, which would preclude the use of the name. Both the prophet Samuel and King Solomon died at the 'young' age of 52, and King Hezekiah passed away at 54, yet traditionally their names have always been used by Jews. If, however, a person died an unnatural death, then, Rabbi Feinstein suggests that the name be altered. It may be for this reason, says *Yam Shel Shlomo (Gittin,* Ch. 4 §30), that many Jews omit the last letter of the name of יְשַׁעְיָהוּ and use the name יְשַׁעְיָה (i.e., Isaiah rather than Isaiahu), since the prophet Isaiah was murdered. If, however, one passed away at a young age without leaving children, this is indeed bad fortune and the name should either be altered or a name added.

HaGaon R' Yaakov Kamenetzky considers the age of sixty the demarcation between young and old. The Talmud (*Moed Katan* 28a) relates that R' Yosef made a party when he reached the age of sixty, celebrating the beginning of his longevity.

BRIS AVOS (8:31) writes that to name a male child after a female who has passed away is an acceptable and honorable custom.

A Male Name from a Female Name Quoting *Midrash Pinchas* (by R' Pinchas of Korets), he cites the example of an infant who was given the name דָּן, *Dan,* after a woman named דִּינָה, *Dinah.* R' Pinchas, a Chassidic great, said that the woman's soul was thereby exalted.

All the letters and vowels of a name are significant. Therefore when adapting a boy's name from a female name, the objective is to use as many letters and vowels as possible. Consequently, בָּרוּךְ, *Baruch,* is the suggested choice for בְּרָכָה, *Brachah,* as is מֶלֶךְ, *Melech,* for מַלְכָּה, *Malkah.*

OFTEN FAMILIES ARE confronted with a choice of naming a child after one of two individuals, for example: one named Eliezer, the

Two Names from Two People other Yaakov. As a compromise they use both names and call their child Eliezer Yaakov. Is the child with this new combination considered to be named for both people? Although this is a

common practice in most communities and is sanctioned by many halachic authorities,[1] there are many who differ on the grounds that one person should not be named after two different people. Some hold that there is no objection to naming people two generations in the same family, for example, if someone was named Yosef *ben* [*son of*] Shimon, a descendant may be named Yosef Shimon. According to this view, names should not be taken from different families. It is reported (*Pe'er HaDor IV* p.200) that the *Chazon Ish* objected to all such combined names, on the ground that such a hybrid name is, in effect, a new name that is unrelated to either of the deceased.

The Right to Choose a Name

AMONG ASHKENAZIC JEWS today, the mother is generally given the right to select her first child's name, with the names of

The First Child

succeeding children being alternated between the two parents. There is a verse in *Genesis*, however, which seemingly indicates that such was not the case in Biblical times.

When the Torah tells (Genesis 38:3, 4) of the birth of Judah's firstborn son, its states: 'And he *named him Er*.' When a second son was born, the Torah writes: 'And she *named him Onan*.' *Da'as Zekeinim* cites an opinion that the custom in those days was that the privilege of selecting the name of the child alternated between father and mother, with the father naming the firstborn, the mother the second, and so on. As the passages above indicate, it was the father — in this case, Judah — who selected a name for the firstborn.[2]

---

1. [*Chasam Sofer* seemingly approved of this practice. In one of his responsa (*Even HaEzer* §18) he cites the origin of the Hebrew name שְׁנִיאוּר, *Schneur*. A couple was unable to agree upon which grandfather their son should be named after. One parent wished to call the baby after one grandfather whose name was מֵאִיר [lightgiver], the other wanted to name him after the other grandfather, יָאִיר [may he shine]. As a compromise the name שְׁנִיאוּר [two lights], derived from the same root as both מֵאִיר and יָאִיר, was coined. *Chasam Sofer* goes on to explain that the baby was not named מֵאִיר יָאִיר or יָאִיר מֵאִיר because in earlier times it was not the custom to give two names. Now, if *Chasam Sofer* was against naming a baby after two people, he would in all probability have raised this point as an additional reason for not giving the baby two names.]

2. There are some who subscribe to this custom today. In a letter (cited in *Shalmei Shmuel*, 10) the present Lubavitcher Rebbe, *Rav Menachem Mendel Schneerson*, שליט״א, writes that where there is no specific custom, the right of naming the first child belongs to the father, the second child to the mother, etc., as indicated in the verses above.

Regarding the present custom of the wife's right to name her first child, *Zocher HaBris* (24:19) offers the following explanation: Because it was a widespread practice among the Jews of Europe for a young couple to be supported by the wife's father while the husband continued his Torah studies, the wife was given the honor of naming the first child born to them. Another suggestion for this privilege may be in deference to the difficult labor and delivery that is usually associated with the birth of the first child.

In Sephardic tradition many families have the custom that both the first son and first daughter are named after the father's parents.

Yiddish and Secular Names

There are many Hebrew names that are seconded by Yiddish names, such as Aryeh Leib, Shlomo Zalman, Tzvi Hirsch, Yitzchak Aizik, Zev Wolf, to name a few. Sometimes the Yiddish name is a translation of the Hebrew — as in Aryeh Leib, respectively the Hebrew and Yiddish words for lion; and Tzvi Hirsch, both of which mean deer. Other Yiddish names are derived from the Hebrew, as is Aizik [similar to Isaac] from Yitzchak, or Zalman [related to Solomon] from Shlomo.

Why were people given, and known by, their Yiddish names as opposed to their Hebrew names?

Yefei To'ar (*Bereishis Rabbah* 82:9) points out that as early as the days of the Patriarchs there was a strong inclination to give only a Hebrew name. He notes that Jacob changed the name of his twelfth son Benjamin (*Genesis* 35:18) even though the dying Rachel had already named him Ben Oni, literally, *son of my sorrow*, a name which the Midrash (ibid.) calls Aramaic. Rachel did not want to use לְשׁוֹן הַקֹדֶשׁ, *the Sacred Tongue*, to perpetuate the memory of her agonizing childbirth which resulted in her death. Jacob, however, wanted all twelve of his children to bear names in the Sacred Tongue, so he altered the name from the Aramaic (*Ben Oni*) to the Hebrew (*Binyamin*).

ON THE OTHER HAND, *Margalios HaYam* (*Sanhedrin* 38b §16) asserts that although Adam named all species of creatures for all

A Sacred Language for Sacred Matters time in Hebrew (see p. 39), he did not use *The Sacred Tongue* in his daily communication with mankind. The holiness of the language warranted its use only on matters

of utmost importance. For day-to-day matters Adam spoke Aramaic.

Rambam, in a responsa, carries this one step further and comments that even the Hebrew script known as *Ksav Ashuris* (used in the writing of a Torah Scroll) also possesses unique holiness. For this reason the Torah-style letters do not appear on any coins of the Holy Temple era. Modern *aleph-beis* script is visually different from the Torah-style letter for this same reason (*Margalios HaYam*, to *Sanhedrin* 21b §38).

Based on these facts, *R' David Cohen* suggests that Jews developed a sensitivity to the holiness inherent in a Hebrew name and began adding a *shem chol* [secular name] to their given Hebrew names. The Hebrew name, the *shem kodesh* (sacred name), would be used solely for religious matters such as being called to the Torah, marriage documents, etc., while the *shem chol* (secular name) would be used in day-to-day affairs. Indeed, in certain European communities it was the custom to announce at the child's *bris*, 'This child shall be called with the *shem kodesh* ... and the *shem chol* ... '

THERE ARE OTHERS, HOWEVER, who speculate that the use of a 'secular' name was simply pragmatic. Long before the Jews migrated

Winds of Anti-Semitism to Europe they found it necessary to have secular names in addition to their Hebraic names. In lands where winds of anti-Semitism blew strong and flames of hatred swept through Jewish towns and villages, a name which did not instantly identify an individual as a Jew was seen to be more practical both for doing business with fellow countrymen and in dealings with local municipalities.

Thus, in the Arab world, the Jewish merchant Avraham became Ibrahim; in Greece the shipping magnate Tovia [God is good] became Ariston and in the Latin West a salesman named Moshe became Moyses. In Hungary a government law forced Jews to select a secular name from an authorized list. These designated names had to be used by Jews in their day-to-day secular affairs and in all government registrations. Hence, a Hungarian Jew may have been called to the Torah as Yehudah, but in business he was known as Jano or Gyula. [Some Hungarian Jews chose names that were similar phonetically to the Hebrew names, such as Miksa for Moshe or Laos for Levi, while others made it a point to choose a secular name that had no connection at all to their Hebrew name, to demonstrate that

their secular name was merely an appendage that was forced upon them.]

It was quite the same with the Jews of Germany and other Yiddish-speaking communities throughout Europe. Since Yiddish is a variation of German, Jews found it was easier to get along with names like Zisskind (sweet child), Rayzel (little rose) or Faivel (light) than with Hebrew names. Mendel was acceptable in Bavarian and Austrian dialects; Baruch, which means blessed, became associated with Bendit, also a form of blessing (as in 'benediction'); and Eliyakim (God sustains) became bound with Getzel (also referring to God).

THERE WAS ONE MAJOR difference, however, between the secular names that Jews had in other countries and the Yiddish names they

Ladino — The Spanish Yiddish

took in Europe. European Jews, over the course of many generations, persisted in giving these Yiddish names to their children, very often without an accompanying Hebrew name. But where Jews spoke Ladino — a Judeo-Spanish dialect that was to Sephardic Jewry what Yiddish is to Ashkenazic Jewry — no child was ever given a Ladino name alone. Rather, a Hebrew and a Ladino name were always given together, e.g., Avraham Alberto or Menachem Miguel.

One can merely speculate that since Yiddish had become the unofficial 'Mother Tongue' of the Jewish people, names in that language were considered as authentic as Hebrew names.

In a recent responsa regarding secular names, *HaGaon Rabbi Moshe Feinstein,* שליט״א (*Igros Moshe, Orach Chaim,* IV §66), writes that if one is naming a child after a grandparent who had (only) a Yiddish name or a secular name which over the years has been accepted by Jews, it is proper to use that exact name for the infant. He notes that using the exact name is especially imperative when one is naming after a deceased parent when the Torah's command *'Honor your father and your mother'* is also a factor.

MANY ARE PUZZLED by the fact that some of our people's greatest sages, primarily the *Amoraim* of the Talmudic era, had and were

The Prominence of Aramaic

known by Aramaic names; Rav Papa, Rav Zevid, Mar Zutra and Mar Keshisha, are but a few examples.

HaGaon Rabbi Moshe Feinstein, שליט״א, in discussing this

problem (ibid.), cites *Yerushalmi Sotah* (7:2) that cautions 'Do not take the Aramaic language lightly, for indeed words of that language appear in all areas of Scripture.' R' Feinstein adds that both the Babylonian and Jerusalem Talmud are written in Aramaic, as is *Targum Onkelos*, and the *Kaddish*.

Thus, he suggests that perhaps names derived from that same language were on a significantly higher plateau than mere secular names.

Prelude to Redemption

שָׁנוּ רַבּוֹתֵינוּ: בִּזְכוּת ד' דְּבָרִים נִגְאֲלוּ יִשְׂרָאֵל מִמִּצְרַיִם: שֶׁלֹּא שִׁנּוּ אֶת שְׁמוֹתָן; שֶׁלֹּא שִׁנּוּ אֶת לְשׁוֹנָם; וְלֹא גִילוּ מִסְטוֹרִין שֶׁלָּהֶם; וְלֹא נִפְרְצוּ בָּעֲרָיוֹת.

> *Our Rabbis taught: In the merit of four acts of restraint were the Jews redeemed from Egypt — they did not change their names; they did not change their language; they did not disclose each other's secrets; and they did not break barriers of morality (Bamidbar Rabbah 20:21).*

In every generation, those who seek to assimilate to 'improve the lot of the Jews' eventually water down their Jewishness until the mixture of contrasting religious cultures and ideas becomes so diluted that the original tenets are no longer discernible. In order to survive, the uniqueness of Israel requires boundaries to assure its purity. Like water and oil, Jews and the nations of the world may exist side by side, but can never mix.

The *Maharal* (*Gevuros Hashem* 43) writes that had the Jews succumbed to social interrelationship with the Egyptians, they never would have left Egypt. Only by their self-imposed barrier of having different names, a different language, maintaining utmost privacy and a higher standard of morality did they merit that first redemption that made them into a nation. They were like the ailing patient whose immunological defense system had broken down. Were his body to weaken to the point that it could offer no resistance to further disease, deterioration would set in and there would be no chance for rehabilitation. Similarly had the unique individuality of Jews in Egypt been worn down, had there been no resistance to the malady of assimilation, the redemption would have been impossible and they could never have attained the holiness of their forefathers.

A MAN'S NAME IS HIS personal identity; his language is his communal bond. For the Jews in Egypt there was no breakdown of

Identity As Community

individual identity, nor was there a breach in communal identity. For this they were worthy of redemption and thus blossomed into nationhood.

While names are not the only way — perhaps not even the most important way — to preserve Jewish identity, the Egyptian experience cannot be ignored. Indeed, many leaders and laymen have worked strenuously to foster the adoption and use of Jewish names, especially in countries where the cultural and commercial pressures toward assimilation are powerful. May the pride in our unique identity bring us one step closer to the final redemption.

A Tapestry of Eights

The ritual of *bris milah*, which normally takes place on the eighth day of a boy's life, is replete with allusions and forthright statements dealing with the number eight.

AS THE INFANT IS brought into the room where the *bris* is to take place, the *mohel* announces בָּרוּךְ הַבָּא [*Baruch haba*], *Blessed is he*

Allusions To Eight *who has come.* The child is thus welcomed into the Jewish community. Numerically, the word הַבָּא, *haba*, is equal to 8 (ה=5; ב=2; א=1), alluding to the command that the *bris* be performed on the eighth day (*Avudraham*).

The knife used by the *mohel* in performing the circumcision is known as the אִזְמֵל, *izmail*. The Hebrew word is a combination of two words: אָז, *then*, and מֵל, *to circumcise*, with the first word again equal to 8 (א=1; ז=7), thereby implying: אָז, *then*, on the *eighth* day, מֵל, *circumcise* the child.

After the *bris*, a סְעוּדַת מִצְוָה, *festive meal in honor of the mitzvah*, is tendered. The source for such a celebration is found in the verse: וַיַּעַשׂ אַבְרָהָם מִשְׁתֶּה גָדוֹל בְּיוֹם הִגָּמֵל אֶת יִצְחָק, *Abraham made a great feast on the day Isaac was weaned* (*Genesis* 21:8). The words, בְּיוֹם הִגָּמֵל, *on the day he was weaned*, are homiletically rendered by *Tosafos* (*Shabbos* 130a) as בְּיוֹם ה"ג מֵל, *on the eighth day* (ה=5 plus ג=3 equals 8), מֵל, *he circumcised*; thus, Abraham made a banquet on the eighth day, when he circumcised Isaac.

The Talmud (*Megillah* 17b) notes that the reason the blessing of healing (רְפָאֵנוּ) was established as the eighth blessing in the daily *Shemoneh Esrei* prayer is that *milah*, which requires a healing process, is performed on the eighth day.

The circumcision itself, which is known as the בְּרִיתוֹ שֶׁל אַבְרָהָם אָבִינוּ, *the Covenant of our father Abraham*, was the eighth of the ten trials with which Abraham was tested to establish his loyalty to God (*Pirkei d'Rabbi Eliezer*, chap. 29).

Milah was the eighth commandment incumbent on Abraham; initially he was responsible for the seven Noachide laws that all people of the world are obligated to observe, but when he was ninety-nine years old, God commanded him with regard to *bris milah* (see *Maharsha, Menachos* 43b).

Why eight? Why is there a constant connection between *bris milah* and the number eight?

The Eighth Day

The Torah does not indicate why God chose the eighth day for *bris milah*. The Midrash (*Devarim Rabbah* 6:1), however, does cite a reason for waiting with the *bris* until that time. 'For God had pity on him, (the child) and waited until he had strength.'

THIS EXPLANATION IS interpreted in two ways. *Ohr HaChayim* (*Vayikra* 12:3 citing the *Zohar*) sees this strength as spiritual in **Spiritual Strength** nature. The child who exists seven full days before his *bris* gains a strength because of his contact with his first Sabbath. The elevation from secular time to spiritual time, that is inherent with the entrance of every Sabbath, gives the child a new-found strength. Having attained this, he is ready for his *bris*.

This is similar to the Midrash (*Vayikra Rabbah* 27:10) that relates a parable of a king who came to a city and decreed that all who wished to visit him would first have to pay their respects to the Queen. So too, all who wish to enter the everlasting covenant with God must first greet the Queen, the Sabbath (see *Shabbos* 119a). Since the law stipulates that the *bris* be on the eighth day, every child will have greeted the Sabbath Queen before having his *bris*.

RAMBAM, THOUGH, INDICATES that this strength is physical. He writes (*Moreh Nevuchim*, 3:49) that all living things are tender **Physical Strength** during the first week of life. Only after the completion of seven days can the child be included among those 'who enjoy the light of the world.' It is then that he has the required vitality to undergo circumcision (see also *Rabbeinu Bachya, Bereishis* 17:13).

Interestingly enough, 'the strength of the child on the eighth day' can be understood with regard to the child's coagulating factors

which classic medical studies have discovered to be at a peak around the eighth day of life.[1]

ADDITIONALLY, THE TALMUD NOTES the Torah's sensitivity to the feelings of the new parents: Why did the Torah ordain *milah* to

Consideration For The New Parents be performed on the eighth day? So that it should not be that all (who attend the *bris* festivities) are joyful while the father and mother are more restrained (*Niddah* 31b). [According to Biblical law conjugal relations are not permitted after the birth of a male child until the eighth day.]

A Deeper Significance

ASIDE FROM THESE reasons which relate specifically to the performance of the *bris* on the eighth day, the number eight has

Past, Present, Future deep spiritual implications as well. There seems to be a remarkable affinity for the number eight in the Jewish community's past, present and future, for the thread of eight is woven in a colorful tapestry of objects, events and regulations of Jewish law and lore.

Consider the following:

— The *tzitzis* (tassels) affixed to the *tallis* contain *eight* strands;
— Chanukah is celebrated for *eight* days;
— Immediately following the seven days of Succos we celebrate *Shemini Atzeres* [the *Eighth* day of Assembly], which is an independent festival (see *Yoma* 3a);
— Joshua, who circumcised the Jews as they entered Israel, (*Joshua* 5:2) was the *eighth* generation from Abraham, with whom

---

1. Factors of coagulation, which are synthesized in the liver, include plasma thromboplastic component (PTC), plasma thromboplastin antecedent (PTA) and prothrombin. Normally, in the full-term infant these factors are slightly below normal at birth. In the period between the second and sixth days of life there occurs a further, though temporary, fall in prothrombin, with the minimum levels at forty-eight to seventy-two hours (second and third days of life).

A gradual rise then begins to take place and by the eighth day the prothrombin level has not only reached the birth level, but surpassed it to above normal levels. Thus circumcision on the eighth day, with regard to blood coagulation, would seem to be the optimum time.

See 13th edition of *Holt's Diseases of Infancy and Childhood*, Holt, McIntosh and Barnet, p. 129 ff; and Owen, Hoffman, Ziffren and Smith, "Coagulation During Infancy," *Proceedings of the Society for Experimental Biology and Medicine*, Vol. 41, 1939, p. 181.

circumcision began (Abraham, Isaac, Jacob, Levi, Kehas, Amram, Moses, Joshua) [interestingly the Talmud (*Bava Basra* 16a) attributes the last *eight* verses of the Torah to Joshua himself];

— King David expressed himself twice (*Psalms* 6:1; 12:1) with the words לַמְנַצֵחַ עַל הַשְׁמִינִית, *To Him who causes victory, on the eight-stringed instrument* (see pp. 120-121);

— David also saw fit to write the longest of his Psalms (*Chapter 119*) with each letter of the Hebrew alphabet represented by *eight* consecutive verses;

— The High Priest was required to wear *eight* special vestments when performing the Temple service;

— An animal must be at least *eight* days old before it be brought as a sacrifice (*Leviticus* 22:27);

— The Talmud relates (*Arachin* 13b) that the harp of the Messiah will be of *eight* strings, as opposed to King David's harp, which had only seven strings.

A study of various events, numerous laws and assorted objects will reveal an understanding of the significance of the number *eight* in Jewish thought.

The Artist Beyond the Canvas

As the Children of Israel stood on the banks of the Sea of Reeds, they reflected upon the awesome events they had just witnessed. The roaring sea had been split asunder, the Jewish people had miraculously marched through two walls of water, and their Egyptians tormentors lay drowned, defeated and destroyed.

Standing there the Jews perceived with utter clarity God's absolute supremacy over all that exists. With the splitting of the sea it became evident that the natural world was totally dependent on the wishes of the One God. Moses was about to lead the Jews in an exuberant song in praise of God. But how does one start? What are the first words one utters when such monumental gratitude is in order?

אָז יָשִׁיר מֹשֶׁה, *Then Moses chose to sing* (*Exodus* 15:1) — the Song at the Sea was introduced with the seemingly simple word אָז, *then. Kli*

One Plus Seven *Yakar* (*Leviticus* 9:1) explains that the word אָז, composed of the letters א (=1) and ז (=7), alludes to the One God who has dominion over the entire universe that He created in seven days. One and seven, equaling

eight, symbolizes God's sovereignty.

Eight thus represents the holiness of God Himself. Unseen, but keenly felt, God is the Artist, and the world His canvas.

Channah, the mother of the prophet Samuel, put it succinctly, אֵין צוּר כֵּאלֹהֵינוּ׳, [literally] *there is no Rock like our God'* (*I Samuel* 2:2), which the Talmud (*Berachos* 10a) understands as אֵין צַיָּיר כֵּאלֹהֵינוּ, *there is no Artist like our God.*

This then is the forerunner of all things *eight*.

A Reminder To Commitment

IN THE COMMANDMENT OF *tzitzis*, one strand of bluish wool, *techeiles*, must appear alongside the seven white strands at each

Techeiles In Tzitzis corner of the four-cornered garment. The *techeiles* was colored with a dye painstakingly processed from a rare amphibian known as *chilazon*, which appeared only once in seventy years (see *Chullin* 89a and *Rashi*). [The identity of this creature is no longer known, which is why we do not wear a blue strand in our *tzitzis* today.]

Blue, the color of the ocean where the *chilazon* is to be found, is similar to the color of the sky where God reigns on His כֵּסֵּא הַכָּבוֹד, *Throne of Glory* (*Menachos* 43b). The blue strand therefore serves as a symbol of God's presence and our duty to him.

The Torah commands us to gaze at the *tzitzis* and thereby remember all the commandments (*Numbers* 15:39). Indeed, the one blue strand and the seven white ones (see *Rambam, Hilchos Tzitzis* 1:6) symbolize that the One God rules over everything in the world created in the Seven Days of Creation, similar to the אָז introducing the song that Moses and Israel sang.

[*Baal HaTurim* suggests that the eight strands serve to remind us to exercise our vigilance over the eight parts of the body that bring man sensations and temptations, and with which he may commit sins: the eyes, ears, nose, mouth, hands, feet, place of gender, and heart. A Jew must always bear in mind his purpose in life — to withstand the temptations of this world and sublimate every fiber of his being towards his service of God.]

Supernatural Wisdom

Maharal (Ner Mitzvah) writes that at the giving of the Torah itself the number eight had a special significance. From the day the

Omer meal-offering was brought in the Temple — the second day of Pesach — forty-nine days are counted. This commandment, known as *Sefiras HaOmer* (Counting of the Omer), culminates with the arrival of Shavuos, the festival that marks the Giving of the Torah at Sinai at the conclusion of a seven-week period following the Exodus.

These seven weeks of counting are to serve as a constant call to introspection and self-improvement for soon we are to reach the apex. Finally at the beginning of the eighth week, on Shavuos itself, we renew our acceptance of the Torah, the ultimate source of knowledge, and proclaim נַעֲשֶׂה וְנִשְׁמַע, *we will do and we will listen*, to the wishes of God, just as our forefathers did at Sinai.

It is interesting to note that just as קַבָּלַת הַתּוֹרָה, *the receiving of the Torah*, is directly related to eight, so too, the festival of Simchas Torah — which is the Celebration of the Torah — also coincides with Shemini Atzeres, which is the eighth day from the beginning of Succos.

MAHARAL WRITES THAT TORAH is the highest form of wisdom, and is unequaled in its profundity. No science from astronomy to

Torah — The Highest Wisdom

zoology, from the study of atoms and electrons to psychological and philosophical analyses, can compare in depth, insight, spiritual power and elevating emotional experience to the study of Torah. It is indeed לְמַעֲלָה מִן הַטֶּבַע, *above the plane of nature*. Thus, the number eight alludes to the Torah in particular and in general, to all things with a higher spiritual purpose. They, too, are on a plane above nature. King David (the *eighth* son of Jesse) symbolized the Torah with eight, for in his longest chapter of Psalms (*Chapter* 119), which speaks of the greatness of Torah, each letter of the Hebrew alphabet, with which the Torah is written, is the initial of eight consecutive verses. Furthermore, in Psalm 19 — after describing in seven verses the wonders of the galaxies in the universe, and the miracles of earth that bespeak the grandeur of God — in the eighth verse King David says that above all the splendor of the world is תּוֹרַת ה' תְּמִימָה מְשִׁיבַת נָפֶשׁ, *the Torah of HASHEM [which] is perfect; it restores the soul.*

Perhaps for this reason, then, Joshua, who was privileged to write a portion of the Torah, was allotted the number of verses that represents the eminence of Torah — eight.

Physical Light and Beyond

Maharal comments that our kindling of the Chanukah lights is not simply a commemoration of the miraculous kindling of the *Menorah* in the Temple, following the Hasmonean victory over the Syrian-Greeks. He understands the kindling of the Temple lights as merely a physical symbol of the true illumination of the nation of Israel, the Torah.

THE SYRIAN-GREEKS HAD NOT permitted the Jews to study Torah. The victory over this enemy meant not merely the freedom to

The Radiance of Chanukah light the *Menorah* daily, but the right to openly study Torah, the light that had served to guide all generations of Jews ever since

Sinai. The rekindling of the lights was not merely the kindling of wicks; it symbolized the resurgence of the Torah's radiance. The flame of Torah lit up the Hasmonean reign, shining through the darkness of despair.

Meiri (Shabbos 21b) and *Abudraham* (citing *Yerushalmi)* write that it took eight days for the *Kohanim* to replenish the supply of olive oil, and therefore God made the newly discovered flask of oil burn for eight days until new oil could be produced. But as the Talmud states: The same God who ordained that oil should burn could have made vinegar burn as well (*Taanis* 25a). He could have made the process of making oil from olives take five days, four days or even ten days — why eight? Because, in the number eight, there lies the symbolic uniqueness and holiness of Torah; thus Chanukah, which in essence is a festival of Torah's illumination, had to be eight days.

A Partner in Holiness

> *R' Shimon bar Yochai said: The Sabbath came before God and said, 'Master of the Universe, for each day of the week there is a partner [Sunday and Monday, Tuesday and Wednesday, etc.], but I have no partner.'*
>
> *God replied, 'The nation of Israel will be your partner' (Bereishis Rabbah 11:8).*

MAHARZU EXPLAINS THAT no man nor creature can exist alone in this universe; everyone and everything is dependent on someone or

Creation Was Complementary something else. For every creature, there is a counterpart to complement it. What one lacks is supplied by another. The shoemaker supplies shoes for the tailor who supplies clothes for the farmer who supplies milk for the shoemaker.

The Sabbath, which is holy, has no counterpart, for the other days of the week are mundane in nature, so God created an embodiment of holiness that would cleave to the holiness of the Sabbath. He created the nation of Israel.

The Jewish nation therefore became the eighth entity — the partner to the seventh entity, which was the Sabbath (*Ramban, Vayikra* 23:36). Soaring above the nations of the world, the holiness of the Jewish people is inextricably bound to the holiness of its partner, the Sabbath. Rising above the mundane, the Jewish nation, like the Sabbath, stands alone among its counterparts as the paragon of holiness that God bequeathed to this world.

The number eight, therefore, epitomizes the Jewish people themselves, the highest level of spirituality.

A Special Fondness

S'fas Emes observes that every Jewish holiday has its own unique *mitzvah* objects. Pesach has *matzah* and *maror;* Shavuos has a special Temple offering consisting of two loaves of wheat; Succos has the four species and the *succah* itself. On Shemini Atzeres, however, God said וְהָיִיתָ אַךְ שָׂמֵחַ, *and you shall be only joyful* (*Deuteronomy* 16:15). The only *mitzvah* of the holiday is happiness, to rejoice with God (see *Succah* 48a).

MIDRASH TANCHUMA (Pinchas 16) depicts Hashem's affection for His people with a beautiful parable:

God's Closest Friend A king made for his people a party which lasted seven days. At the end of the seven days he called his close friend and said, 'We have fulfilled our obligation to our countrymen. Now you remain here with me, and we will find a little food to share — just you and me.' So too, God said to Israel, 'The seventy *mussaf* sacrifices that you offered these past seven days of Succos were to benefit the nations of the world. And now, on the eighth day, Shemini Atzeres, bring just one sacrifice and you and I will enjoy it together.'

On Succos, judgment is passed on the world's rainfall (see *Rosh*

Hashanah 16a). The reservoirs of the cities, the irrigation systems of the farms, the nations' crops, the storms and the tides, are needed by all elements of the world (hence the seventy sacrifices representing the seventy nations of the world who are the recipients of God's beneficence). Shemini Atzeres, however, is reserved for the unique love between God and the Jewish nation alone.

SHEM MISHMUEL NOTES that Shemini Atzeres foreshadows the Messianic era when God will rejoice in intimacy with His people. **'Remain** The seven days of Succos, like the seven days of **With Me'** Creation, deal with the entire world; they represent the cycles of life before the coming of the Messiah. The eighth day, Shemini Atzeres, crystallizes the relationship between God and His people — 'Remain with Me one more day.'

It is natural, then, that on this day we, the bride, celebrate with the 'ring' that God, the Groom, has given us — His Torah. It is for this reason that Simchas Torah, a time of rejoicing with the Torah, coincides with Shemini Atzeres (S'fas Emes).

Thus, there is new meaning to the phrase: קוּדְשָׁא בְּרִיךְ הוּא אוֹרַיְתָא וְיִשְׂרָאֵל חַד הוּא, God, the Torah and Israel are one (Zohar, Acharei 73a). They are all intertwined through the concept of 'eight', manifesting together the bond of love between God and His nation (R' David Cohen).

The Eighth Generation Comes Home

A condition of the covenant of milah that God made with Abraham stipulated that if the Jews observed the mitzvah of circumcision they would be given the land of Israel (Genesis 17:8). Thus the arrival of the Jews in Eretz Yisrael fulfilled God's promise to a people that had observed its obligation to Him.

STARTING WITH ABRAHAM, THE Jews had practiced bris milah for seven generations (Abraham, Isaac, Jacob, Levi, Kehas, Amram, **Abraham to** Moses). Although many Jews in the desert did **Joshua** not circumcise their children because of the unique health hazard that existed there (see Yevamos 71b-72a), the Levites scrupulously maintained the unbroken chain of observance. Now, as Israel entered the Promised Land, Joshua, who led the eighth generation, organized them all, to continue the observance of this great precept (see Joshua 5).

This historical phenomenon is used to interpret an enigmatic verse: תֶּן חֵלֶק לְשִׁבְעָה וְגַם לִשְׁמוֹנָה, *Bestow distinction to seven and also to eight* (*Ecclesiastes* 11:2). The *Midrash* suggests that *seven* refers to the generation that Moses circumcised, for just before the Exodus, Moses ordered the circumcision of that entire generation. It was in that merit that they were redeemed on the first night of Passover (see *Shemos Rabbah* 17:3 and 19:5). That generation was the seventh from Abraham, while *eight* refers to the next generation, the one that Joshua circumcised, the first people to live in Israel as Jews.

How beautiful it must have been to be among those very first people who savored the sweet thrill of a promise fulfilled! What joy and ecstasy they must have experienced when they fulfilled the *mitzvah* in whose merit they had come home.

Eight — the number that depicts the bond between God and His people, the number that implies holiness, that betokens the perfection that Jews strive for — was the number of the generation that entered Israel. It was fitting, then, that Joshua, the new leader and teacher of Israel who himself had merited recording eight verses in the Bible, should be the one to perform *bris milah*, the eighth-day *mitzvah*.

Symphony of Redemption

There is a beautiful Yiddish melody that poses the question which Jews have sought to answer for generations: וואָס וועט זיין וועט זיין וועט מָשִׁיחַ וועט קומען?, *What will be when the Messiah will come?* Many Biblical verses and Talmudic passages offer us a glimpse of the hallowed Messianic era.

The Talmud (*Arachin* 13b) teaches that the harp of the Messiah will be of eight strings, as opposed to the conventional harp used in the Temple which was of seven strings. To understand the significance of the additional string one must first comprehend the meaning of seven.

FROM MARRIAGE WHICH IS celebrated with seven blessings on each day of seven days following the wedding, to death which is

Cycles of Seven observed with seven days of mourning, a cycle that is complete is represented by seven. The Midrash (*Genesis* 32:7) relates that, for seven days prior to the Flood, God Himself mourned the impending destruction of His creations.

A week is seven days; the *shmittah* cycle is seven years; there are seven heavens; man goes through seven stages of life (see *Tanchuma Pikudei* 3); and King Solomon wrote that there are seven pillars of wisdom (*Proverbs* 9:1).

In the physical world, a cycle, a full measure, is seven. In the metaphysical, the higher spiritual plane is represented by eight (see R' *Hirsch, Timeless Torah* p. 404). In the Messianic era the world will attain spiritual perfection when Man's Evil Inclination ceases to exist. This future epoch will herald a sublime existence far and beyond the life we now know. It will be an existence superior to that which the number seven represents; it will be perfect, like things represented by eight.[1]

Maharsha (Arachin 13b) writes that the additional string on the harp of the Messiah represents the new rapture that will be enjoyed by Jews in the Messianic era. The freedom from subservience to the nations of the world (שִׁעְבּוּד מַלְכָיּוֹת), a phenomenon unknown to them throughout the millennia of Exile, will bring 'music to their ears.'

Israel will be free to dedicate itself to a purely spiritual life. It will not have to concern itself with opinion polls in the democracies of the West, or the whims and wishes of the tyrant politicians of the East. The Jewish Nation will be dependent solely on the will of God. This new dimension is represented by the eighth string.

The world, as we know it, will have run its course like the first seven notes in the musical scale. Beyond that is the eighth note, an octave higher. It is similar in sound to the first note, but is on a higher level. Similarly, when the Messiah comes, the world will continue to function but on a higher level of existence.

YET, THERE WAS A TIME when Jews enjoyed a higher level of intimacy with God, during the period of the Holy Temple, the

Eights in the Temple dwelling place of the Divine Presence. *Rabbeinu Bachya* notes (*Leviticus* 9:1) that the number eight had great significance among various items in the Temple service. The High Priest wore eight vestments; eight musical instruments accompanied the Levites in the singing of the

---

1. It is noteworthy that the word תָּמִים, *perfect*, is used in several verses that relate to the number eight:

הִתְהַלֵּךְ לְפָנַי וֶהְיֵה תָמִים, *Go before Me and be perfect* (*Genesis* 17:1), refers to *bris milah*;

תָּמִים יַקְרִיבֶנּוּ לִפְנֵי ה', *perfect* [i.e., without physical blemish] *shall he bring it before*

Psalms; animals could be offered as sacrifices only after they were eight days old; there were eight poles for carrying the vessels in the sanctuary; and there were eight varieties of spices used in the making of the שֶׁמֶן הַמִּשְׁחָה, *anointment oil.*

It was for this reason, suggests *Kli Yakar,* that the inauguration of Aaron and his sons as *Kohanim* took place on the eighth day of the Tabernacle's dedication. Aaron and his sons learned in seven days all that was necessary to know regarding the performance of the Divine service. It was only because of the inherent holiness of the *eighth day* that their inauguration was held then.

Eight thus indicates an elevated level of life dedicated to God and the Jewish nation (*R' Hirsch*).

Bris Milah — Epitome of Eight

THE TALMUD RELATES that King David felt secure surrounded by seven *mitzvos:* the *mezuzah* on his doorpost, the two *tefillin* on his

Surrounded by Mitzvos hand and head, and the four fringes of his *tzitzis.* But when he entered the bath house, there was no *mezuzah,* and he could not wear his *tefillin* or *tzitzis.* Suddenly he felt insecure, devoid of *mitzvos.*

Then he remembered the eighth *mitzvah,* that was always with him — *bris milah.* When King David emerged from the bath house he exclaimed, לַמְנַצֵּחַ עַל הַשְּׁמִינִית, *To Him Who causes victory because of the eighth* (Psalms 12:1) — i.e., the *mitzvah* of *milah* [in which the number eight figures so prominently] indelibly sealed on his body forever (*Maharsha, Menachos* 43b).

The act of *milah* vividly portrays the eternal bond between God and His people. By bearing the irrevocable sign of the covenant throughout one's life, the Jew remains aware that the moral perfection demanded of the members of the family of Abraham is of a higher standard than that expected from the rest of mankind. A Jew must not perceive of himself as one who belongs to the heavens in spirit, but to the earth with his body. Serving God merely with intellect while allowing one's body to succumb to his baser desires is a negation of the intent of *bris milah* (*R' Hirsch, Timeless Torah*).

HASHEM (*Leviticus* 3:1), refers to a Temple sacrifice which is required to be at least eight days old (see *Leviticus* 22:27);

תּוֹרַת ה' תְּמִימָה מְשִׁיבַת נָפֶשׁ, *The Torah of* HASHEM *is perfect; it restores the soul* (*Psalms* 19:8), refers to Torah, which as explained above is represented by the number eight.

PLACING THE אוֹת בְּרִית קוֹדֶשׁ, *the sign of the Holy Covenant,* in an area of the body that responds to man's strongest physical desire is

The Message of Milah not contradictory at all. To the contrary, the message is to be aware of the potential pitfalls, and by conscious effort strive for perfection by overcoming them.

God's Dominion as implied in the word אָז; *spirituality* as envisioned in the creation of Israel; *the loving bond* as indicated by Shemini Atzeres; *living above our natural instincts* as indicated by Torah — these are concepts that are portrayed in entities of eight. Because they are all inherent in the act and understanding of *milah,* the *bris* warrants being performed on the eighth day.

Abraham was called אָב לִשְׁמוֹנָה, *the father to eight,* firstly, because he was the first one to perform *bris milah* on the eighth day (when circumcising his son Isaac); secondly, because he had eight children, Ishmael, Isaac, and six children from Keturah (*Midrash Shochar Tov* 5:5); and perhaps most of all, because he mastered the symbolism of eight, living a life of perfection and of an elevated status.

Our adherence to this basic precept of *bris milah* merited our first redemption, from Egypt. Our continued adherence to it will merit our final redemption as well (*Pirkei d'Rabbi Eliezer* 29).

It will thus be at this future redemption, that all Jews, like musicians in an orchestra, will follow in perfect harmony the great conductor, the Messiah, who will perform his composition of glory on his harp of eight strings.

❊ ❊ ❊

The Sandak's Role:
A Study in Contrasts

At every *bris milah* one man is honored with the role of *sandak*. This man has been given the highest and most prestigious honor of the *bris milah* ceremony, namely, to hold the child during the *bris*.

THE FUNCTION OF *SANDAK* is not merely a technical one of assisting the *mohel* by holding the child in place. Through his

A Shield of Holiness

participation, the *sandak* bridges the centuries since the commandment of *milah* was given by God to Abraham. Cradling the infant on his lap and engulfing him in his *tallis*, the *sandak* casts a shield of holiness that binds the infant irrevocably to the great heritage of his forefathers.

The *Maharil* (cited by *Rama, Yoreh Deah* 265:11) writes that the role of the *sandak* is of such prominence that it is akin to the *Kohen* burning the קְטֹרֶת [*ketores*], *incense*, on the Temple Altar. But why should the *sandak's* seemingly simple task be equated with the *ketores*, a service that the Torah (*Exodus* 30:10) terms 'Holiest of Holies?' And conversely, how is the Divine service of incense burning similar to the act of *bris milah*?

A Crowning Glory

As the rays of the rising sun began to cast their glow over the holy city of Jerusalem, the *Kohen* in the Temple inaugurated each new day with the morning *ketores* offering. The sweet aroma that permeated the Temple signified a new day of service and closeness to God (see *Pesachim* 59a).

At day's end, as the sun dipped westward over Jerusalem, a similar *ketores* offering was made. This time the *ketores* was a culmination rather than an inaugural; it was a final act that crowned the Divine service that had come before it.

Indeed, the very first time *ketores* was brought on the Altar, it was an act of culmination. Moses had completed construction of the Tabernacle in the Wilderness, the utensils had been crafted, the sacrifices had been brought and set on the Altar, the table with its twelve loaves of *Panim* Bread had been arranged, the Menorah lit...but still there was a void, for the Divine Presence did not descend until the *ketores* was burned (*Midrash Tanchuma, Tetzaveh* 15).

An Act of Culmination...

The very first time a *bris milah* was performed, it too was an act of culmination. God told Abraham (*Genesis* 17:1): 'Go before me and be תָמִים, *perfect.*' Up to that point Abraham had lived most of his life in acknowledgment and service to God. His life of benevolent kindness to mankind was inspirational to all who benefited from it. Yet only with this final act of *bris milah* did he merit that God called him 'perfect.' All that had come before it would be crowned with the act of circumcision — the בְּרִית קֹדֶשׁ, *bris kodesh* (holy covenant).

THE *BRIS* ON AN infant is the culmination of his creation. First there is the wonder of conception; then the miracle of the formation

The Wonder of Creation of the embryo as the mother nurtures the new being within her, and finally a child is born. The child is complete, but he is not yet תָמִים, *perfect.* For this too-often-taken-for-granted miracle of birth to be considered perfect, there is one final step, *bris milah.*

The construction of the Tabernacle with all its genius and grandeur did not receive the Divine Presence until the final act of the *ketores* offering by Moses. Similarly the construction of man does not achieve the status of perfection until the act of *milah,* the sign of the holy covenant, is implanted on the body.

...And Inauguration

Yet, like the morning *ketores,* the *bris* is an inaugural ceremony as well. It is not an end but a beginning — the start of the child's spiritual development and the beginning of his fulfillment of God's life-designation for man, the adherence to Torah and *mitzvos.*

A PHILOSOPHER ONCE ASKED Rabbi Hoshaya, 'If *milah* is so favorable in God's eyes, why isn't man born circumcised?' Rabbi Hoshaya replied that everything that was created requires development. Plants must be sweetened, wheat must be milled and even man needs to be perfected (*Bereishis Rabbah* 11:6).

Born Circumcised

Thus the message of *bris milah* is that man must strive, improve and refine. At the outset of a Jew's life, the amending process begins. For Abraham the act of *milah* was a conclusion — the attainment of perfection. To later generations, it was אוֹת בְּרִית, *a sign of the covenant*, that God made with Abraham, that reminds us to strive towards the perfection that Abraham reached.

Like the *Kohen* who offers the *ketores* on the Temple's inner Altar, the *sandak* presents the child for circumcision as he holds him for the *mohel*. Both the *Kohen* and the *sandak* participate in proceedings that simultaneously reflect back and look forward.

The Elevation and the Unity

When Abraham circumcised himself and his entire household, he left the foreskins in the sun. Although they rotted, God considered their odor to be like the fragrance of קְטֹרֶת, *frankincense*, that was burned upon the Altar.

God said, 'When the descendants of this man commit transgressions and evil deeds, I will remember this odor in their favor and will be filled with compassion for them and convert the Attribute of Justice into the Attribute of Mercy' (*Shir HaShirim Rabbah* 4:6).

We know that God metes out recompense to humanity with the principle of מִדָּה כְּנֶגֶד מִדָּה, *measure for measure*. What is it then about *bris milah* that causes the turnabout from harsh judgment to soft compassion? Why and how does this holy covenant cause God to look away from the evil of man and extend His benevolence to him?

ONE OF THE ELEVEN SPICES and herbs required for the incense mixture was חֶלְבְּנָה, *galbanum* (*Exodus* 30:34), a foul-smelling substance. One would think that its inclusion in the incense should have been considered disgraceful to God. However, the

A Blend of Opposites

Torah prescribed that galbanum be included with the pleasantly scented spices.

R' Bachya (Exodus 30:34) compares the inclusion of galbanum in the incense to that of the *aravah* [willow twigs] among the four species used on Succos (see *Vayikra Rabbah* 30:12). The *esrog*, which has both a sweet odor and a good taste, represents the Jew who has both Torah and good deeds; the date palm from which the *lulav* is taken has tasteful fruit but no smell, symbolizing those who possess Torah knowledge but lack in good deeds. The *hadas* [myrtle twig], with its pleasant smell and no taste, refers to people of good deeds but no Torah knowledge. The willow, which has neither taste nor odor, alludes to those Jews who have neither Torah knowledge nor good deeds. Nevertheless, God said, 'Bind them all together in one unit, and one will atone for the other. If you do so, I shall be exalted'; for, as the Midrash interprets the verse, *Amos* 9:6: 'The Builder of Heaven is exalted when the disparate groups of humanity are united' (see *Maharzu, Vayikra Rabbah* 30:12).

The Hebrew root קשר means *to bind*; its Aramaic equivalent is קטר [see, e.g., *Targum* to *Genesis* 38:28], a word reminiscent of קְטֹרֶת. Thus *ketores* may be interpreted homiletically as the binding and uniting of all aspects.

R' Bachya explains that this follows the dictum of the Sages, כָּל יִשְׂרָאֵל עֲרֵבִים זֶה לָזֶה, *all Israel is responsible for one another.* All Jews, collectively, are like the limbs of a single body, each affected by the action of another. Consequently, the righteous Jew cannot turn his back on the sinner, but must reach out and include him as part of the congregation that stands before God. This in turn will bring the sinner to repentance and thereby exalt God. For He is exalted when evil recognizes the truth of goodness and changes for the better.

This same sentence (*Amos* ibid.) is used by the Talmud (*Kreisos*, 6b) to explain the inclusion of galbanum in the incense. Galbanum, too, symbolizes the sinner in Jewish society; and it is imperative that he be included along with the righteous as they stand before Him.

All Jewry As One

IT IS FOR THIS REASON also that at the start of the *Kol Nidre* service on Yom Kippur eve the *chazzan* begins with the introduction: עַל דַּעַת הַמָּקוֹם, וְעַל דַּעַת הַקָּהָל, אָנוּ מַתִּירִין לְהִתְפַּלֵּל עִם הָעֲבַרְיָנִים, *With the consent of the Omnipresent, and with the consent of the congregation, we permit ourselves to pray together with the transgressors* (see *Tur Orach Chaim* 619).

A Fusion of Forces

The act of *bris milah* likewise is a symbiosis of bad and good, an inherent bonding of two diametrically opposed forces, which fuse to exalt God.

The Evil Inclination of licentiousness and the desire for sensual gratification lead to the breakdown of barriers of decency and the dissipation of standards of morality. Man's first sin, eating from the Tree of Knowledge, was brought about by the cunning design of a lustful serpent for Eve. He therefore coaxed her to disobey her Creator (see *Rashi, Genesis* 3:1).

YET, A BY-PRODUCT OF this very same drive is that man has the ability to accomplish something that is beyond the power of any **A Most Powerful Drive** other human function — to draw a soul down to this world and produce a living human being (see *Waters of Eden*, by R' Aryeh Kaplan, p. 43).

God therefore commanded Abraham to place the holy mark of circumcision on the organ through which the perpetuation of life is accomplished, because Abraham and his descendants, the chosen people, would bring the holiest souls down to this earth.

Rambam (Moreh Nevuchim 3:49) writes that the removal of the foreskin lessens the desire for sensual gratification. *Milah* thus represents the potential within every Jew to dominate his physical desires and direct them toward the purpose for which God intended them (*Ramban, Genesis* 17:9).

KING DAVID EXCLAIMED (*Psalms* 119:162), שָׂשׂ אָנֹכִי עַל אִמְרָתֶךָ כְּמוֹצֵא שָׁלָל רָב, *I rejoice over Your word like one who finds abundant* **Man's Loftiest Purpose** *spoils.* The Talmud (*Shabbos* 130a) homiletically interprets this as referring to *milah.* *Meshech Chochmah (Lech Lecha)* explains that the acquisition of booty is a greater cause for joy than the mere discovery of treasure; the latter brings its discoverer new-found wealth, while the former not only accomplishes that, but also depletes the enemy's resources. Thus, *milah*, as understood by *Rambam* (ibid.), represents man's loftiest purpose — to sublimate that which seems inherently evil and direct it toward a spiritual accomplishment.

It was for this reason that the odor emitted by the foreskins of Abraham and his household was akin to that of *ketores*, whose smell was fragrant, despite the fact that it included the putrid galbanum. For like the Jew combining the *aravah* among the Four Species, and like the *chazzan* on Yom Kippur including the transgressor in his prayers, both the *sandak* offering the infant for *milah* and the *Kohen* offering the *ketores* on the Altar represent this kind of elevation to goodness. In this turnabout lies the cause of God's conversion of harsh judgment to soft compassion.

May our generation be among those which benefit from this generosity.

חנוך לנער ‏

Chanoch Lanaar

• Insights and Allusions

* ע״ש זקני הרב חנוך העניך בן הרב בן ציון זצ״ל

שָׁלוֹם זָכָר / Shalom Zachar

(See *Laws* §19-21)

On the first Friday night after a boy is born, it is customary to gather in the home of the newborn for a שָׁלוֹם זָכָר, *Shalom Zachar*, i.e., a celebration in honor of the newborn. There are some today, however, who hold the *Shalom Zachar* in a synagogue or at the home of a grandparent.

Some relate the *Shalom Zachar* to the celebration known in the talmud (*Bava Kama* 80a) as *Yeshua HaBen, the salvation of the son* from the rigors of birth (see *Taz, Yoreh Deah* 265:13).

Various reasons have been suggested for the origin of this custom and the name *Shalom Zachar*:

• The name is based on the Talmudic dictum (*Niddah* 31b): When a *zachar* [male] is born, *shalom* [peace] comes to the world. Hence, the name *Shalom Zachar* (*Edus LeYisrael;* see *Maharsha* to *Niddah* 31b).

• Every Jewish male has the potential to develop into a Torah scholar. And as the Talmud (*Berachos* 64a) states: Torah scholars bring an abundance of peace [*shalom*] to the world. Thus, on the Sabbath, when we enjoy restful peace and tranquillity, we celebrate with the hope that through this *zachar* and his study of Torah the world will merit the blessing of *shalom*.

• While a baby develops within the womb, an angel teaches him the entire Torah. Just before birth, the angel touches the child on his mouth causing him to forget all that he has learned (*Niddah* 30b). The gathering in the home of the newborn is to console him for the Torah that he has forgotten (*Taz* ibid.). And since the baby is 'in mourning' for the Torah he has lost, lentils or beans (*kitniyos*) are usually served at the *Shalom Zachar*, since these foods are customarily eaten by mourners (*Zocher HaBris* 3:6). It is for this reason that *arbes* (chick peas) are commonly served at a *Shalom Zachar*.

Additionally, nuts are served, in accordance with *Tikunei Zohar* (*Tikun* 24) which compares the foreskin removed by circumcision to the shell which surrounds the nut [and is subsequently discarded].

• Some speculate that the proper name of the celebration is שָׁלוֹם זָכוֹר, *Shalom Zachor* [lit. *peace, remembering*]. Based on the Talmudic teaching cited above that the baby is made to forget his Torah, we gather at the home of the infant on the Sabbath — about which is

written: זָכוֹר, *Remember the day of Sabbath (Exodus 20:8)* — and pray that he will indeed study the Torah and 'Remember' what he has forgotten *(Migdal Oz, intro. §15)*.

• The *Shalom Zachar* is held on Friday night for that is when people are more apt to be at home, [and available to participate in the gathering] *(Terumas HaDeshen 269)*.

Additionally, the Midrash *(Vayikra Rabbah 27:10)* relates the parable of a king who visited a province and decreed that anyone wishing to have an audience with him personally, must first pay respects to the royal matron. So too, one who wishes to enter into everlasting covenant with God [the King] must first celebrate with the Sabbath Queen *(Taz ibid.)*.

⊱§ לֵיל שִׁימוּרִים / Vach Nacht
The Night Before the Bris
(See *Laws* §23-28)

⊷§ Traditionally, the night before the *bris* is known as לֵיל שׁמוּרים or *Vach Nacht* [Night of the Vigil]. The 'vigil' is held to ward off anything that may interfere with the *bris*, for as the *Midrash* states: The merit of *bris milah* is so great that it safeguards Jews from *Gehinnom (Tana Dvei Eliyahu Zuta, 25)*, therefore the Accuser [Satan] and his cohort of מַזִּיקִין, *evil* or *harmful spirits*, wish that the *bris* not be performed *(Bris Avos)*.

• As part of this vigil, the men of the family study Torah in the house where the infant sleeps. A list of passages that are related to *milah*, and apropos for study on the *Vach Nacht* follows:

SCRIPTURE	TALMUD
Genesis chapter 17	Shabbos chapter 19 / 130a-137b
Genesis 21:1-8	Nedarim 3:1 / 31b-32a
Exodus 4:24-26	Yevamos 8:1 / 70a-74a
Exodus 19:5	
Leviticus 12:1-3	
Numbers 23:10	MIDRASH RABBAH
Numbers 25:10-12	Bereishis chapters 45,47,48
Deuteronomy 10:16	Shemos 15:12
Deuteronomy 30:6	Shemos 17:3
Deuteronomy 33:8-11	Shemos 19:4,5
Joshua 5:1-9	Vayikra 27:10
	Bamidbar 12:8
SHULCHAN ARUCH	Bamidbar 14:12
Yoreh Deah chapters 260-268	Bamidbar 15:12
Orach Chaim 331	Devarim 6:1

• Children are brought to the crib of the infant, where they recite the first chapter of the *Shema* and the verse הַמַּלְאָךְ הַגֹּאֵל, *May the angel who redeems ...* (*Genesis* 48:16). The children are then given candies, other sweets and, sometimes, coins.

The Talmud (*Berachos* 5a) teaches : If one recites the *Shema* at his bedside, it is as if he holds a double-edged sword in his hand, i.e., the *Shema* serves as a protection against harmful spirits (*Rashi*, ibid.). The Talmud derives this from the verse רוֹמְמוֹת אֵל בִּגְרוֹנָם וְחֶרֶב פִּיפִיּוֹת בְּיָדָם, *The lofty praises of God are in their throat,* [i.e., they recite the *Shema*] and a double-edged sword is in their hand (*Psalms* 149:6). This same verse alludes to the *izmail,* the *milah* knife, which traditionally is doubled-edged (see below, page 98).

• Some customarily place the *izmail* under the pillow of the infant the night before the *bris,* reasoning that this is a protection against harmful spirits.

Others contend that the custom of placing the *izmail* under the infant began because it is commendable to begin preparations at night for a *mitzvah* that will take place the following morning. Furthermore, by always bringing the *izmail* to the home of the infant the night before the *bris,* one avoids the problem that could arise if a *mohel* forgot to bring it there on Friday in preparation for a Sabbath *bris.* Since it is not permitted to carry in a public thoroughfare on the Sabbath, it is a precautionary measure to always bring the *izmail* the night before (*Bris Avos*).

נֵרוֹת / Candles

(See *Laws* §30-31)

It is customary to have candles burning at the *bris* ceremony. This adds dignity and beauty to the *mitzvah* and is a universal tradition.

• The candles are also a commemoration of the times when Jews, because of persecution, could not make public announcements regarding a *bris.* Instead, they placed candles in the windows of their home as a covert signal that a *bris* was to take place there (see *Sanhedrin* 32b, with *Rashi* and *Tosafos*). The candles thus symbolize the courage and dedication that Jews have always had for the *mitzvah* of *milah* (*Edus LeYisrael*).

• Some cite a reason for candles based on the verse לַיְּהוּדִים הָיְתָה אוֹרָה ... וְשָׂשׂן, *For the Jews there was light ... and joy* (*Esther* 8:16). The word 'joy' refers to the *mitzvah* of *milah* (see below s.v. *Tefillin*) and the word 'light' is a reference to candles (*Migdal Oz*).

• Every child is a new spark of life, and the spark within a human being is his God-given soul. Thus the verse, נֵר ה' נִשְׁמַת אָדָם, *The candle of God*

is the soul of man (Proverbs 20:27), may be an additional source for lighting candles at a *bris,* for it commemorates the entrance of the newborn's soul into this world (see *Tanchuma, Behaalosecha, 3; Zohar, Shelach).*

⋞ Wimple

⋞ In German communities, the infant to be circumcised is brought into the room where the *bris* will take place with a long rectangular cloth wrapped around his clothes or over the pillow on which he lays. This special piece of material is eventually made into a *wimple.*

In the weeks and months following the *bris,* this piece of material is painted or embroidered with ornate designs. These include the child's name and numerous Judaic artifacts such as a *succah,* a marriage canopy, Torah Scroll, etc. It may even contain Scriptural verses.

When the child is old enough, he is brought to the synagogue (this is known as *Shulentragen*) on a day when the Torah is read and his father and grandfather are honored with the raising or rolling together of the Torah Scroll. The small boy then presents the wimple to the *golel* (the one who rolls together and binds the Scroll) who wraps and ties the Torah Scroll with it. The child is then brought to the rabbi for a blessing. The wimples are stored in the synagogue where they are used, in rotation, for tying the Torah scrolls.

⋞ Kvatter and Kvatterin
Colloquially: Godparents
(See *Laws* §36-39)

⋞ Two people — one male, the other female (usually a married couple) — are customarily given the honor of bringing the child to the room where the *bris* will take place, and then returning him to his mother after the *bris.* They are known as the *kvatter* and *kvatterin.*

• The origin of the word *kvatter* is unclear. Several etymologies have been suggested:

• Some derive the word *kvatter* from the German term *Gevatter* which means 'intimate friend' (*Zocher HaBris* 19:1). [The word *Gevatter* in German is also used to mean godfather and for this reason many people mistakenly refer to the *kvatter* and *kvatterin* as godfather and godmother. It should be noted, however, that the words *Gevatter* and 'godfather,' despite their phonetic similarity, are totally unrelated etymologically. And certainly there are neither legal nor traditional ramifications or responsibilities that go along with this honor.]

• Another possible etymology is based on the tradition that those

involved with the *bris* are likened to the *Kohen* who performed the incense-burning in the Temple (see p. 65). The Talmud (*Kreisos* 6b) describes the incense as קוֹטֵר וְעוֹלֶה [*koter v'oleh*], *burning and ascending to heaven.* Perhaps, over a period of time, the Hebrew word קוֹטֵר [which was printed without vowels] was misread as קוּוְטֵר with an additional וּ, resulting in the term *kvatter* (*Aruch HaShulchan, Yoreh Deah* 265:35).

• *Bris Avos* finds the roots of this word in the *mohel's* practice of wrapping the child's legs in diapers or small sheets so that he would not kick and interfere with the circumcision. These wrappings, traditionally supplied by those honored with bringing the baby to the *bris,* were called קְפוֹטוֹרִין [see *Tanchuma, Mikeitz* §10 for a similar use of this word] or *kafotrin gezeug* [wrapping materials] which became corrupted to *kvatterin gezeug,* leading to the names *kvatter* and *kvatterin* for the bearers.

• Another opinion is that the word *kvatter* is actually a conjunction of two words, one Hebrew, the other Yiddish: כָּבוֹד [*kavod*], *honor,* and טיר [*tir*], door. This is a reference to one who is given honor at the door, from where he brings the child into the room where the *bris* will take place (*Levushei Michlol,* cited in *Ohel Rachel*).

כִּסֵּא שֶׁל אֵלִיָהוּ / Throne of Elijah

(See *Laws* §40-43)

◆§ The custom of designating a Throne of Elijah dates back to the Geonic period (6th-10th centuries) and is based on *Pirkei d'Rabbi Eliezer* (ch. 29). From the time that the Jews entered *Eretz Yisrael* under the leadership of Joshua, they had been diligent in the practice of *bris milah.* However, after King Solomon died, and the Jewish kingdom was divided in two, the division living in Samaria, known as the kingdom of Ephraim, ceased circumcising their infants.

Elijah, a prophet of the time, was incensed at his fellow Jews and cried out to God, '*They have forsaken Your covenant*' (*I Kings* 19:10). Elijah then swore that he would restrain the heavens from giving rain or dew. God acceded to his oath, and told Elijah that because he had championed the *mitzvah* of circumcision, he would be privileged to be present at every *bris* that Jews would perform (*Prishah, Yoreh Deah* 265:25).

• Others interpret Elijah's presence at every *bris* as a form of rebuke. Because Elijah spoke harshly of God's people, he would be forced to attend every *bris,* where he would see that Jews indeed do fulfill the *mitzvah* of *bris milah* diligently (*Zohar, Lech Lecha*).

• *Bnei Yisaschar* writes (*Tishrei* §4):
   I have heard in the name of the Midrash, although I have been unable

to locate the source, that Elijah agreed to come to all circumcisions with the understanding that he would be given the power to forgive the sins of all those present. God agreed, and therefore anyone near the Throne of Elijah has his sins forgiven.

• It is related that when R' Nissim Gaon was to be circumcised, his father R' Yaakov brought him to the synagogue, where he held him in his arms and sat on the designated chair after which R' Yaakov placed him on the *sandak's* knees. The assembled, having never witnessed this custom before, questioned R' Yaakov. He replied that it was a tradition from the sages of long ago that Elijah sat on the chair designated for him, at the *bris,* and so he had sat there with his child so that they would be blessed by Elijah. [A similar story is told regarding R' Yitzchak Luria, the famed *Arizal.*]

• R' Shlomo Kluger once attended a *bris,* but the family seemed in no hurry to begin the procedure. There was no apparent reason for their delay for the *mohel* and baby were both present. The rav inquired about the delay and was told that the father of the child was incurably ill and very near death, and that local custom called for delaying the *bris,* until the last possible minute, so that if the father died, the baby would bear his name.

The rav grew upset and insisted that the baby immediately be taken to the father's bedside and that the *bris* be performed there without delay. After the *bris,* the father began his recovery which eventually was complete. When people started speaking of the miraculous cure effected by R' Shlomo Kluger, the rav replied: 'I am no miracle worker, it is merely that when Elijah, the angel of the covenant, came to heal the child, he healed the sick father as well.'

◈§ סַנְדָּק / Sandak ◈§

(See *Laws* §54-58)

◈§ The word *sandak* originates from the Greek word *suntekos,* which means 'companion of child,' or from *sundikos,* 'patron of child.'

• The *sandak's* role is based on *Midrash Tehillim* (35): King David said to God, 'With all parts of my physical substance I serve You. On my head I wear *tefillin* ... with my lips I pray ... upon my neck I wear *tzitzis* ... and as *sandak,* I place children on my knees during their circumcisions ...'

• Furthermore, the role of the *sandak* at a *bris* is equated with that of the *Kohen* who offered the daily incense [קְטוֹרֶת] on the Temple Altar (*Rama, Yoreh Deah* 265:11, citing *R' Peretz* and *Maharil;* see *Darkei Moshe* ibid.; see also above, page 65).

• This comparison of the *sandak* to the *Kohen* has generated a dispute

between halachic authorities: Based on the proximity of two phrases (*Deuteronomy* 33:10-11) — יָשִׂימוּ קְטוֹרָה בְּאַפֶּךָ ... בָּרֵךְ ה' חֵילוֹ ... — [*the Kohanim*] *place incense before You ... May God bless his possessions* — the Talmud (*Yoma* 26a) derives that the *Kohen* performing the incense offering would be blessed with wealth as a result. Therefore, in fairness to the other *Kohanim*, once a *Kohen* performed the incense offering he was not chosen for this service another time. [It is noteworthy that the words וּבְרִיתְךָ יִנְצֹרוּ, *and Your covenant they guard* (*Deuteronomy* 33:9), appear just before the verses cited above. This is an additional allusion to the relationship of *bris milah* to the incense offering.]

Since the roles of *sandak* and *Kohen* are equated, concludes *Rama* (et al., ibid.), it has become customary that one father not honor the same person to act as *sandak* at the circumcisions of two of his sons.

• Not all authorities agree with *Rama*, however. Some see the comparison of *sandak* to *Kohen* as limited to the homiletical lessons to be derived therefrom. *Noda B'Yehudah* (*Yoreh Deah* §86) writes: As a matter of fact the rabbi of the community was always *sandak*, even in one family; in Poland the opinion of not being the *sandak* for two brothers was disregarded.

Chasam Sofer (*Orach Chaim* §158-159) refutes *Noda B'Yehudah*, arguing that the fact that the community rabbi was always *sandak* was similiar to the *Kohen Gadol* [High Priest] who had the prerogative of performing the incense-offering as often as he wished. Therefore the rabbi, too, is an exception to the rule. However, concludes *Chasam Sofer*, a lay person should not be the *sandak* for two brothers.

• *Vilna Gaon* agrees with *Rama's* decision that one man not be *sandak* for two brothers, but disagrees with *Rama's* reason. For, as *Vilna Gaon* states, if one is enjoined from serving twice in the capacity of *sandak* in order to enable others to have a chance at this *mitzvah*, then what difference does it make whether he is *sandak* for two brothers or for two strangers? (*Beur HaGra, Yoreh Deah* 265:46). Moreover, continues the Gaon, 'We have never seen anyone attain wealth because he had been a *sandak*.' Rather, the custom derives from the testament of *R' Yehudah HaChassid*, who cites the custom but offers no reason (ibid.). *Aruch HaShulchan* (Y.D. 265:34) elucidates further and states that the practice has roots in Kabbalistic teachings.

אִזְמֵל / Izmail-Milah Knife

(See *Laws* §49-50)

◄§ A metal knife called an אִזְמֵל, *izmail,* is used to perform the circumcision.

• The use of a metal knife is based on the verse in *Joshua* (5:2) in which God says: עֲשֵׂה לְךָ חַרְבוֹת צֻרִים וְשׁוּב מֹל אֶת בְּנֵי יִשְׂרָאֵל, *Make sharp knives*

for yourself and return and circumcise the Children of Israel. If God commanded Joshua to use a knife, obviously that is the ideal implement. This is not contradicted by the fact that Zipporah used a stone to circumcise (*Exodus* 4:25), for since Moses and his family were traveling, the stone was the only sharp instrument available *(Aruch HaShulchan, Yoreh Deah* 264:15).

• Others base the preference for metal on the Midrash which states that when Goliath's metal helmet split to allow the stone from David's sling to kill Goliath *(I Samuel 17:49),* God rewarded metal with the promise that it would forever after be used in the performance of *milah (Prishah, Yoreh Deah* 264:7).

The connection between David's killing of Goliath and circumcision can be understood in light of David's description of the haughty Goliath as, *the uncircumcised one* (ibid. 17:36).

David rid Israel of the menace of the 'uncircumcised one' with the assistance of Goliath's metal helmet, and therefore God rewarded metal by enjoining man to use it to excise the foreskin of the uncircumcised in all generations *(R' Kolman Krohn; R' Naftoli Bassman).*

• The traditional *izmail* is sharp on both edges, to eliminate the possibility of cutting with a blunt edge that could hurt the child without excising the foreskin *(Derech Pikudecha).*

• Homiletically, the two-edged knife is referred to in the verse, וְחֶרֶב פִּיפִיּוֹת בְּיָדָם, *a two-edged sword is in their hand (Psalms* 149:6; *Derech Pekudecha).*

עָרְלָה / The Foreskin

◄§ The foreskin that is cut away during circumcision is referred to in Scripture as the עָרְלָה, *orlah.* In general the word עָרְלָה has the connotation of something that is restricted or uncontrolled. The removal of the foreskin therefore symbolizes the idea of control. Through the act of *milah,* a Jew indicates that he can control the pattern of his life. Cutting away the foreskin is a removal of a defilement which could restrict man's sacred and spiritual development.

Additionally, an uncircumcised state is considered a state of spiritual shame. Jacob's sons, in referring to the people of Shechem *(Genesis* 34:14), deemed those who had a foreskin as disgraceful. When God told Joshua *(Joshua* 5:2) to circumcise all Jews who had not been circumcised throughout their sojourn in the desert, He said that by removing their foreskins Joshua would be removing the shame of the Egyptians that Jews still bore with them (see *Malbim, Joshua* 5:9).

• The term עָרְלָה when used by itself refers to the foreskin. [The implication is that one who has a foreskin will suffer restrictions in his

spiritual growth.] However, if the term עָרְלָה is used in conjunction with another word such as עָרְלַת לְבַבְכֶם, *orlah of the heart,* (*Deuteronomy* 10:16) its meaning is indicated by the context (*Ibn Ezra, Vayikra* 12:3). The following are some examples:

• When Moses hesitated to obey God's command that he return to Egypt and talk to Pharaoh so that he could lead the Jewish people out of bondage, he said to God, 'אֲנִי עֲרַל שְׂפָתָיִם, *I am one of uncontrolled lips,*' i.e., hindered speech (*Exodus* 6:12). The term עָרֵל connotes an inability to control that which by nature should be under one's command. Moses did not feel secure with his ability to express himself. Hence the term עֲרַל שְׂפָתָיִם, *uncontrolled lips* (*R' S.R. Hirsch*).

• It is understood that when one plants an orchard, he desires to enjoy the fruits of his labor. Scripture (*Leviticus* 19:23), however, states that the first three years of fruit growth are to be years of עֲרַלְתֶּם אֶת פִּרְיוֹ, *its restriction [of] its fruit.* All fruits grown during those years may not be eaten nor may one have financial gain therefrom. Here, too, one is restricted from receiving benefit from them (see *Rashi* and *Ramban,*ibid.).

• Moses' exhortation to the Jews (*Deuteronomy* 10:16), וּמַלְתֶּם אֶת עָרְלַת לְבַבְכֶם, *And you shall rid yourselves of the insubordination* [lit. *circumcise the orlah] of your hearts,* reiterates the same idea. A heart that is insubordinate to the words of God is restricted in its performance of good; because of its uncontrolled passion for sin, it requires a spiritual circumcision that will rid the heart of its tendency towards evil.

⋟ The excised foreskin is customarily placed in earth or sand. The origin of this custom may be traced to Israel's forty-year sojourn in the wilderness. Each time a child was circumcised during that period, his foreskin and the circumcision blood would be covered with earth. When the gentile prophet Balaam proclaimed: מִי מָנָה עֲפַר יַעֲקֹב, *Who can count the dust of Jacob?* (*Numbers* 23:10), he was referring to the merit of *milah,* i.e., the foreskins that were lying in the dust, which rendered him incapable of pronouncing a curse on the Jews (*Pirkei d'R'Eliezer* 29; see also *Tosafos, Yevamos* 71b, s.v. מאי טעמא; *Beur HaGra, Yoreh Deah* 265:41).

• Others find the roots of this custom even earlier in history. Abraham, in his great humility, declared before God, וְאָנֹכִי עָפָר וָאֵפֶר, *and I am merely earth and ashes* (*Genesis* 18:27).Thus, placing the foreskin in the sand serves to evoke the merit of Abraham.

• In Kabbalah, the foreskin is viewed as an object of impurity stemming from the נָחָשׁ, *serpent,* who is considered the spiritual enemy of mankind for having induced Eve to sin. In light of the advice of King Solomon (*Proverbs* 25:21), אִם רָעֵב שֹׂנַאֲךָ הַאֲכִילֵהוּ לָחֶם, *If your enemy is*

hungry feed him bread [to placate him], the foreskin is consigned to earth, which is the food of the serpent [as it is written *(Genesis 3:14)*: *God said to the serpent ... 'Earth shall you eat all the days of your life']* *(Levush 255:10)*.

It is for this reason that when Moses was lax in circumcising his son, and his child still bore the 'impure' foreskin, Moses was attacked by a serpent, the symbol of sin and impurity *(Zohar, Pikudei 266; see also Rashi, Exodus 4:25; see p. 156)*.

• *Baal HaTurim (Numbers* 23:10) points out that the word עָפָר, *earth,* is numerically equal to עָרְלָה בְּחוֹל, *the foreskin in sand.*

⋖§ בְּרִיתוֹ שֶׁל אַבְרָהָם / The Covenant of Abraham ⋗

⋖§ Although the Patriarch Abraham fulfilled all the commandments of the Torah (see *Yoma* 28b) he did not circumcise himself until he was specifically commanded to do so. Various reasons are offered for Abraham's different approach to *milah*:

• The Talmud *(Kiddushin* 31a) states: He who is commanded and fulfills a command [מְצֻוֶּה וְעוֹשֶׂה] is greater than he who fulfills it though not commanded. This is because man's reward is commensurate with the degree of effort needed to fulfill any given *mitzvah*. Man's Evil Inclination is stronger when it is challenged by a decree issued by God than when there is no such command.

Although God had not actually commanded him to adhere to the Torah's precepts, Abraham nevertheless kept them, out of love for God. Should God later instruct him to perform the *mitzvos,* he would continue to observe them, in fulfillment of God's command.

However, *bris milah,* by its very nature, can only be performed once on an individual. Abraham therefore waited until God commanded him, otherwise the opportunity to fulfill the *mitzvah* as one who is 'commanded and fulfills' would be lost forever *(Sifsei Chachamim, Bereishis* 18:1).

• The act of *milah* entails some pain and some loss of blood. It is against Torah law to inflict unnecessary pain on any creature, even oneself. Thus Abraham was hesitant to perform an act that could perhaps be a violation of God's will *(Ksav Sofer* to *Lech Lecha* 17:1).

• The act of *milah* was a בְּרִית, *covenant,* between man and God. A covenant, by definition, is a formal binding *agreement.* It has no validity unless the parties involved have expressed consent to its terms. Hence, Abraham could not possibly have performed the act of the covenant without the other party, i.e., God, having expressed agreement.

קְרִיאַת הַשֵּׁם ‎ / Naming the Baby

‎•§ The custom of naming a boy at his *bris* is based on the fact that it was in conjunction with the commandment of *milah* that God changed Abram's name to Abraham. The name אַבְרָהָם was much more than an old name with a new letter added; it symbolized a totally new identity (*Zichron Bris LaRishonim;* see also *Zohar, Lech Lecha* 93a; see page 35).

• An additional source for this custom is *Pirkei d'R' Eliezer* (chap. 48) which states that Moses was named at his *bris.*[1] [The name he was given at that time was *Yekusiel.* The name Moses (מֹשֶׁה) was given to him by Pharaoh's daughter when she "drew him" (מְשִׁיתִהוּ) out of the river (see *Exodus* 2:20).]

• *Ramban (Exodus* 4:20) notes that when Moses' son Eliezer was born, Moses was preoccupied with fulfilling God's command regarding his return to Egypt for the sake of the Jewish people, and hence, he neither circumcised nor named his newborn son.

The relationship of *bris* and naming the child may be based on the fact that an article can be named only after it has been completed. According to Kabbalah, the removal of the foreskin rids an individual of a certain degree of impurity, allowing him to attain the full sanctity of his soul [יְסוֹד הַנְּשָׁמָה] (*Chessed LeAvraham,* see *Zohar, Shelach*). The *Zohar* (*Shemos* 86a) writes that it is only after the removal of his foreskin that a child can be called אָדָם, *man.* Thus, with his physical and spiritual creation now complete, he attains the holiness of an Israelite (see *R' Yaakov HaGozer,* p. 94, and commentary to *Targum Yonasan, Bereishis* 48:20). It is fitting, then, that at that time he be given his Hebrew name.

• My son, Avrohom Zelig, has suggested a Scriptural source for the custom of not naming a boy before his *bris.* King David married Bathsheba and she bore him a son (*II Samuel* 11:27). However, the verse does not give the child's name. In the following chapter (12:14,18), Scripture records that the prophet Nassan forewarned David, *'The son who was born to you will die.'* The verse continues: HASHEM *smote the boy ... David prayed for the lad ... And on the seventh day* [of his life] *the boy died.* Nowhere is the child mentioned by name. This is perhaps so because since he did not live to his *bris* on the eighth day, he was never given a name.[2]

---

1. According to those who contend that Moses was born circumcised (*Sotah* 12a; *Avos d'R' Nassan,* ch. 1) he was named at his *hatofas dam bris* (see page 92, Laws §2) which took place when he was eight days old (*Radal* §38 to *Pirkei d'R' Eliezer,* Chap. 48).

2. Today, if a child, God forbid, expires before he has had his *bris,* he is circumcised and given a name before his interment. This is done so that God may have mercy on him at the time of

סְעוּדַת מִצְוָה / Festive Meal

(See Laws §71-77)

◄§ The Talmud states (*Shabbos* 130a) that because *bris milah* is one of the precepts that Jews accepted with joy, it is celebrated to this very day with great joy. *Rashi* (ibid.) notes that this happiness is manifested through the tendering of a festive meal. *Tosafos* (ibid.) observes that this special party is alluded to in *Genesis* 21:8: וַיַּעַשׂ אַבְרָהָם מִשְׁתֶּה גָדוֹל בְּיוֹם הִגָּמֵל אֶת יִצְחָק, *Abraham made a great feast on the day Isaac was weaned*. Midrashically the word הִגָּמֵל, *was weaned*, is interpreted as two words — ה''ג מָל, *he circumcised on the eighth day* [ה(5) + ג(3) = 8].

• *Tosafos'* interpretation presents a difficulty. Since the verse specifically states that the feast took place on the day Isaac was weaned, how can it be deduced that the feast made by Abraham was in honor of the *bris* of his son? The answer is based on the fact that circumcision was an unpopular procedure when Abraham performed it on Isaac. Had Abraham held a feast on the day of the *bris,* it would have seemed to the world that he was insensitive to the discomfort Isaac suffered due to the circumcision. However, once Isaac was weaned, and it became clear to all that the circumcision had done him no harm, only then did Abraham celebrate with a festive gathering in retroactive honor of the circumcision (*Chasam Sofer, Vayeira*).

• Some perceive the father's act of bringing his son into the covenant of circumcision as akin to bringing an offering upon the Altar. Just as one celebrates the Temple offering with a festive meal, so does one celebrate the *milah* 'offering' with a festive meal (*Yalkut Shimoni, Lech Lecha* §81).

• Another allusion to the circumcision feast is found in *Psalms* (50:5), אִסְפוּ לִי חֲסִידָי כֹּרְתֵי בְרִיתִי עֲלֵי זָבַח, *Gather Me, My devout one, sealers of My covenant through sacrifice*. The word זָבַח, generally refers to a peace-offering, most of which is eaten by its owner and his guests, usually at a feast (*Sefer HaManhig*). Additionally, *Eretz HaChaim* points out, the cost of the feast is considered a sacrifice, for just as one gives of his possessions to the Temple Altar, so does the father provide for this meal.

◄§ Circumcision and Tefillin

(See Law §33)

◄§ If one is wearing *tefillin* and a *bris* is to take place, he should not remove them until after the *bris,* for just as *tefillin* are referred to as אוֹת, *a sign*

the Resuscitation of the Dead (*Y.D.* 263:5). At that time, his name will serve to identify him with his family (see *Korban Nesanel, Moed Katan* 3:88:20).

(see *Exodus* 13:9), so is *bris milah* designated as an אוֹת (see *Genesis* 17:11). Therefore it is appropriate to wear tefillin during the performance of a *bris (Shach, Yoreh Deah 265:24)*.

The question is raised that this seems to contradict the Talmud (*Menachos* 36b), which states that on the Sabbath one does not wear *tefillin* inasmuch as the Sabbath itself is an אוֹת, (see *Exodus* 31:13, 17) hence the additional sign of *tefillin* is unnecessary. Why, then, does the *Shach* assert that *bris milah* should be accompanied by the presence of the sign of *tefillin*?

The answer is that a Jew requires two signs each day as witnesses of his loyalty to God, for in Torah law, testimony must be substantiated by two witnesses. Thus, on weekdays, when the sign of the covenant is ever present on one's body, the additional sign of *tefillin* is appropriate. However, on the Sabbath, when the sign of the covenant and the sign of the day itself [Sabbath] are both present, the additional sign of *tefillin* is unnecessary *(Pri Megadim, Orach Chaim, 29)*.

• A Scriptural source for this custom may be found in *Esther* 8:16, which reads: לַיְּהוּדִים הָיְתָה אוֹרָה וְשִׂמְחָה וְשָׂשׂוֹן וִיקָר, *The Jews had light and gladness and joy and honor*. The Talmud (*Megillah* 16b) interprets this passage as referring to four *mitzvos:* אוֹרָה is the *light* of Torah; שִׂמְחָה is the *gladness* of the Festivals; שָׂשׂוֹן is the *joy* with which one brings his son into the covenant of circumcision; and יְקָר is the *honor* of the *tefillin*. The juxtaposition of *bris* and *tefillin* implies a connection in the performance of these two *mitzvos (Zocher HaBris 21:22)*.

�ᵴ Circumcision and Torah

�ᵴ Akilas (some say Onkelos) sought to convert to Judaism but was afraid to antagonize his anti-Semitic uncle Hadrian, the Roman emperor. Akilas went to Hadrian to seek counsel. 'I wish to do business and get acquainted with people of the world,' said the nephew. 'What do you advise?'

'Seek that which is low [in value] now, but will eventually go up, and then you will profit,' instructed the emperor.

Akilas set out for Israel, had himself circumcised and began to study Torah. A while later he was visited by his uncle who, upon seeing his nephew, became furious. 'What has happened to you?' he raged. 'Your face and demeanor have changed!'

'I followed your advice,' answered Akilas. 'I searched among all the nations for that which is considered the lowest commodity and discovered that it is the Jewish people. Yet *Isaiah* (49:7) proclaimed that God has assured these same ridiculed Jews that one day they will be kings and rulers, before whom all people will stand up and bow.'

'But you could have just studied Torah; why did you have to circumcise youself?' asked the frustrated king.

Replied Akilas, 'Are the spoils of war allocated to warriors who have not borne arms?'

Similarly, the [rewards of] Torah cannot be dispensed to anyone who has not carried out the commandment of circumcision. As King David said, מַגִּיד דְּבָרָיו לְיַעֲקֹב, *He declares His word to Jacob (Psalms* 147:19); God bequeathed His words of Torah only to those who have been circumcised, as was Jacob (*Tanchuma, Mishpatim,* §5).

◅§ On the Sabbath

(See *Laws* §78-84)

◅§ As a general rule, an act which causes bleeding is a violation of Sabbath (*Shabbos* 106a). However, because the Torah specifies the day of *milah* — וּבַיּוֹם הַשְּׁמִינִי יִמּוֹל בְּשַׂר עָרְלָתוֹ, *And on the eighth day, the flesh of his foreskin shall be circumcised (Leviticus* 12:2) — the Talmud (*Shabbos* 132a; *Sanhedrin* 59b) derives that the act of *milah* in its proper time (i.e., on the eighth day) supersedes the Sabbath.

• The Midrash likens this to the story of two noblewomen who were standing together. A passerby observing them was unable to distinguish which of them was of a higher rank. When one stepped aside in deference to the other it became obvious who was the more prominent of the two. So too, the Sabbath 'steps aside' for *milah* so that the *bris* may take place on the eighth day, indicating the loftiness of the *mitzvah* of *milah* (*Yalkut Shimoni, Yirmiyahu* 33).

Allusions

Throughout the voluminous writings on *bris milah,* there exists a myriad of acronyms, *gematriaos* (numerical equivalencies) and *ramazim* (allegorical illustrations) that have both halachic and homiletical applications. The following is a sampling:

◄§ Acronyms

◄§ Many Scriptural verses contain allusions to circumcision, with the word מִילָה appearing in the initial letters (רָאשֵׁי תֵּיבוֹת) of a phrase. Some examples are:

• An allusion to naming a child at his *bris* is found in the verse: וַיָּבֵא אֶל הָאָדָם לִרְאוֹת מַה יִּקְרָא לוֹ, *And He [God] brought them* [all the species of the animal kingdom] *to Adam, to see what he would call them* (Genesis 2:19). The initials of the words הָאָדָם לִרְאוֹת מַה יִּקְרָא can be rearranged to spell the word מִילָה (*Even Shlomo*).

• *Mateh Moshe* writes that it is impossible for one who is uncircumcised to comprehend the duty of service to God and to emulate His ways. This is hinted at in the verse מִי יַעֲלֶה לָּנוּ הַשָּׁמַיְמָה, *Who will go up for us to Heaven?* (Deuteronomy 30:12). The first letters of these words spell מִילָה, the final letters spell the Divine Four-Letter Name of HASHEM (*Baal HaTurim*).

• *King David* wrote the twelfth psalm in honor of *milah* (see *Menachos* 43b, and below, pp. 120-121). The opening phrase, לַמְנַצֵּחַ עַל הַשְּׁמִינִית, is understood to mean: *To the one who grants victory,* [regarding the *mitzvah* performed] *on the eighth day.* The words that follow immediately thereafter are, מִזְמוֹר לְדָוִד יְ־הֹ־וֹ־ה הוֹשִׁיעָה, *A psalm of David, O HASHEM save...* The initials of these words form the word מִילָה (*Chida*).

• לְבַד מֵאֲשֶׁר יוֹשִׁיט לוֹ הַמֶּלֶךְ אֶת שַׁרְבִיט הַזָּהָב וְחָיָה, *Except for the one to whom the king shall extend the golden scepter so that he may live* (*Esther* 4:11). The initials of the phrase מֵאֲשֶׁר יוֹשִׁיט לוֹ הַמֶּלֶךְ spell the word מִילָה (*R' Shlomo Garmiza*). This indicates a special royal favor that the King proffers only to the circumcised.

•§ The word מִילָה, *circumcision,* also serves as an acronym for:

• מוֹהֵל יוֹרֵד לִפְנֵי הַתֵּיבָה, *The mohel goes before the Ark,* i.e., he leads the *Shacharis* prayers *(Mateh Moshe).* In the German community the *mohel* acts as *chazzan* during *Pesukei D'zimrah* (which contains the phrase וְכָרוֹת עִמּוֹ הַבְּרִית), and after *Shemoneh Esrei* (when וַאֲנִי זֹאת בְּרִיתִי is recited in וּבָא לְצִיּוֹן).

• מִשְׁתֶּה יַעֲשֶׂה לְכָל הַקְּרוּאִים, *A festive meal is tendered for all the invited guests (Mateh Moshe).*

• מַלְאָךְ יוֹשֵׁב לִפְנֵי הָאָרוֹן, *An angel [Elijah] sits before the Ark,* i.e., when the *bris* takes place in the synagogue.

•§ The exalted status of the *bris* is often alluded to in the final letters (סוֹפֵי תֵיבוֹת) of a Scriptural passage. Among these are:

• Milah is alluded to in the verse: בָּרוּךְ אֱלֹהִים אֱלֹהֵי יִשְׂרָאֵל עֹשֵׂה נִפְלָאוֹת לְבַדּוֹ, *Blessed is* HASHEM, *God, the God of Israel, Who alone does wonders (Psalms 72:18).* The final letters of the four words אֱלֹהִים אֱלֹהֵי יִשְׂרָאֵל עֹשֵׂה form the word מִילָה *(R' Shlomo Garmiza).*

• וּשְׁמַרְתֶּם אֶת בְּרִיתִי וִהְיִיתֶם לִי סְגֻלָּה מִכָּל הָעַמִּים, *And you shall guard My covenant, and you shall be to Me a treasure from among all the nations (Exodus 19:5).* The final letters of וִהְיִיתֶם לִי סְגֻלָּה מִכָּל form the word מִילָה *(Baal HaTurim).* [Interestingly this acrostic follows the word בְּרִיתִי, *My covenant.]* Homiletically, God informs Israel that only by upholding the covenant of circumcision will they merit to be 'His treasure.'

• *Milah* is a unique source of merit. It was because of their adherence to the commandment of circumcision that the Jews merited redemption from Egypt (see *Ezekiel* 16:6; *Shemos Rabbah* 19:5). This is hinted to in the very first verse in the book of *Exodus* where the final letters of וְאֵלֶּה שְׁמוֹת] בְּנֵי יִשְׂרָאֵל הַבָּאִים מִצְרָיְמָה, *[And these are the names of] the Children of Israel who came to Egypt,* can be rearranged to form the word מִילָה *(Derashos Chasam Sofer §107).* *Baal HaTurim* sees this message in the first and final letters of the words יִשְׂרָאֵל הַבָּאִים, for they, too, spell the word מִילָה.

• The Midrash *(Bereishis Rabbah* 18:8) teaches that Abraham sits at the entrance of *Gehinnom* and does not allow anyone who is circumcised to descend there. An allusion to this is found in the verse: שָׁם בְּעִמְקֵי שְׁאוֹל קְרֻאֶיהָ, *There, in the depths of the Lower World are her summoned ones (Proverbs 9:18).* The last letters of these words are מִילָה *(Zichron Bris LaRishonim).*

•§ Allusions to other aspects of *milah* are also found:

• The *mohel* should wear fine festive clothes in honor of a *bris,* for the day is a holiday for him. This is alluded to in the words מְאֹד הוֹד

וְהָדָר לָבָשְׁתָּ, much; You have donned majesty and splendor (Psalms 104:1). The initials of these words spell מוֹהֵל, mohel (Mateh Moshe).

• Candles are lit at the festive meal that accompanies the bris. Candles are also lit on certain other festive occasions and holidays. A symbol for these occasions that call for lighting candles is found in the verse, עָרַכְתִּי נֵר לִמְשִׁיחִי, I have prepared a lamp for My anointed (Psalms 132:17). The word מְשִׁיחִי, My anointed, is an acronym for מִילָה, circumcision; שַׁבָּת, the Sabbath; יוֹם טוֹב, a holiday; חֲנוּכָּה, Chanukah; and יוֹלֶדֶת, a new mother (Zichron Bris LaRishonim). [Following the birth of each child many women customarily add a candle to the number lit in honor of the Sabbath. Additionally, in some communities, it was customary for a new mother to donate money designated for the purchase of candles for the synagogue.]

• וְאֶת בְּרִיתִי אָקִים אֶת יִצְחָק, And My Covenant I will establish with Isaac (Genesis 17:21). The word אָקִים is an acronym for the words אֲשֶׁר קִדֵּשׁ יְדִיד מִבֶּטֶן, Who sanctified the beloved one from birth, the first words in the blessing recited after the bris (Baal HaTurim).

• Esau rejected the covenant of circumcision. According to one view (Daas Zekeinim, Bereishis 25:25), Esau's father Isaac was forced to postpone his son's circumcision because of health considerations. Eventually when Isaac was ready to perform the bris, Esau refused to be circumcised (see p. 134).

Others contend that during Isaac's lifetime Esau and his children did observe the covenant. However, when Isaac passed away, Esau's family discontinued their practice of circumcision (Yalkut Shimoni, Toldos §116; see also Sanhedrin 59b; Yerushalmi Nedarim 3:8; Rambam,Melachim 10:7).

Although not mentioned explicitly in Scripture, Esau's rejection and callousness towards milah is alluded to in his statement: וְלָמָה זֶּה לִי, What use is this to me? (Genesis 25:32). The word וְלָמָה has the identical letters as the word מָהוּל, circumcised (R' Shlomo Garmiza).

⤠§ Gematria

⤠§ Another form of allusion is known as gematria. Each Hebrew letter is assigned a numerical equivalent. If the numerical value of the letters of two words or phrases are the same, they are sometimes interpreted as relating to one another, homiletically or, at times, even halachically. Examples of gematriaos that allude to milah are:

• The Talmud (Nedarim 32a) states that milah is equal to all other 612 mitzvos combined. According to Machzor Vitry, this is one of the reasons for which milah is often called בְּרִית, bris. The numerical

value of the word בְּרִית is 612 [ב(2) + ר(200) + י(10) + ת(400) = 612].

• The Talmud (Nedarim 31b) emphasizes the importance of milah by noting that the word בְּרִית, bris, or covenant, is mentioned in the chapter of milah (Genesis 17) thirteen times. The number thirteen symbolizes unity and oneness because the numerical value of the word אֶחָד, one, is thirteen [א(1) + ח(8) + ד(4) = 13]. Thus the unity of God and His people is symbolized through the covenant of milah (Maharal).

• R' Shlomo Garmiza (p. 284) notes that the reverse of the word עָרֵל, uncircumcised one, is לָרַע, to evil, symbolizing that those who remain uncircumcised will be attracted to evil. He also notes the Talmudic (Succah 52a) teaching that one of the names of the יֵצֶר הָרָע, Evil Inclination, is עָרֵל. In addition, the numerical values of יֵצֶר [י(10) + צ(90) + ר(200)] and עָרֵל [ע(70) + ר(200) + ל(30)] are the same, 300.

• The mohel's blessing at a bris concludes with the words עַל הַמִּילָה, regarding circumcision. The numerical value of the words עַל [ע(70) + ל(30)], 100, and הַמִּילָה [ה(5) + מ(40) + י(10) + ל(30) + ה(5)], 90, correspond to the ages of Abraham (100) and Sarah (90) at the time their son Isaac was circumcised. Thus in the blessing there is an allusion to the first bris performed for an eight-day-old Jewish child.

After many childless years, Channah, the mother of the prophet Samuel, gave birth to her son. When her long-awaited dream was fulfilled, she exulted in gratitude, עָלַץ לִבִּי בַּה', My heart rejoices with God (I Samuel 2:1). The numerical value of עָלַץ, rejoices, is 190 [ע(70) + ל(30) + ץ(90)]. This alludes to Channah's twofold thanks. First, she, like Abraham and Sarah after many childless years, was granted the miracle of bearing a child. Second, she bore a male child and was thus given the opportunity to have the blessing of עַל הַמִּילָה (also equaling 190) recited over her child's circumcision (Zichron Bris LaRishonim).

ידיד אברהם ‎§

Yedid Avrohom

• The Laws

◆§ The Laws

This digest of laws and customs has been prepared to serve a twofold purpose: to familiarize the layman with the basic laws of *bris milah*, and to facilitate the planning of a *bris*.

The reader should be aware that this section is by no means all-inclusive, either halachically or medically; nor should it be viewed as rendering final halachic decisions. Many situations require the counsel of either the *mohel*, the doctor or a rabbinical halachic authority, and some require the advice of all three.

The laws have been culled primarily from the *Shulchan Aruch Yoreh Deah* (here abbreviated Y.D.), *Shulchan Aruch Orach Chaim*, (O.C.) and from the *Mishnah Berurah* (M.B.). Numerous halachic decisions rendered by leading contemporary Torah authorities are included as well.

The rationale underlying many of the customs mentioned in this section appears in the Insights and Background section. I have named the Laws and the Ritual sections of this work יְדִיד אַבְרָהָם, *Yedid Avrohom*, in memory of my beloved father, הרב אברהם זעליג בן הרב חנוך העניך זצ״ל, RABBI ABRAHAM Z. KROHN, of blessed memory, who was pleasing to God and pleasing to man.

Suggested sources for a more comprehensive treatment of the laws and customs pertaining to *bris milah* are *Zocher HaBris* by R' Asher Anshel Greenwald and the encyclopedic *Sefer HaBris* by Rabbi Moshe Bunim Pirutinsky.

◆§ Which Day?

1. A *bris* is performed on the eighth day of a child's life, with his day of birth counting as the first day. Thus, if a child is born on a Monday, his *bris* would be on the following Monday. However, since in Jewish tradition the day begins with the preceding nightfall (see *Genesis* 1:6), if a boy is born Monday night, his *bris* would be on the following Tuesday.

2. A *bris* that was performed before the eighth day is invalid and requires *hatafas dam bris* [the drawing of a speck of blood, a token circumcision] on the eighth day (*Shach*, Y.D. 262:2).

3. A child must be born before sundown for that day to be counted as the first day. However, the halachic definition of sundown is not necessarily the same as the time of sunset as given in the newspaper or almanac. Indeed, there is a period of time between sunset and nightfall that is called בֵּין הַשְּׁמָשׁוֹת, *twilight*, part of which may belong to the previous day and part to the following day. There are divergent views as to how much, if any, of this

time frame belongs to each of these days. The laws regarding the day of *milah* of a baby born during this twilight period are complicated and detailed, and are not within the purview of this compilation of laws. If a child is born anytime between the 'listed' sundown and seventy-two minutes thereafter, a rabbi must be consulted as to the proper day of the *bris*. [See O.C. 261:2 with M.B. and *Beur Halachah*; O.C. 331:5; see also *Igros Moshe*, O.C. Vol. 4 §62.]

[The rabbi will either determine that: (a) the time of birth is halachically considered as belonging to the previous day, so that, in our example, the *bris* should be on the next Monday; (b) the time of birth is halachically considered as belonging to the following day, so that the *bris* should unquestionably be on the next Tuesday; or (c) the time of birth cannot be assigned definitely to either of the two days. In this last case the *bris* will be made on the next Tuesday, not because it is unquestionably the eighth day, but because the *bris* cannot be performed on Monday, which may only be the seventh day from the baby's birth. The reason for the assignment of Tuesday as

the proper date of the *bris* has ramifications when that day is a Festival (see below).]

4. A *bris* that has been postponed to after the eighth day [for any reason whatsoever] may not take place on a Sabbath or Festival. [With regard to this rule the word Festival includes: the first two and last two days of Pesach; Shavuos; Rosh Hashanah; Yom Kippur; the first two days of Succos; Shemini Atzeres and Simchas Torah.]

5. A *bris* can take place on the Sabbath only if the child was born on the previous Sabbath, at a time which halachically is definitely Sabbath. Similarly, it may not take place on a Festival unless it is definitely the eighth day from birth. Consequently, if a baby was born during the twilight on Friday, for example, it may be halachically doubtful whether the birth took place on the Sabbath or on Friday. If the birth was indeed on Friday, it would be forbidden to perform the *bris* on the Sabbath. In such a doubtful case, the *bris* would have to be put off until Sunday (Y.D. 266:8-9).

6. By Biblical injunction, only the *bris* of a baby born by normal delivery overrides the Sabbath or a Festival. Therefore, a child born by Caesarean section may not have his *bris* performed on the Sabbath. In this case it is postponed until Sunday (Y.D. 266:10).

7. A *bris* that is being performed for the purpose of conversion may not take place on the Sabbath or a Festival (Y.D. 266:13).

ᴥᴥ Medical Causes for Postponement

8. A *bris* may not be performed on an ill child until he is fully recovered (Y.D. 262:2). The slightest ailment or the least pain, as determined by the *mohel*, rabbi, or doctor, may be cause enough to have a *bris* postponed until the child is healed (*Shach*, Y.D. 262:2).

9. There are two types of illness that may cause a delay of the *bris*: a systemic illness that affects the entire body and a localized ailment that affects only a specific part of the body.

If an infant contracts an illness, such as fever, which affects the entire body, he must be completely cured for seven full days (i.e., seven twenty-four-hour periods) before the *bris* may be performed (ibid.). If, for example, the child was pronounced healthy at 3:00 p.m., Tuesday, the *bris* may not take place any earlier than 3:00 p.m. of the following Tuesday.

However, an illness affecting a specific part of the body needs no waiting period and the *bris* may be performed promptly after full recovery (ibid.).

10. The most common cause for delaying a *bris* is a condition known as jaundice.[1] This is manifested by the skin of the child becoming a shade of yellow (referred to in Y.D. 263:1 as יֵרוֹק). The generally accepted opinion is that as soon as the jaundiced condition clears up the child can be circumcised. However, if the condition is serious enough to warrant a blood

---

1. The following is a simplified explanation of jaundice, and why it affects the timing of a circumcision:

Every human body contains millions of red blood cells. These cells have life-spans of approximately 120 days. After this period, the cells are broken down in the body, and form a substance called bilirubin. The bilirubin travels through the liver where it is processed, broken down further and finally excreted through the urine.

The infant has had blood cells from the fourth month of his conception, and these, too, must be broken down. Until birth, his mother's liver has been doing this function for him, but after birth he must rely on his own body. In a newborn, however, the liver is somewhat immature and often unready to function properly in processing the bilirubin. This is not a disease since it is only a matter of time and maturity until the liver will begin to function as it should.

When bilirubin is not processed properly it is deposited in the tissues of the body and the skin takes on a yellowish tint — a condition known as jaundice. In an infant, jaundice is

transfusion, the *bris* must wait a full seven days from the time of recovery.

11. There are congenital (birth) defects of the penis that may cause a postponement of the *bris* or even prevent one from being performed. Consultation between the doctor, *mohel*, and rabbi is necessary in such cases to determine when the child may have his *bris*.

12. An underweight baby may not be circumcised. Doctors have different opinions as to the minimum weight required before an infant may be circumcised (usually five pounds). However, once the desired weight is reached, there is no waiting period, and the *bris* should be performed as soon as possible, unless other health considerations warrant delay.

13. If the child was placed in an incubator (because of a health factor) he must wait seven full days from the time he is released until he can have his *bris*. Similarly, a child that required a blood transfusion must wait seven days, even if medical opinion holds that he can have his *bris* sooner (*Igros Moshe*, Y.D. II §121).

14. A *bris* may not be delayed to another day simply for the sake of convenience.

15. If a *bris* must be postponed for a considerable length of time, one should consult a rabbi regarding when to give the child his Hebrew name.

✥§ What Time of Day?

16. A *bris* should not be performed before sunrise of the eighth day of the child's life. If the *bris* was performed before sunrise, but after dawn, which is halachically given as

seventy-two minutes before sunrise, then *post facto* [בְּדִיעֲבַד] it is considered valid. A *bris* that has been performed at night is invalid and requires *hatafas dam bris* (Y.D. 262:1; see above §2).

17. The *bris* may be performed anytime until sunset, but since it is preferable that *mitzvos* be performed with alacrity, it is meritorious that the *bris* be performed in the morning (Y.D. 262:1).

At least, one should not delay the *bris* past midday, if possible (see *Aruch HaShulchan*, Y.D. 262:8).

18. If there is a more experienced *mohel* who will not be available until the afternoon of the *bris* date, one need not engage a less qualified *mohel* simply to perform that *bris* in the morning (*Zocher HaBris* 4:5).

✥§ The Shalom Zachar

19. On the first Friday night after a boy is born, it is customary to gather in the home of the newborn for a שָׁלוֹם זָכָר, *Shalom Zachar*, i.e., a celebration in honor of the newborn (see p. 73). [There are some today, however, who hold the *Shalom Zachar* in a synagogue or at the home of a grandparent.] The *Shalom Zachar* has the status of a *seudas mitzvah* i.e., a *mitzvah* feast (Y.D. 265:12).

20. If a child is born on Friday evening after sundown, his *bris* will be held on the following Sabbath or Sunday (see above, §3, 5). Hence, there would be two Friday nights available to celebrate the *Shalom Zachar*. Authorities differ regarding the proper day for the *Shalom Zachar*. *Pri Megadim* (*Mishbetzos* 444:9) is of the opinion that it is held on the first Friday night. However, most follow the

usually physiological, meaning that it is a normal occurrence in the body, while in an adult, jaundice is usually symptomatic of a pathological condition which must be dealt with medically.

The bilirubin level [or count] indicates how much of this substance is in the blood and will subsequently be deposited in the tissues. If the level is high it is an indication that the child's liver may not yet be functioning adequately, the body may have less resistance and the child may be prone to infection or may not heal as quickly as normal. Furthermore, the liver helps to

opinion of *Chachmas Adam* (149:24) who says that it should be held on the second Friday night. *Sefer HaBris* (265:80) explains this on practical grounds because it would be difficult to inform people of the *Shalom Zachar* on the first Friday night, the night of the child's birth. Furthermore the second Friday night is the *Vach Nacht* (see below) which, in many communities,is customarily a night of celebration.

21. Even if the child's *bris* definitely will not be performed during the coming week (due to premature birth, illness, etc.) the *Shalom Zachar* is still held (*Zocher HaBris* 3:7).

22. It is customary to serve lentils and other beans (such as *arbes*, chick peas), as well as nuts, at the *Shalom Zachar* (*Zocher HaBris* 3:5-7; see p. 73).

◄§ Vach Nacht/The Night Before the Bris

23. Traditionally, the night before the *bris* is known as *Vach Nacht* [*Night of the Vigil*]. The 'vigil' is held to ward off anything that may interfere with the *bris*, for as the *Midrash* states: The merit of *bris milah* is so great that it safeguards Jews from *Gehinnom* (*Tana Dvei Eliyahu Zuta*, 25), therefore the Accuser [Satan] wishes that the *bris* not be performed (*Bris Avos*).

24. As part of this vigil, in some communities the men of the family and their colleagues remain awake studying Torah throughout the night, or at least until midnight, in the house where the infant sleeps (*Bris Avos*). Laws and customs pertaining and relating to *bris milah* are usually studied. *Siddur Bais Yaakov* offers a list of Torah sections that are apropos for study and recital. See page 108 for

prayers; page 74 for suggested study.

25. This vigil is omitted on Friday night, the first two nights of Passover and on the eve of Yom Kippur (*Zocher HaBris* 3:20). This is because the unique character of each of these nights offers its own special protection.

26. Children are brought to the crib of the infant where they recite the first chapter of the *Shema* and the verse הַמַּלְאָךְ הַגּוֹאֵל, *May the angel who redeems ... (Genesis* 48:16; see p. 108). The children are then given candies and other sweets.

27. In many communities a celebration is held the night before a *bris*, with a festive meal, dance and song (*Zocher HaBris* 3:8). However, this celebration (based on *Zohar, Lech Lecha* 93a-b) is not classified as a *seudas mitzvah* [mitzvah feast] (*Magen Avraham*, O.C. 640:13; see also *Shaarei Teshuvah*, O.C. 551:36).

28. In some Sephardic communities, family and friends would come to the home of the *sandak* and then, with torches, candles and musical instruments, all would march to the home of the infant where a celebration would be held and the *chacham* [rabbi] would deliver a Torah discourse (*Sefer HaBris* 265:118).

◄§ Shacharis Services

29. It is customary in many congregations during the *Shacharis* prayers for the *mohel* and the congregation (or, in some congregations, the *mohel* and the *sandak*) to recite alternate phrases from וְכָרוֹת עִמּוֹ הַבְּרִית until the end of the אָז יָשִׁיר [see page 110] (see *Mogen Avraham*, O.C. 51:9, and *Machatzis HaShekel; Radal* on *Shemos Rabbah* 23:12; *Zocher HaBris* 21:10).

produce the clotting factors of the blood, and since it is imperative that the blood clot after circumcision, the *halachah* rules that if there is even a slight suspicion that the liver is not functioning properly, it is forbidden to perform the *bris*.

Cases of jaundice vary and it is the doctor's duty to pass pertinent medical information to the *mohel*, who, in consultation with the doctor and a competent halachic authority, will make the decision as to when the child may be circumcised.

30. On the morning of the day on which a *bris* is to be performed, the *Tachanun* prayers are omitted by the *minyan* in which one of the three principals of the *bris* [*mohel, sandak* or father] is praying (*Ba'er Haitev*, O.C. 131:12). Additionally, the three principals do not recite *Tachanun* at *Minchah* (M.B. 131:25). If the *bris* is to be performed after *Minchah*, then the *Tachanun* prayers are omitted from both *Shacharis* and *Minchah*.

31. Although *Tachanun* is omitted, אָבִינוּ מַלְכֵּנוּ is recited on those days that it normally would be, even though the *bris* will take place immediately after *Shacharis*. On days when the Torah is read, the priorities for being called to the Torah are *sandak*, father and *mohel* (*Mogen Avraham* O.C. 282:18). Others hold that the father has priority over the *sandak* (see *Sefer HaBris* 265:141).

32. לַמְנַצֵּחַ (*Psalm* 20) that is recited every weekday contains the phrase, *May Hashem answer you on the day of distress*. *Maharil* contends that despite this phrase the psalm is recited even on the day of a *bris*, for our rejoicing is not complete because the child may experience some pain. Additionally, *Midrash Shocher Tov* notes that the nine verses of לַמְנַצֵּחַ allude to the nine months of pregnancy (*Shach*, Y.D. 265:24).

However, the Sephardic custom [also followed by Chabad/Lubavitch] is to omit לַמְנַצֵּחַ whenever *Tachanun* is omitted. Consequently, it is omitted on the day of a *bris*.

✍§ Tefillin

33. If one is wearing *tefillin* and a *bris* is to take place, he should not remove them until after the *bris* (*Shach*, Y.D. 365:24; *Mogen Abraham*, O.C. 25:28). *Shach* explains that just as *tefillin* are referred to as an אוֹת, *a sign* (see *Exodus* 13:9), so too is *bris milah* designated as an אוֹת, *sign* (see *Genesis* 17:11). Therefore it is appropriate to wear *tefillin* during the performance of a *bris*.

Os Chaim (25:18) notes that certain great chassidic leaders such as the Ziditchover and Sassover Rebbes removed their *tefillin* before a *bris*. They based their practice on the Talmudic passage (*Menachos* 36b), which states that one does not wear *tefillin* on the Sabbath, being that they are both אוֹתוֹת, *signs*; so too, reasoned these chassidic leaders, one does not need the sign of *tefillin*, when the sign of *bris milah* is being performed.

Os Chaim disagrees with this reasoning, however, and cites *Zohar* which says that a person should bear two אוֹתוֹת, *signs*, each day (see page 84).

✍§ Candles

34. It is customary to have candles at the *bris* ceremony (see Y.D. 265:5). This custom adds dignity and beauty to the *mitzvah* and is a tradition that is practiced universally (see page 75). The number of candles lit is subject to local custom.

Machzor Vitri suggests lighting one candle. For twins, one candle is lit for each child (Y.D. 265:5). Others suggest the lighting of thirteen candles at each *bris* corresponding to the thirteen times that the word *bris* is mentioned in the seventeenth chapter of *Genesis* with reference to *milah*.

35. In certain German communities a special candle made with thirteen wicks was lit at each *bris* and was then put away until the child's wedding day, when it would be used at his *marriage ceremony*.

Additionally, in these communities when the *bris* took place in the synagogue twelve candles would be lit around a central candle. The twelve candles symbolized the twelve tribes and the middle candle represented the child himself. These candles are called the שְׁלִישִׁי לְמִילָה, literally, *third after milah*, because the middle candle was left to burn for three days so that the people who saw it would pray for

the health of the circumcised child.[1]

◆§ Kvatter and Kvatterin
(Colloquially:Godparents)

36. Two people — one male, the other female (usually a married couple) — are customarily given the honor of bringing the child to the room where the *bris* will take place, and then returning him to his mother after the *bris*. They are known as the *kvatter* and *kvatterin* (see *Rama*, Y.D. 265:11).

37. It is customary to delegate the honor of *kvatter* and *kvatterin* to a couple seeking to have a child. This custom is probably based on the Midrash (*Bamidbar Rabbah* 14:2) which states that God rewards measure for measure those participating in particular *mitzvos*. For example, regarding those who give charity, though they have few possessions, and those circumcising [or participating in a *bris*] though they have no children of their own, God says, 'It is My obligation to compensate them with money, children …'. (See also *Vayikra Rabbah*, 27:2.)

38. Some do not permit a pregnant woman to be *kvatterin* lest she become frightened by the *bris*, and cause harm to her unborn baby (*Zocher HaBris* 19:13).

39. Anyone can be chosen as *kvatter* or *kvatterin*. In some families the baby is held by many people each bringing him a bit closer to where the *bris* will take place (see *Aruch HaShulchan* 265:35; *Migdal Oz Nachal* 9:4).

◆§ Throne of Elijah

40. At the *bris* a chair is set aside in honor of אֵלִיָּהוּ הַנָּבִיא, *Elijah the Prophet*, who is called the מַלְאַךְ הַבְּרִית, *Angel of the Covenant* (Y.D. 265:11). This chair is known as כִּסֵּא שֶׁל אֵלִיָּהוּ, *the Throne of Elijah*.
The *sandak's* chair is placed to the

left of Elijah's, following the Talmudic teaching that a student walks on his teacher's left (*Derech Pekudecha*).

In some Sephardic communities one chair serves a dual purpose and the *sandak* sits on the Throne of Elijah.

41. One of the assembled is honored with placing the infant on the Throne of Elijah, so that Elijah should bless the child (*Sefer HaRokeach*).

42. It is customary to bedeck the Throne of Elijah with beautiful sheets or pillows (*Zocher HaBris* 20:3 citing *Zohar*, *Terumah* 149). *Zecher David* writes that in some communities the curtain of the Ark was used to bedeck the Throne, symbolizing that the Divine Presence which rests upon the Ark also manifests itself upon the Throne.

43. When the *bris* is performed in the synagogue, some leave the Throne of Elijah in place for three days thereafter (*Mateh Moshe*, *Milah* 7:7), as a reminder to all to pray for the health of both mother and child.

◆§ The Mohel

44. The *bris* should be performed by a male (Y.D. 264:1).

45. Since the act imprints the 'seal of the covenant' on the child, it must be done by one who is himself a member of the covenant. Therefore, a gentile may not perform a *bris*. If a gentile does circumcise a Jewish child, the circumcision is invalid and the child requires *hatafas dam bris* [see §2 above] (*Rama*, Y.D. 264:1). [It is the act of circumcision itself, not merely the recitation of the blessings that must be performed by a Jew. Thus, even if a Jew recited the blessings, the *bris* is invalid if performed by gentile.]

46. One should appoint a *mohel* who is a God-fearing, observant Jew of exemplary character (Y.D. 264:1).

---

1. In the distinguished Khal Adas Yeshurun in the Washington Heights section of New York (a congregation that adheres strictly to the ancient customs of the Frankfurt am Main community) the middle candle has been replaced by an electric light.

47. Once a *mohel* has been designated to perform a *bris*, one may not subsequently reject him in favor of a different *mohel* (*Y.D.* 264:1). However, if the second *mohel* is a close friend of the family, or is an exceptionally righteous person, and it is obvious that he would have been called in the first place had the family known he was available, the family may withdraw its original choice (*Taz, Y.D.* 264:5).

48. It is essential to stress that *bris milah* is a religious observance and not a medical procedure. Consequently, although some physicians are qualified *mohalim* — indeed, *Rashi* (*Sanhedrin* 17b) notes that doctors would perform a *bris* in Talmudic times — one may use a physician only if he is qualified to be a *mohel* entirely apart from his medical expertise. In order to avoid a trend toward having *bris milah* performed by doctors who are not qualified *mohalim*, some authorities have expressed the view that even religious doctors should desist from performing *bris milah* (*Sefer HaBris* 264:30).

◈§ The Izmail

49. A metal knife is used to perform the circumcision (*Y.D.* 264:2). The knife used is usually referred to as an אִזְמֵל, *izmail.*

50. The traditional *izmail* is sharp on both edges. It is made in this fashion to eliminate the possibility of cutting with a blunt edge that could hurt the child without excising the foreskin (*Derech Pikudecha*).

◈§ The Father's Role

51. It is customary for the father to stand by the *mohel* and verbally appoint him to act in his behalf in performing the *bris*, inasmuch as it is actually the father who is commanded by the Torah to circumcise his son (*Y.D.* 265:9).

52. There is a custom in some places that the father hands the *izmail* to the *mohel*, thereby signifying that he appoints him to act as his agent (*Zocher HaBris* 18:20).

53. During the *bris*, the father recites a blessing (see below §62). If the father is not present at the *bris*, or if he cannot, for whatever reason, recite the blessing, then the *sandak* recites the blessing for him (*Y.D.* 265:1). Others hold that the rabbi of the community recites the blessing (*Os Sholom* 265:5).

◈§ The Sandak

54. At every *bris* an individual known as the *sandak* is designated to hold the child as the *mohel* performs the *bris*. The designation of being *sandak* is considered the most prominent honor of the *bris* ceremony; indeed the *sandak* is often referred to as בַּעַל בְּרִית, *principal participant of the bris.*

55. It is proper to seek and designate a God-fearing, righteous man to the role of *sandak* (*Rama, Y.D.* 264:1). Since one is obligated to honor his father and father-in-law, it is customary to accord one of them the honor of *sandak*. This is so unless they express a preference that the child's great-grandfather be given this honor instead (*Leket Yosher*). In many communities it is customary to give the rabbi this honor (*Noda BeYehudah, Kama, Y.D.* §86).

Divrei Malkiel (*Responsa, sec. V,* §86) suggests that the father of the child should himself be the *sandak*, for since the *mitzvah* to circumcise the child is incumbent upon him, he should assist in the ceremony in every way possible. This, indeed, is the custom in many Sephardic communities.

56. The *sandak* should wear clothes suitable for the Sabbath, inasmuch as this day is halachically deemed a holiday for him (see §98).

57. The *sandak* wears a *tallis* which he partially overlaps on the forehead of the child. However, if a *tallis* is not available, the *bris* should not be delayed in order to obtain one (*Kores HaBris*).

58. There are differing customs, based on opposing halachic views, regarding one person serving as *sandak* for two children of the same parents. Some maintain that just as a *Kohen* was not appointed to perform the incense ritual more than one time, so is one person not designated by the same father to serve as *sandak* for two of his sons (*Rama, Y.D.* 265:11; see page 65 for the connection between the *sandak* and the incense ritual). Others understand the *sandak*/incense relationship as purely homiletical, and thus permit the same person to function as *sandak* repeatedly (*Noda BeYehudah, Kama, Y.D.* §86). Still others differentiate between the rabbi of a community and a layman as *sandak*, permitting the rabbi to be so honored more than once, while limiting the layman to one time (*Chasam Sofer, O.C.* §158-159).

⋅§ The Others Present

59. It is preferable, but not mandatory, that a *minyan* be present at a *bris* (*Y.D.* 265:6).

60. Some maintain that all who are present in the room [with the exception of the *sandak*] where the *bris* is taking place should stand. This is alluded to in the verse (*II Kings* 23:3): וַיַּעֲמֹד כָּל הָעָם בַּבְּרִית, *and the entire nation stood at the covenant* [when King Josiah renewed Israel's commitment to the Torah] (*Y.D.* 265:1; see however *Beur HaGra*).

⋅§ The Milah

61. Just before performing the circumcision, the *mohel* recites the blessing: בָּרוּךְ אַתָּה ה' אֱלֹהֵינוּ מֶלֶךְ הָעוֹלָם, אֲשֶׁר קִדְּשָׁנוּ בְּמִצְוֹתָיו, וְצִוָּנוּ עַל הַמִּילָה, to which all present respond אָמֵן (*Y.D.* 265:1; see p. 122).

62. As the *mohel* performs the *milah*, the father of the baby recites the blessing: בָּרוּךְ אַתָּה ה' אֱלֹהֵינוּ מֶלֶךְ הָעוֹלָם, אֲשֶׁר קִדְּשָׁנוּ בְּמִצְוֹתָיו, וְצִוָּנוּ לְהַכְנִיסוֹ בִּבְרִיתוֹ שֶׁל אַבְרָהָם אָבִינוּ, and all present respond אָמֵן, then add: כְּשֵׁם שֶׁנִּכְנַס לַבְּרִית, כֵּן יִכָּנֵס לְתוֹרָה וּלְחֻפָּה וּלְמַעֲשִׂים טוֹבִים (*Y.D.* 265:1).

63. The *milah* consists of three acts: חִיתוּךְ, excision (see below, §64); פְּרִיעָה, uncovering (see below, §65); and מְצִיצָה, drawing (see below, §66).

64. חִיתוּךְ, excision: The entire foreskin covering the glans (head of the penis) is excised with the *izmail*. Halachah requires that the *mohel* must remove the foreskin so that the entire glans, including the coronal sulcus, is visible (*Beis Yosef* to *Tur Y.D.* 264; see also *Shach, Y.D.* 264:12).

65. פְּרִיעָה, uncovering: The thin membrane that usually adheres to the glans is removed or folded back so that it uncovers the glans and remains behind the corona.

66. מְצִיצָה [*metzitzah*], drawing: Blood is extracted from the wound. The Talmud considers *metzitzah* to be a therapeutic imperative (*Shabbos* 133b; see *O.C.* 331:3 with *M.B.* notes 4 and 36). It strongly admonishes those who delete this part of the *bris*, warning that any *mohel* refraining from performing *metzitzah* is to be removed from his practice. Additionally, *Zohar* bases the reason for *metzitzah* on Kabbalistic considerations (see *Ohr HaChaim, Leviticus* 12:3; and *Midgal Oz*).

There is controversy regarding the exact method of performing *metzitzah*. Many feel that it should be done only בְּפֶה, orally, while there are those who contend that other means are acceptable as well. [For a detailed discussion on the halachic ramifications and historical background to the controversy, see *Kuntrus HaMetzitzah*, in *Sdei Chemed*; *Sefer HaBris* p. 213-226; see also *Beur Halachah* to *O.C.* 331:1.]

67. The excised foreskin is customarily covered with earth or sand (*Y.D.* 265:10; see p. 81).

⋅§ Twins

68. When two boys [whether twins or from two different families] are circumcised at the same ceremony, they are brought into the room

separately, so that each child receives the honor due him (*Shach*, *Y.D.* 265:15).

69. If one of the circumcisions is not on the eighth day, regardless of the reason for postponement, the eighth-day circumcision is performed first. Otherwise, it is customary to perform the older child's *bris* first (*Pischei Teshuvah*, *Y.D.* 265:9).

70. At a *bris* of twin boys, verses such as ...הַמַּלְאָךְ הַגּוֹאֵל, *the angel who redeems* ...are recited between the two circumcisions in order to make an obvious separation between the two ceremonies. Because of this separation the blessing recited at the first *bris* is not valid for the second, and a new blessing is recited (*Pischei Teshuvah*, *Y.D.* 265:10).

◆§ The Circumcision Meal

71. It is customary to make a festive meal following the *bris* ceremony (*Y.D.* 265:12).

72. There are those who contend that the Talmudic dictum אֵין שִׂמְחָה אֶלָּא בְּבָשָׂר, *there can be no celebration without* [the eating of] *meat* (*Pesachim* 109a), is applicable today and therefore maintain that it is incumbent to serve a meat meal (see *Magen Avraham O.C.* 249:6 and *Machatzis HaShekel*). Others hold that fish as well as chicken fulfill this requirement (*Os Bris* 265:12 cited by *Zocher HaBris* 25:7, based on *Magen Avraham* 552:2).

Others contend that this dictum was applicable only during the Temple era when it was fulfilled through the eating of sacrificial meat (*Levush*; *Shaagas Aryeh* 65,68). This then is the basis for the many who serve a dairy or pareve meal at a *bris* (*Os Bris*, 265:12).

73. Bread and wine should be served (see *Yam Shel Shlomo*, *Beitzah* 2:5; *Chochmas Adam* 149:24; *Sefer HaBris* 265:161).

74. In times of economic difficulty one should not be ostentatious in the presentation of his meal so as not to embarrass those who are less fortunate. In Safed there was a rabbinic decree to serve fish and not meat at the circumcision meal because of the vast difference in price between the two foods (*Zocher HaBris* 25:7).

75. It is customary not to invite anyone explicitly to the circumcision meal, for one may not refuse to participate once he has been invited (*Pesachim* 113b). Consequently, instead of formally inviting his guests, one merely informs them that a meal will be tendered (*Zocher HaBris* 25:10).

76. Candles should be lit during the *bris* meal. However, if the meal takes place on the Sabbath one may not call a gentile to light these candles (*Zocher HaBris* 25:13).

77. Various *piyuttim* (liturgical songs) are sung during the meal and *Bircas HaMazon* (see pages 138, 148, and 160).

◆§ On the Sabbath or a Festival

78. As a general rule, an act which causes bleeding is a violation of the Sabbath (*Shabbos* 106a). However, because the Torah specifies the day of *milah* — וּבַיּוֹם הַשְּׁמִינִי יִמּוֹל בְּשַׂר עָרְלָתוֹ, *And on the eighth day, the flesh of his foreskin shall be circumcised* (*Leviticus* 12:3) — the Talmud (*Shabbos* 132a; *Sanhedrin* 59b) derives that the act of *bris milah* in its proper time (i.e., on the eighth day) supersedes the Sabbath and Festivals (even Yom Kippur). However, a *bris* that has been delayed for any reason (underweight, ill health, etc.) cannot be rescheduled for a Sabbath or Festival.

79. The *bris* of a child born by Caesarean section, or one being done for the purpose of conversion, may not be performed on the Sabbath or a Festival, because the provision for a Sabbath *bris* refers only to the eighth day and only to a normal birth (*Y.D.* 266:10; *O.C.* 331:5, and *M.B.* §18).

80. *Hatafas dam bris* (see above, §2), may not be done on the Sabbath, even if it is the eighth day (*O.C.* 331:5; see *M.B.* §15).

81. A child born Friday or Sabbath during the twilight period (see above, §3) may not have his *bris* performed on the Sabbath (*O.C.* 331:5; see *M.B.* §14; see also above §5).

Similarly, one born during the twilight period eight days before a Festival may not have his *bris* performed on the Festival.

82. On the Sabbath or Yom Kippur it is forbidden to carry a child through a public domain to the place where the *bris* is to be performed, unless there is an *eruv*. This holds true even if the carrying is done by a gentile (*M.B.* 331:20). Although most authorities disagree, some permit such carrying by a gentile under certain conditions (see *Shulchan Aruch HaRav* 331:7-8).

83. The אַב הָרַחֲמִים prayer which usually precedes the Sabbath *Mussaf* service is omitted in the presence of the *sandak*, *mohel* or father of the baby whose *bris* will take place on that Sabbath (*O.C.* 284:7). However, it is customary to recite אַב הָרַחֲמִים during the days of *Sefiras HaOmer*, between Pesach and Shavuos, even on the day of the *bris* (*M.B.* §18).

84. If the Sabbath or Festival *bris* takes place before one has recited *Kiddush*, the blessing recited over wine following the *bris* may be reckoned for *Kiddush* as well [because the wine blessing alone, without any scriptural verses, is sufficient for *Kiddush* (see *Pesachim* 106b)]. The one who recites the blessing should have a piece of cake [or wash for the meal] right after he has tasted the wine to fulfill the requirement of קִידּוּשׁ בִּמְקוֹם סְעוּדָה, *Kiddush in the same location as the meal* (see *O.C.* 273:5; *M.B.* §25).

◆§ On Rosh Hoshanah

85. See above §78-81 and 84, all of which apply to Rosh Hashanah also.

86. On Rosh Hashanah if the *bris* is to be performed in the synagogue, it should take place after the reading of the Torah [so that the Divine Presence that attends Torah reading should be with the child as well, when he is being circumcised (*Rokeach* §217)], but before the blowing of the *shofar*. One of the many reasons for the commandment to use a ram's horn for the blowing of the *shofar* is to invoke the merit of the *Akeidas Yitzchak* [binding of Isaac], in whose place a ram was sacrificed (see *Genesis* 22:13). Historically, the circumcision of Abraham occurred before the *Akeidah*; it is thus proper for the *bris* to precede the blowing of the *shofar*. Additionally, the *Vilna Gaon* notes that since *bris milah* occurs more often throughout the year than the *mitzvah* of *shofar*, the *bris* is performed first. This is so because of the axiom: תָּדִיר וְשֶׁאֵינוֹ תָּדִיר, תָּדִיר קוֹדֶם, *mitzvos that occur regularly take precedence to those that occur only occasionally* (*O.C.* 584:4; *M.B.* §11).

If the *bris* is to be held in the child's home which is a distance from the synagogue, then it is preferable for it to take place after the services so as not to inconvenience the congregation by having them leave the synagogue and then return for the *Mussaf* prayers (*M.B.* 584:11).

87. During the Ten Days of Awe, between Rosh Hashanah and Yom Kippur, אָבִינוּ מַלְכֵּנוּ is recited (*Shach* 265:24).

◆§ On Yom Kippur

88. See above §78-82, all of which apply to Yom Kippur also.

89. If the *bris* is to be held in the synagogue, it should take place after the Torah reading, before the Torah is returned to the Ark (see above, §86). It is best to perform the *bris* before the recitation of *Ashrei* (*O.C.* 621:2; *M.B.* §7). If the *bris* is to be performed outside the synagogue, it should take place after the Torah has been returned to the Ark, before the *Mussaf* service (*O.C.* 621:2).

90. Sephardim omit the customary cup of wine at a *bris* which is performed on Yom Kippur (*O.C.* 621:3). Ashkenazim do use the customary wine and give the circumcised infant a taste of the wine (*Rama,* ibid.). If, however, the mother of the child is not fasting (upon her doctor's and rabbi's advice that it may be dangerous for her), it is better that she should drink from the wine [provided of course that she heard the wine blessing and had in mind to drink] (*O.C.* 621:3, *M.B.* §12; *Shaar HaTziun* §5). Children should not be given the wine, lest they become accustomed to drink on Yom Kippur (ibid.).

◄§ On Erev Pesach

91. The day before Passover — Erev Pesach — is a fast day for all בכורים, *firstborn adult* males (see *O.C.* 470). [This is in commemoration of the miracle in which all Jewish firstborns were spared from death during the Plague of the Firstborns in which all Egyptian firstborns died.]

If a firstborn attends a circumcision meal on this day he is permitted to partake of it and is thus exempt from fasting (*O.C.* 470:1-2 with *M.B.* §1, 10).

92. *Chametz* may not be eaten after the first third of the daylight period of Erev Pesach (*O.C.* 471:1). [It is therefore of utmost importance that, if *chametz* is to be served at the meal following the *bris,* the *bris* be performed very early, in order to allow enough time for the completion of the meal before the restrictions on *chametz* take effect.]

◄§ During the Nine Days

93. The mourning period over the Temple's destruction commences with the fast of the Seventeenth of Tammuz and reaches its climax with the fast of the Ninth of Av [Tishah B'Av]. During this three-week period some of the laws of mourning are observed [e.g., marriages do not take place; one does not take a haircut; new clothing are

neither purchased nor worn for the first time]. The arrival of Rosh Chodesh Av signals an intensification of the mourning restrictions. During the first nine days of Av, commonly referred to as the 'Nine Days,' one refrains from drinking wine or eating meat, except on the Sabbath (see *O.C.* 551). The occasion of a *bris,* however, provides specific exemptions from these restrictions for certain participants. Regarding these exemptions, the Nine Days themselves are subdivided into two periods: (a) from Rosh Chodesh until Sunday of the week in which Tishah B'Av falls; and (b) the week of Tishah B'Av, the more stringent of the two periods.

94. Prior to the week of Tishah B'Av, the principal participants in the *bris* (father, mother, mohel and *sandak*) may shave or take a haircut in honor of the occasion. *Chasam Sofer* (*O.C.* 158), however, is of the opinion that they may do so even during the week of Tishah B'Av. Nevertheless, many other authorities disagree (see *Shaarei Teshuvah,* *O.C.* 551:3).

95. Prior to the week of Tishah B'Av, all relatives and friends who attend the circumcision meal may drink wine and eat meat (*O.C.* 551:10). However, during the week of Tishah B'Av only the principal participants, including the *kvatters* (*Shaar HaTziun* note 85), close relatives [up to and including first cousins; see *M.B.* 551:77] and a *minyan* (quorum of ten) of friends may participate in the meat meal. The other guests may partake only of dairy and pareve products.

If a meat meal is served at a *bris* performed on Erev Tishah B'Av, the meal should be concluded by midday (*M.B.* 551:78).

96. Throughout the Nine Days, only the principal participants may wear special Sabbath attire at a *bris* (*O.C.* 555:1). However, the custom is that the *kvatterin* (the woman who carries the child in) may also wear Sabbath attire, for that is her main role

in the ceremony (*M.B.* 551:3). Grand-parents of the child also customarily wear Sabbath attire (*Shaarei Teshuvah* 551:3). However, none may don new clothes for a *bris* during the Nine Days (*M.B.* 551, §9).

⋅§ On Tishah B'Av

97. A *bris* on Tishah B'Av should be performed after the recital of *Kinos*, the elegies recited on Tishah B'Av in mourning for the Temple (*O.C.* 559:7).

98. The infant's parents, the *sandak* and the *mohel* may dress in Sabbath clothes in honor of the *bris*, but must change into weekday clothing after its conclusion. They may not wear new clothes (*M.B.* 559:32-34), nor may they wear leather shoes (*Beur Halachah* 559, s.v. ומותר).

99. If the mother of the child is not fasting, only she is permitted to drink from the wine [provided that she heard the wine blessing and had in mind to drink]. If the mother is not present or if she is fasting, then a young child should drink the wine (*O.C.* 559 with *M.B.* §30).

This differs from the rule of Yom Kippur (see above §90), on which young children may not be given the wine (see *O.C.* 621:3). This is so because the laws of Yom Kippur are more stringent, since that day is biblically ordained as a fast (*Magen Avraham* 559:9).

100. If Tishah B'Av falls on the Sab-bath, the fast is postponed until Sunday. If there is a *bris* on this Sunday, the parents, the *sandak* and the *mohel* may pray the *Minchah* service after midday, bathe [even before the *bris*] and [after the *bris*] participate in a small meal in honor of the *bris* (*O.C.* with *M.B.* 559:36). [A large festive meal may be held in the evening following the conclusion of the fast (*Shaar HaTziun* 559:37).] The *havdalah*, which is normally delayed in such a case until the fast ends on Sunday night, must be recited before they eat (ibid.). Although they are required to fast until after the *bris*, those who partake of the meal need not resume fasting after the meal, for it is a holiday for them (*O.C.* 559:9).

⋅§ On Other Fast Days

101. In the presence of the *mohel*, *sandak* or father of a baby whose *bris* will take place on a fast day [Tzom Gedaliah (3 Tishrei), Tenth of Teves, Taanis Esther (13 Adar), Seventeenth of Tammuz], the regular *Selichos* are recited during the morning prayers, but *Tachanun* is omitted (*Y.D.* 265:13).

102. Taanis Esther is considered the least stringent of the fasts. Thus if a *bris* occurs on this day the father, mother, *mohel* and *sandak* need not fast (*Shaar HaTziun* 686:16 based on *Gra*; however, see other views cited there).

103. Regarding the other three fasts, the principal participants are not exempt from fasting (see, however, view of *Gra*, cited in *Shaar HaTziun* ibid.). However, if the fast day was a *nidchah*, i.e., the actual date of the fast fell on the Sabbath, causing the fast to be postponed until Sunday, the principal participants are exempt from fasting (ibid.).

104. Regarding the drinking of the wine, the law is the same as on Tishah B'Av, see above, §99.

⋅§ Adoption / Conversion

105. A non-Jewish male who wishes to convert to Judaism must undergo circumcision and ritual immer-sion [in a *mikveh*], in addition to acceptance of the responsibility of observing the entire Torah and all of its commandments.

106. A *bris* performed for the pur-pose of conversion cannot take place on the Sabbath or a Festival (*Y.D.* 266:13). Therefore, the son of a Jewish man by a non-Jewish woman — since

his circumcision is part of his conversion process — may not be circumcised on the Sabbath or a Festival, even if it is the eighth day from his birth.

107. If the convert, child or adult, was circumcised for medical reasons prior to his *bris milah* ceremony, he requires *hatafas dam bris* (see above, §2), however, no blessing is recited (*Y.D.* 265:3, and 268:1, *Shach* ibid. §1; see also *Aruch HaShulchan* 265:18; *Sefer HaBris* 265:62).

108. If the convert requires a full circumcision (see above, §107) the following blessings are recited (*Y.D.* 268:5; *Taz* §12; *Shach* §15):

בָּרוּךְ אַתָּה יהוה אֱלֹהֵינוּ מֶלֶךְ הָעוֹלָם, אֲשֶׁר קִדְּשָׁנוּ בְּמִצְוֹתָיו, וְצִוָּנוּ לָמוּל אֶת הַגֵּרִים.

בָּרוּךְ אַתָּה יהוה אֱלֹהֵינוּ מֶלֶךְ הָעוֹלָם, בּוֹרֵא פְּרִי הַגָּפֶן.

בָּרוּךְ אַתָּה יהוה אֱלֹהֵינוּ מֶלֶךְ הָעוֹלָם, אֲשֶׁר קִדְּשָׁנוּ בְּמִצְוֹתָיו, וְצִוָּנוּ לָמוּל אֶת הַגֵּרִים, וּלְהַטִּיף מֵהֶם דַּם בְּרִית, שֶׁאִלְמָלֵא דַּם בְּרִית לֹא נִתְקַיְּמוּ שָׁמַיִם וָאָרֶץ, שֶׁנֶּאֱמַר: אִם לֹא בְרִיתִי יוֹמָם וָלַיְלָה חֻקּוֹת שָׁמַיִם וָאָרֶץ לֹא שָׂמְתִּי. בָּרוּךְ אַתָּה יהוה, כּוֹרֵת הַבְּרִית.

109. If the male child of a non-Jewish mother has been adopted by a Jew, the baby's *bris* must be performed with the intent of conversion. This must be followed later by the acceptance, on the part of his adoptive parents, that the child will be committed to a life of Torah and *mitzvos*, and then by ritual immersion in a *mikveh*. A Jewish tribunal *(beis din)* of three males is required at both the *bris* and the ritual immersion (*Y.D.* 268:3).

110. Prior to the child's reaching majority, there is an obligation to inform him of his prerogative to either accept or reject the commitment to Judaism which his adoptive parents made on his behalf.

111. The laws governing adoption and conversion are extremely delicate and complex. Before people undertake the adoption of a child, they should consult a rabbi whose proficiency in halachah is beyond reproach regarding the many halachic ramifications that may be involved.

112. Customarily a convert is given the name Abraham (*Zohar, Lech Lecha* 96a). Additionally he is referred to as *ben Avraham Avinu* (the son of our forefather Abraham), for he, Abraham, was the first to convert others to Judaism *(Zichron Bris LaRishonim,* p. 135; see also *Rashi* and *Targum Yerushalmi, Genesis* 12:5). Abraham was also considered to be the first convert (*Chagigah* 3a).

The name Ovadiah has also been suggested for the new convert —Ovadiah being a combination of the words *Ovaid Yah* (a servant of God) — because he came of his own free will to accept the Torah and *mitzvos (Edus LeYisrael* p. 151).

113. According to *Zichron Bris LaRishonim,* the convert is given his Hebrew name at his *bris.* The following formula (ibid. p. 135; see, however, *Zocher HaBris* 22:25) is used:

אֱלֹהֵינוּ וֵאלֹהֵי אֲבוֹתֵינוּ, קַיֵּם אֶת הָאִישׁ הַזֶּה בְּתוֹרַת אֵל וּבְמִצְוֹתָיו, וְיִקָּרֵא שְׁמוֹ בְּיִשְׂרָאֵל פב״פ יִשְׂמַח בְּתוֹרָה וְיָגֵל בְּמִצְוֹת, הוֹדוּ ...פְּלוֹנִי זֶה בֶּן אַבְרָהָם גָּדוֹל יִהְיֶה, כֵּן יִכָּנֵס בְּתוֹרַת אֵל וּבְמִצְוֹתָיו וּבְמַעֲשִׂים טוֹבִים.

Igros Moshe (*Y.D.* I §161) maintains that the preferred time for naming a convert is at the ritual immersion, for only after the immersion is he considered a part of the Congregation of Israel. In the case of a newborn, however, if the family wishes to name the child at his *bris,* they may do so. According to this opinion two different formulas are used.

(a) If the name is given at the *bris* —

אֱלֹהֵינוּ וֵאלֹהֵי אֲבוֹתֵינוּ, קַיֵּם אֶת הַיֶּלֶד הַזֶּה, וְיִקָּרֵא שְׁמוֹ פְּלוֹנִי בֶּן אַבְרָהָם אָבִינוּ. הוֹדוּ לַיהוה כִּי טוֹב, כִּי לְעוֹלָם חַסְדּוֹ. הוֹדוּ לַיהוה כִּי טוֹב, כִּי לְעוֹלָם חַסְדּוֹ. פְּלוֹנִי זֶה הַקָּטָן גָּדוֹל יִהְיֶה, וְיִכָּנֵס לִטְבִילָה לִקְדוּשַׁת יִשְׂרָאֵל וּלְתוֹרָה וּלְחֻפָּה וּלְמַעֲשִׂים טוֹבִים.

(b) If the name is given at the immersion in the *mikveh* —

אֱלֹהֵינוּ וֵאלֹהֵי אֲבוֹתֵינוּ, קַיֵּם אֶת הַיֶּלֶד הַזֶּה לְיִשְׂרָאֵל, וְיִקָּרֵא שְׁמוֹ בְּיִשְׂרָאֵל פְּלוֹנִי בֶּן אַבְרָהָם אָבִינוּ. הוֹדוּ לַיהוה כִּי טוֹב, כִּי לְעוֹלָם חַסְדּוֹ. הוֹדוּ לַיהוה כִּי טוֹב, כִּי לְעוֹלָם חַסְדּוֹ. פְּלוֹנִי זֶה הַקָּטָן גָּדוֹל יִהְיֶה. וְיִכָּנֵס לַתּוֹרָה וּלְחֻפָּה וּלְמַעֲשִׂים טוֹבִים.

114. If the family wishes to call the child, 'so and so, the son of (the adopting father),' instead of 'the son of our forefather Abraham,' they may do so (*Igros Moshe, Y.D.* I §161; see *Targum Yonasan* and *Daas Zekeinim* to *Bereishis* 41:45, and *Pirkei d'R' Eliezer* 38, regarding Aserath, daughter of Potiphera; see also *Choshen Mishpat* 42:15, and *Shemos Rabbah* 46:5).

৺ During a Mourning Period

115. The general rule is that a mourner may attend a *bris milah.* However, before permitting a mourner to participate in the festive meal served in honor of the *bris,* numerous factors must be taken into consideration (see *Y.D.* 391:2, 393:2,3):

(a) The mourner's relationship to the deceased — for one mourning a parent the laws are more stringent than for one mourning a spouse, sibling or child (see *Taz* 391:3);

(b) the time frame of the mourning period — *shivah,* the first week, which is further divided between the first three days and the remainder of the week; *shloshim,* the first month; or the first year (see *Y.D.* 393:2,3 and *Shach* §4);

(c) the mourner's role in the *bris,* i.e., if he is a principal participant [*mohel, sandak,* parent, and, according to some, grandparent] (see *Y.D.* ibid.; *Aruch HaShulchan* 391:11).

Because of the divergent halachic opinions relating to each of these factors, any mourner wishing to attend the *bris* meal should consult with a halachic authority before doing so.

HONORS BESTOWED AT A BRIS

Honor	Functions and Significance
קְוָואטֶערִין מַכְנִיס וּמוֹצִיא Kvatterin (colloquially-Godmother)	Carries baby from mother to *bris* room and, after the *bris,* back to mother. This is the one formal honor bestowed upon a woman at a *bris.* Often, the *Kvatterin* and *Kvatter* are a couple seeking to have a child, as this honor is deemed propitious for this purpose. In some communities baby is passed from woman to woman, each bringing him closer (הַגָּשׁוֹת) to *bris* room.
קְוָואטֶער מַכְנִיס וּמוֹצִיא Kvatter (Godfather)	Carries baby from *Kvatterin* to *bris* area and, after the *bris,* back to her. In some communities the baby is passed from man to man, each bringing the baby closer (הַגָּשׁוֹת) to the *bris* area.
כִּסֵּא שֶׁל אֵלִיָּהוּ Throne of Elijah	Places baby on chair designated as Throne of Elijah. Some place great emphasis on this honor.
מִיַּד הַכִּסֵּא * From the Throne	Takes baby from Throne of Elijah and (gives him to father who) places him on *sandak's* lap.
סַנְדָּק Sandak	Holds baby during *bris.* Highest honor at *bris,* the *sandak* is equated with *kohen* burning incense offering in the *Beis HaMikdash.* Many single out the Rabbi or the grandfather for this honor.
מִן הַכִּסֵּא * From the Throne	Takes the baby from *sandak* at conclusion of circumcision and gives him to the standing *sandak* (see below).
מְבָרֵךְ—Reader of the Blessings	Recites two blessings said following *bris.* This honor is often bestowed on *mohel* or *sandak.*
סַנְדָּק מְעוּמָד עֲמִידָה עַל הַבְּרָכָה Standing Sandak	Holds baby while abovementioned blessings are recited. *Arizal* considered this an important honor.
קְרִיאַת הַשֵּׁם Giving the Name	Recites Prayer during which baby is given his Hebrew name. Many consider this the second highest honor at *bris* and designate the Rabbi if he did not serve as *sandak.* This honor is often combined with that of reader of the blessings.
עֲמִידָה שְׁנִיָּה Second Standing Sandek	Holds baby during the giving of the name. This honor is often combined with that of standing *sandak.*
מְזַמֵּן Leader of Bircas HaMazon	*Recites zimun/inivitation before Bircas HaMazon fol-*lowing festive meal; recites הָרַחֲמָן prayers. In some communities *mohel* is accorded this honor. In others, a different person recites each הָרַחֲמָן prayer.

* Honors marked with an asterisk are optional, and are often performed by the *mohel.*

‎ידיד אברהם‎ ‏ﯗ‏

Yedid Avrohom

• The Ritual

❧וואַך נאַכט❧

PRAYERS AND STUDY ON THE NIGHT PRECEDING THE BRIS

It is customary on the night before the *bris* to have children come to the cribside of the infant to recite the first paragraph of the *Shema* and Jacob's prayer, הַמַּלְאָךְ, *May the angel*. The children are then given sweets or candies. See *Laws §26*.

שְׁמַע יִשְׂרָאֵל, יהוה אֱלֹהֵינוּ, יהוה אֶחָד:

In an undertone—בָּרוּךְ שֵׁם כְּבוֹד מַלְכוּתוֹ לְעוֹלָם וָעֶד.

וְאָהַבְתָּ אֵת יהוה אֱלֹהֶיךָ, בְּכָל לְבָבְךָ, וּבְכָל נַפְשְׁךָ, וּבְכָל מְאֹדֶךָ. וְהָיוּ הַדְּבָרִים הָאֵלֶּה, אֲשֶׁר אָנֹכִי מְצַוְּךָ הַיּוֹם, עַל לְבָבֶךָ. וְשִׁנַּנְתָּם לְבָנֶיךָ, וְדִבַּרְתָּ בָּם, בְּשִׁבְתְּךָ בְּבֵיתֶךָ, וּבְלֶכְתְּךָ בַדֶּרֶךְ, וּבְשָׁכְבְּךָ וּבְקוּמֶךָ. וּקְשַׁרְתָּם לְאוֹת עַל יָדֶךָ, וְהָיוּ לְטֹטָפֹת בֵּין עֵינֶיךָ. וּכְתַבְתָּם עַל מְזֻזוֹת בֵּיתֶךָ, וּבִשְׁעָרֶיךָ.

הַמַּלְאָךְ הַגֹּאֵל אֹתִי מִכָּל רָע יְבָרֵךְ אֶת הַנְּעָרִים, וְיִקָּרֵא בָהֶם שְׁמִי, וְשֵׁם אֲבֹתַי אַבְרָהָם וְיִצְחָק, וְיִדְגּוּ לָרֹב בְּקֶרֶב הָאָרֶץ.

It is customary on this evening for the men of the household to study portions of the Torah and Talmud that are relevant to *bris milah* (a list of suggested passages, appears on p. 74). Some study until midnight while some study the entire night (see *Laws §23-25*).

Some recite the following prayer before the study begins:

יְהִי רָצוֹן מִלְּפָנֶיךָ יהוה אֱלֹהֵינוּ וֵאלֹהֵי אֲבוֹתֵינוּ, הַבּוֹחֵר בְּאַבְרָהָם אוֹהֲבוֹ וּבְזַרְעוֹ אַחֲרָיו, שֶׁתָּפֵן בְּרַחֲמִים אֶל לְמוּדֵנוּ, וְתִמְשׁוֹךְ חוּט שֶׁל חֶסֶד עַל הַיֶּלֶד הַזֶּה, לִהְיוֹת חָזָק וּבָרִיא, כְּדֵי לְהַכְנִיסוֹ לִבְרִית מִצְוַת מִילָה בִּזְמַנּוֹ. וְתִזְכֶּה אוֹתוֹ לִהְיוֹת נִמּוֹל כְּהוֹגֶן וּכְשׁוּרָה וּבְכַוָּנָה הָרְאוּיָה, וּתְהֵא חֲשׁוּבָה וּמְרֻצָּה מִצְוָה זוּ לְפָנֶיךָ כְּקָרְבָּן עַל מִזְבַּחֲךָ, וְכַעֲקֵדַת יִצְחָק, וְלֹא יְסֻכַּן חַס וְשָׁלוֹם מֵחֲמַת הַמִּילָה. וְתִשְׁלַח רְפוּאָה וְחַיִּים לַיֶּלֶד הַזֶּה וּלְאִמּוֹ, כִּרְפוּאַת חִזְקִיָּהוּ מֶלֶךְ יְהוּדָה מֵחָלְיוֹ, וּכְמִרְיָם הַנְּבִיאָה מִצָּרַעְתָּהּ, וּכְנַעֲמָן מִצָּרַעְתּוֹ, וּכְמֵי מָרָה עַל יְדֵי מֹשֶׁה רַבֵּנוּ, וּכְמֵי יְרִיחוֹ עַל יְדֵי אֱלִישָׁע.

וּכְשֵׁם שֶׁתִּכְנְנוֹס אוֹתוֹ לַבְּרִית, כֵּן תְּזַכֶּה אֶת אָבִיו וְאֶת אִמּוֹ לְגַדְּלוֹ וּלְהַכְנִיסוֹ לְתוֹרָתְךָ וְלַעֲבוֹדָתֶךָ, וְקַדֵּשׁ שִׁמְךָ עָלָיו עַד כִּי יִרְאוּ כָל בָּשָׂר כִּי שֵׁם יהוה נִקְרָא עָלָיו וְיִרְאוּ מִמֶּנּוּ. וּתְהֵא עִם פִּיו בְּעֵת הַטִּיפוֹ, וְעִם יָדָיו בְּעֵת מַעֲבָדָיו, וְיִהְיוּ פָנָיו מַצְהִיבוֹת וְקוֹמָתוֹ נָאָה, וְאֵימָתוֹ מוּטֶלֶת עַל הַבְּרִיּוֹת. וְיִהְיֶה אָהוּב לְמַעְלָה, וְנֶחְמָד לְמַטָּה. וְיִזְכּוּ לִרְאוֹת בְּשִׂמְחָתוֹ וּבְשִׂמְחַת בְּנֵי בָנָיו, שֶׁיִּהְיוּ עוֹסְקִים בַּתּוֹרָה וּבְמִצְוֹת, וְשָׁלוֹם עַל יִשְׂרָאֵל. בָּרוּךְ אַתָּה יהוה, לַמְּדֵנִי חֻקֶּיךָ.

The Ritual / Vach Nacht [108]

PRAYERS AND STUDY ON THE NIGHT PRECEDING THE BRIS

It is customary on the night before the *bris* to have children come to the cribside of the infant to recite the first paragraph of the *Shema* and Jacob's prayer, הַמַּלְאָךְ, *May the angel.* The children are then given sweets or candies. See *Laws* §26.

Hear, O Israel: HASHEM is our God, HASHEM, the One and Only.

In an undertone—Blessed is the Name of His glorious kingdom for all eternity.

וְאָהַבְתָּ *You shall love HASHEM, your God, with all your heart, with all your soul and with all your resources. Let these matters that I command you today be upon your heart. Teach them thoroughly to your children and speak of them while you sit in your home, while you walk on the way, when you retire and when you arise. Bind them as a sign upon your arm and let them be tefillin between your eyes. And write them on the doorposts of your house and upon your gates.*

הַמַּלְאָךְ *May the angel who redeems me from all evil bless the lads, and may my name be declared upon them — and the names of my forefathers Abraham and Isaac — and may they proliferate abundantly like fish within the land.*

It is customary on this evening for the men of the household to study portions of the Torah and Talmud that are relevant to *bris milah* (a list of suggested passages appears on p. 74). Some study until midnight while some study the entire night (see *Laws* §23-25).

Some recite the following prayer before the study begins:

יְהִי רָצוֹן *May it be Your will, HASHEM, our God and God of our forefathers, who has chosen Abraham His beloved, and his offspring after him, that You turn with compassion to our study, and extend a thread of kindness upon this child; that he be strong and healthy, in order that he may be brought into the covenant of the mitzvah of circumcision, in its proper time. May You grant that he be circumcised properly and accurately — with the proper intent. May the performance of this mitzvah be worthy and acceptable before You as a sacrifice upon Your Altar and as the binding of Isaac. And may he not be endangered, Heaven forbid, due to the circumcision. May You send healing and life to this child and to his mother, like the healing of Hezekiah, King of Judah, from his illness; like Miriam the prophetess from her tzaraas; like Naaman from his tzaraas; like the waters of Marah through the hand of our teacher Moses; and like the waters of Jericho through the hands of Elisha.*

Just as You shall enter him into the covenant, so may You privilege his father and mother to raise him and to enter him into a life of Your Torah and Your service. Sanctify Your Name upon him, until all mankind sees that the Name of Hashem is called upon him and they will thus hold him in reverence. Be with his mouth when he speaks, and with his hands when he works. May his face be radiant, his stature beautiful, and his awe cast upon all living creatures. May he be loved Above and desired below. And may they [his parents] merit to see his happiness and the happiness of his grandchildren, that they may be involved in Torah study and mitzvos, and [may there be] peace upon Israel. Blessed are You, HASHEM, teach me Your statutes.

‏שירת הים‏ ‏⊰⊱‏

During *Shacharis* before a circumcision, in many congregations the *mohel* and congregation recite the verses of the Song of the Sea responsively.

‏Mohel—וְכָרוֹת עִמּוֹ הַבְּרִית לָתֵת אֶת אֶרֶץ הַכְּנַעֲנִי‏

‏Cong.—הַחִתִּי הָאֱמֹרִי וְהַפְּרִזִּי וְהַיְבוּסִי וְהַגִּרְגָּשִׁי, לָתֵת לְזַרְעוֹ,‏

‏Mohel—וַתָּקֶם אֶת דְּבָרֶיךָ, כִּי צַדִּיק אָתָּה.‏

‏Cong.—וַתֵּרֶא אֶת עֳנִי אֲבֹתֵינוּ בְּמִצְרָיִם, וְאֶת זַעֲקָתָם שָׁמַעְתָּ עַל יַם‏
‏סוּף.‏

‏Mohel—וַתִּתֵּן אֹתֹת וּמֹפְתִים בְּפַרְעֹה וּבְכָל עֲבָדָיו וּבְכָל עַם אַרְצוֹ,‏

‏Cong.—כִּי יָדַעְתָּ כִּי הֵזִידוּ עֲלֵיהֶם, וַתַּעַשׂ לְךָ שֵׁם כְּהַיּוֹם הַזֶּה.‏

‏Mohel—וְהַיָּם בָּקַעְתָּ לִפְנֵיהֶם, וַיַּעַבְרוּ בְתוֹךְ הַיָּם בַּיַּבָּשָׁה,‏

‏Cong.—וְאֶת רֹדְפֵיהֶם הִשְׁלַכְתָּ בִמְצוֹלֹת, כְּמוֹ אֶבֶן בְּמַיִם עַזִּים.‏

‏Mohel—וַיּוֹשַׁע יהוה בַּיּוֹם הַהוּא אֶת יִשְׂרָאֵל מִיַּד מִצְרָיִם,‏

‏Cong.—וַיַּרְא יִשְׂרָאֵל אֶת מִצְרַיִם מֵת עַל שְׂפַת הַיָּם.‏

‏Mohel—וַיַּרְא יִשְׂרָאֵל אֶת הַיָּד הַגְּדֹלָה אֲשֶׁר עָשָׂה יהוה בְּמִצְרַיִם,‏
‏וַיִּירְאוּ הָעָם אֶת יהוה,‏

‏Cong.—וַיַּאֲמִינוּ בַּיהוה וּבְמֹשֶׁה עַבְדּוֹ.‏

‏Mohel—אָז יָשִׁיר מֹשֶׁה וּבְנֵי יִשְׂרָאֵל אֶת הַשִּׁירָה הַזֹּאת לַיהוה,‏
‏וַיֹּאמְרוּ לֵאמֹר,‏

‏⊰⊱ שִׁירַת הַיָּם‏/The Song at the Sea

During *Shacharis* on the day of a *bris* many congregations place special emphasis on the recital of ‏וְכָרוֹת עִמּוֹ‏ ‏הַבְּרִית‏, by reciting the verses responsively. Customs vary regarding the number of verses, who recites them, and the manner of their recitation. Some follow the full format given above [taken from *Siddur Tefillah Yesharah Berditchev* and *Siddur Otzar HaTefillos*], while others follow different divisions [see, e.g., *Siddur Avodas Yisrael*]. The responsive reading as indicated here continues until the end of ‏אָז יָשִׁיר‏ and this is the present practice in some congregations. However, in a majority of Eastern European communities an abridged version of this custom was followed, and the responsive reading concluded with ‏בְּמַיִם עַזִּים‏. Most congregations today follow this shorter custom. In some congregations the *mohel* merely recites the paragraph ‏וְכָרוֹת‏ aloud with no communual response.

Although in most *siddurim* the recitation is divided between *mohel* and congregation, an ancient custom [still followed in German-Jewish congregations] has the *mohel* and *sandak* alternating phrases, rather than *mohel* and congregation (see *Machatzis HaShekel, Orach Chaim* 51:9).

Magen Avraham (*Orach Chaim* 51:9) questions the custom of reciting these passages in phrases rather than complete verses; for the Talmud states: Any verse that Moses did not divide, we may

❈ THE SONG AT THE SEA ❈

During *Shacharis* before a circumcision, in many congregations the *mohel*
and congregation recite the verses of the Song at the Sea responsively.

Mohel — *And You established the covenant with him to give the land of the
Canaanite,*

Cong. — *Hittite, Emorite, Perizzite, Jebusite, and Girgashite, to give it to
his offspring;*

Mohel — *and You affirmed Your word, for You are righteous.*

Cong. — *You observed the sufferings of our forefathers in Egypt and their
outcry You heard at the Sea of Reeds.*

Mohel — *You imposed signs and wonders upon Pharaoh and upon all his
servants, and upon all the people of his land.*

Cong. — *For You knew that they sinned flagrantly against them, and You
brought Yourself renown as clear as this very day.*

Mohel — *You split the Sea before them and they crossed in the midst of the
Sea on dry land,*

Cong. — *but their pursuers You hurled into the depths, like a stone into
turbulent waters.*

Mohel — HASHEM *saved on that day Israel from the hand of Egypt,*

Cong. — *and Israel saw the Egyptians dead on the seashore,*

Mohel — *Israel saw the great hand that* HASHEM *inflicted upon Egypt, and
the people feared* HASHEM,

Cong. — *and they had faith in* HASHEM *and in Moses, His servant.*

Mohel — *Then Moses and the Children of Israel chose to sing this song to*
HASHEM, *and they said the following:*

---

not divide (*Megillah* 22a). He suggests
that we are permitted to recite it this
way because the original song was sung
by Moses and Israel in phrases rather
than verses (see three views in *Sotah*
30b). Regarding וְכָרוֹת, which is not part
of the song itself, he speculates that
only verses of the Five Books of Moses
may not be divided; since וְכָרוֹת is not
from the Pentateuch but from
Nechemiah (9:6-11), the law of not
dividing verses does not apply (see
Magen Avraham, O.C. 422:4).

The problem of dividing the verses is
circumvented by some by having each
party recite the entire passage, his
phrases aloud and his counterpart's
silently (*Zocher HaBris* 21:10; *Otzar
HaTefillos*).

וְכָרוֹת עִמּוֹ הַבְּרִית — *And You established*
[lit. *cut*] *the covenant with him.* The
recitation begins with this phrase
because it alludes to the covenant of
Abraham. The Midrash (*Bereishis
Rabbah* 49:2) relates when Abraham
took the knife in his hand to circumcise
himself, he became frightened and
unsure, so God took his hand and
helped him. The verse therefore reads:
וְכָרוֹת עִמּוֹ הַבְּרִית, *and* [*God*] *established
the covenant with him* [*Abraham*], i.e.,
they did it together (*Emek Brachah*, p.
226).

אָז — *Then.* Several interpretations have
been offered regarding the relationship
between the Song at the Sea and *bris
milah*:

אָשִׁירָה לַיהוה כִּי גָאֹה גָּאָה, סוּס וְרֹכְבוֹ רָמָה בַיָּם. —Cong.

עָזִּי וְזִמְרָת יָהּ וַיְהִי לִי לִישׁוּעָה, —Mohel

זֶה אֵלִי וְאַנְוֵהוּ, אֱלֹהֵי אָבִי וַאֲרֹמְמֶנְהוּ. —Cong.

יהוה אִישׁ מִלְחָמָה, יהוה שְׁמוֹ. —Mohel

מַרְכְּבֹת פַּרְעֹה וְחֵילוֹ יָרָה בַיָּם, —Cong.

וּמִבְחַר שָׁלִשָׁיו טֻבְּעוּ בְיַם סוּף. —Mohel

תְּהֹמֹת יְכַסְיֻמוּ, יָרְדוּ בִמְצוֹלֹת כְּמוֹ אָבֶן. —Cong.

יְמִינְךָ יהוה נֶאְדָּרִי בַּכֹּחַ, יְמִינְךָ יהוה תִּרְעַץ אוֹיֵב. —Mohel

וּבְרֹב גְּאוֹנְךָ תַּהֲרֹס קָמֶיךָ, תְּשַׁלַּח חֲרֹנְךָ יֹאכְלֵמוֹ כַּקַּשׁ. —Cong.

וּבְרוּחַ אַפֶּיךָ נֶעֶרְמוּ מַיִם, נִצְּבוּ כְמוֹ נֵד נֹזְלִים, קָפְאוּ תְהֹמֹת בְּלֶב יָם. —Mohel

אָמַר אוֹיֵב, אֶרְדֹּף אַשִּׂיג אֲחַלֵּק שָׁלָל, —Cong.

תִּמְלָאֵמוֹ נַפְשִׁי, אָרִיק חַרְבִּי, תּוֹרִישֵׁמוֹ יָדִי. —Mohel

נָשַׁפְתָּ בְרוּחֲךָ כִּסָּמוֹ יָם, צָלֲלוּ כַּעוֹפֶרֶת בְּמַיִם, אַדִּירִים. —Cong.

מִי כָמֹכָה בָּאֵלִם יהוה, מִי כָּמֹכָה נֶאְדָּר בַּקֹּדֶשׁ, נוֹרָא תְהִלֹּת עֹשֵׂה פֶלֶא. —Mohel

נָטִיתָ יְמִינְךָ, תִּבְלָעֵמוֹ אָרֶץ. —Cong.

נָחִיתָ בְחַסְדְּךָ עַם זוּ גָּאָלְתָּ, —Mohel

נֵהַלְתָּ בְעָזְּךָ אֶל נְוֵה קָדְשֶׁךָ. —Cong.

שָׁמְעוּ עַמִּים יִרְגָּזוּן, חִיל אָחַז יֹשְׁבֵי פְּלָשֶׁת. —Mohel

אָז נִבְהֲלוּ אַלּוּפֵי אֱדוֹם, אֵילֵי מוֹאָב יֹאחֲזֵמוֹ רָעַד, —Cong.

נָמֹגוּ כֹּל יֹשְׁבֵי כְנָעַן. —Mohel

תִּפֹּל עֲלֵיהֶם אֵימָתָה וָפַחַד, בִּגְדֹל זְרוֹעֲךָ יִדְּמוּ כָּאָבֶן, —Cong.

עַד יַעֲבֹר עַמְּךָ יהוה, עַד יַעֲבֹר עַם זוּ קָנִיתָ. —Mohel

תְּבִאֵמוֹ וְתִטָּעֵמוֹ בְּהַר נַחֲלָתְךָ, מָכוֹן לְשִׁבְתְּךָ פָּעַלְתָּ יהוה, —Cong.

מִקְּדָשׁ אֲדֹנָי כּוֹנְנוּ יָדֶיךָ. —Mohel

יהוה יִמְלֹךְ לְעֹלָם וָעֶד. —Cong.

יהוה | יִמְלֹךְ לְעֹלָם וָעֶד. —Mohel

Mechilta (see *Yalkut Shimoni II*, 321) notes that because the Jews performed the rite of circumcision before they left Egypt, they merited that God should split the sea for them. This is homiletically referred to in the first words of the Song at the Sea, אָז יָשִׁיר מֹשֶׁה, *Then Moses sang*. The numerical value of the word אָז is eight [א=1, ז=7]. Thus the phrase implies: אָז, because of

Cong. — *I shall sing to HASHEM for He is exalted above the arrogant, having hurled horse with its rider into the sea.*

Mohel — *God is my might and my praise, and He was a salvation for me.*

Cong. — *This is my God, and I will build Him a Sanctuary; the God of my father, and I will exalt Him.*

Mohel — *HASHEM is Master of war, through His Name HASHEM.*

Cong. — *Pharaoh's chariots and army He threw into the sea;*

Mohel — *and the pick of his officers were mired in the Sea of Reeds.*

Cong. — *Deep waters covered them; they descended in the depths like stone.*

Mohel — *Your right hand, HASHEM, is adorned with strength; Your right hand, HASHEM, smashes the enemy.*

Cong. — *In Your abundant grandeur You shatter Your opponents; You dispatch Your wrath, it consumes them like straw.*

Mohel — *At a blast from Your nostrils the waters were heaped up; straight as a wall stood the running water, the deep waters congealed in the heart of the sea.*

Cong. — *The enemy declared: 'I will pursue, I will overtake, I will divide plunder;*

Mohel — *I will satisfy myself with them; I will unsheathe my sword, my hand will impoverish them.'*

Cong. — *You blew with Your wind — the sea enshrouded them; the mighty ones sank like lead in the waters.*

Mohel — *Who is like You among the heavenly powers, HASHEM! Who is like You, mighty in holiness, too awesome for praise, doing wonders!*

Cong. — *You stretched out Your right hand — the earth swallowed them.*

Mohel — *You guided in Your kindness this people that You redeemed;*

Cong. — *You led with Your might to Your holy abode.*

Mohel — *People heard — they were agitated; convulsive terror gripped the dwellers of Philistia.*

Cong. — *Then the chieftains of Edom were confounded, trembling gripped the powers of Moab,*

Mohel — *all the dwellers of Canaan dissolved.*

Cong. — *May fear and terror befall them, at the greatness of Your arm may they be as still as stone,*

Mohel — *until Your people passes through, HASHEM, until this people You have acquired passes through.*

Cong. — *You shall bring them and implant them on the mount of Your heritage, the foundation of Your dwelling place, which You, HASHEM, have made:*

Mohel — *the Sanctuary, my Lord, that Your hands established.*

Cong. — *HASHEM shall reign for all eternity.*

Mohel — *HASHEM shall reign for all eternity.*

the eighth-day mitzvah, *milah*, Moses and the people were able to sing of the miracles that happened at the sea. Additionally the Midrash notes the

תְּפִלּוֹת קוֹדֶם הַבְּרִית

תְּפִלַּת הָאָב

The following prayer from *Avodas HaKodesh (Chida)*
is recited by the infant's father before the *bris*.

לְשֵׁם יִחוּד קוּדְשָׁא בְּרִיךְ הוּא וּשְׁכִינְתֵּהּ בִּדְחִילוּ וּרְחִימוּ וּרְחִימוּ וּדְחִילוּ לְיַחֵד שֵׁם י״ה בו״ה בְּיִחוּדָא שְׁלִים, בְּשֵׁם כָּל יִשְׂרָאֵל.

הִנֵּה אָנֹכִי בָּא לְקַיֵּם מִצְוַת עֲשֵׂה: וּבַיּוֹם הַשְּׁמִינִי יִמּוֹל בְּשַׂר עָרְלָתוֹ.[1] לְתַקֵּן אֶת שָׁרְשָׁהּ בִּמְקוֹם עֶלְיוֹן. וַהֲרֵינִי מוֹסֵר בְּנִי לַמּוֹהֵל, וַאֲנִי מְמַנֶּה אוֹתוֹ שָׁלִיחַ גָּמוּר, שֶׁיָּמוֹל אֶת בְּנִי כְּדַת מַה לַּעֲשׂוֹת.

וִיהִי רָצוֹן מִלְּפָנֶיךָ, יהוה אֱלֹהַי וֵאלֹהֵי אֲבוֹתַי, שֶׁתַּעֲלֶה עָלַי כְּאִלּוּ קִיַּמְתִּי מִצְוָה זוֹ עִם כָּל הַכַּוָּנוֹת הָרְאוּיוֹת לְכַוֵּן בְּמִצְוַת מִילָה וּפְרִיעָה וּמְצִיצָה. וְיִתְגַּלּוּ הַחֲסָדִים בְּמִשְׁפַּט הָאוֹרִים. וּתְהֵא מִצְוָה זוֹ חֲשׁוּבָה לְפָנֶיךָ כְּרֵיחַ נִיחוֹחַ.

וְתַשְׁפִּיעַ נְשָׁמָה קְדוֹשָׁה לַיֶּלֶד. וְאֵלִיָּהוּ הַנָּבִיא זָכוּר לַטּוֹב, יִשְׁמוֹר הַיֶּלֶד, לְשָׁמְרוֹ בְּרִיתוֹ, וְשֶׁלֹּא יֶחְטָא כְּלָל. וּתְזַכֵּנִי לִי וּלְאִמּוֹ, לְגַדְּלוֹ לַתּוֹרָה וּלְמִצְוֹת, וְיִהְיֶה חָכָם וְחָסִיד וּבַעַל מִדּוֹת טוֹבוֹת, וּבַרְיָא מַזְלֵיהּ. וְנִשְׂמַח בּוֹ וּבְתוֹרָתוֹ. וְנַגִּיעֵהוּ לְחוּפָּה.

וְעַתָּה הִנֵּה הֵבֵאתִי אֶת רֵאשִׁית פְּרִי הָאֲדָמָה אֲשֶׁר נָתַתָּ לִי לְקַיֵּם מִצְוֹתֶיךָ. בְּיִרְאָה וּבְאַהֲבָה וְשִׂמְחָה רַבָּה בָּאתִי הַיּוֹם לַעֲשׂוֹת רְצוֹנֶךְ. וְאַתָּה בְּרוֹב רַחֲמֶיךָ תְּבָרְכֵנוּ מִבִּרְכוֹתֶיךָ, וּתְשַׂמְּחֵנוּ בַּעֲבוֹדָתֶךְ. וְתַצִּילֵנוּ מִכָּל חֵטְא. וּתְזַכֵּנוּ לְקַיֵּם כָּל הַמִּצְוֹת שֶׁבַּתּוֹרָה.

חַנֵּנִי אֲדֹנָי כִּי אֵלֶיךָ אֶקְרָא כָּל הַיּוֹם.[2] עָזְרֵנוּ אֱלֹהֵי יִשְׁעֵנוּ עַל דְּבַר כְּבוֹד שְׁמֶךָ, וְהַצִּילֵנוּ וְכַפֵּר עַל חַטֹּאתֵנוּ לְמַעַן שְׁמֶךָ.[3]

וִיהִי נֹעַם אֲדֹנָי אֱלֹהֵינוּ עָלֵינוּ, וּמַעֲשֵׂה יָדֵינוּ כּוֹנְנָה עָלֵינוּ, וּמַעֲשֵׂה יָדֵינוּ כּוֹנְנֵהוּ.[4]

word זֹאת, *this*, appears both in the Song at the Sea — הַשִּׁירָה הַזֹּאת, *this song* — and in God's instructions to Abraham regarding *bris milah* — זֹאת בְּרִיתִי, *this is My covenant* (Genesis 17:10). At the sea, the Jews said to God, 'We are now fit to sing הַשִּׁירָה הַזֹּאת, *this song*, for we have rid ourselves of defilement by having been circumcised and observing Your instructions of זֹאת בְּרִיתִי, *this is My covenant*' (*Shemos Rabbah* 23:12 with *Radal*).

Olelos Ephraim suggests a relevancy

based on the homiletic interpretation of the verse לְגֹזֵר יַם סוּף לִגְזָרִים, *To Him who divides the Sea of Reeds into parts* (Psalms 136:13). The word לִגְזָרִים could be vowelized לִגְזוּרִים, Aramaic for *those who are circumcised*. Hence the implied meaning in the verse is: To Him who divides the Sea of Reeds, for the sake of the circumcised.

◆§ לְשֵׁם יִחוּד — *For the sake of the unification.* This preliminary formulation serves two purposes. It is a

❄{ PRAYERS BEFORE THE BRIS }❄

THE FATHER'S PRAYER

The following prayer from Avodas HaKodesh (Chida)
is recited by the infant's father before the bris.

לְשֵׁם יִחוּד *For the sake of the unification of the Holy One, Blessed is He, and His Presence, in fear and love, and love and fear, to unify the Name — yud-kei with vav-kei — in perfect unity, in the name of all Israel.*

Behold I come to fulfill the positive commandment: 'And on the eighth day shall you circumcise the flesh of his foreskin',¹ to perfect its source from on High.

I hereby give my son to the mohel, and I appoint him absolute proxy to circumcise my son according to halachic requirement.

May it be Your will, HASHEM, my God and the God of my forefathers, that it be considered for me as if I have fulfilled this commandment with all the proper intentions one must have for the commandments of circumcision, revealing and drawing. May Your kindness be revealed in luminous judgment. May this commandment be reckoned before You as the delightful fragrance (of a sacrifice).

Bestow a sacred soul to this child and may Elijah the Prophet — who is remembered for good — guard this child to protect his covenant, and that he never sin. Grant me, together with his mother, the privilege of rearing him to [the study of] Torah, and [the performance of] mitzvos; that he be wise, pious, of exemplary character and good fortune, May we rejoice in him and his Torah [knowledge] and may we bring him to his marriage canopy.

Now, I have presented the first of my fruits which You have given me to fulfill Your commandments. With awe, with love and with joy I have come today, to fulfill Your will. May You, in Your abundant compassion, bless us from Your bountiful blessings and gladden us with Your service. Save us from all sins and grant us the privilege of fulfilling all the Torah's commandments.

Favor me, HASHEM, for I call to You throughout the day.² Assist us, O God of our salvation, for the sake of Your Name's glory; rescue us and atone for our sins for Your Name's sake.³

May the pleasantness of my Lord, our God, be upon us, our handiwork may He establish for us; our handiwork may He establish.⁴

---

(1) *Leviticus* 12:3. (2) *Psalms* 86:3. (3) 79:9. (4) 90:17.

statement of intent that the act about to be performed is to fulfill the Torah's commandment. The second purpose, indicated by the mystical references, is a prayer that the Kabbalistic spiritual qualities of the commandment be realized.

לְיַחֵד שֵׁם ... — *To unify the Name* ... The first half of the Divine Name, formed of the letters *yud* and *hei*, symbolizes the Attribute of Judgment, while the second half, formed of the letters *vav* and *hei*, symbolizes the Attribute of Mercy. The blend of both attributes leads to His desired goal for Creation. Since these letters form the sacred Four-Letter Name that is not to be uttered as it is spelled, and since many commentators maintain that this prohibition extends even to uttering the four letters of the Name, the commonly used pronunciation of these letters in the לְשֵׁם יִחוּד prayer is *yud-kei b'vav kei.*

תפלת המוהל

The following Kabbalistic prayer from *Zecher David* is recited by the *mohel* before the *bris*. Some *siddurim*, notably *Beis Yaakov* and *Otzar HaTefillos*, have much longer versions.

לְשֵׁם יִחוּד קוּדְשָׁא בְּרִיךְ הוּא וּשְׁכִינְתֵּהּ בִּדְחִילוּ וּרְחִימוּ וּרְחִימוּ וּדְחִילוּ לְיַחֵד שֵׁם י״ה בְּו״ה בְּיִחוּדָא שְׁלִים בְּשֵׁם כָּל יִשְׂרָאֵל.

הִנְנִי בָא לָמוּל °תִּינוֹק זֶה [אֶת בְּנִי—If the father serves as *mohel* he substitutes°]
לְקַיֵּם מִצְוַת עֲשֵׂה, כְּמָה שֶׁנֶּאֱמַר: זֹאת בְּרִיתִי אֲשֶׁר תִּשְׁמְרוּ בֵּינִי וּבֵינֵיכֶם וּבֵין זַרְעֲךָ אַחֲרֶיךָ, הִמּוֹל לָכֶם כָּל זָכָר.[1] לְהַכְנִיסוֹ בִּבְרִיתוֹ שֶׁל אַבְרָהָם אָבִינוּ, וּלְהַכְנִיסוֹ בְּחוּלָקָא טָבָא דְקוּדְשָׁא בְּרִיךְ הוּא, דִּכְתִיב: וְצַדִּיק יְסוֹד עוֹלָם.[2]

יְהֵא רַעֲוָא דְקוּדְשָׁא בְּרִיךְ הוּא בְּהַאי קָרְבָּנָא, וְיִתְרְעֵי בֵּיהּ, וְיִזְכֶּה לַעֲשֶׂר חֻפּוֹת שֶׁעָתִיד קוּדְשָׁא בְּרִיךְ הוּא לְמֶעְבַּד לַצַּדִּיקִים לְעָלְמָא דְאָתֵי, כְּדִכְתִיב: אַשְׁרֵי תִּבְחַר וּתְקָרֵב יִשְׁכֹּן חֲצֵרֶיךָ נִשְׂבְּעָה בְּטוּב בֵּיתֶךָ קְדוֹשׁ הֵיכָלֶךָ.[3]

וְעַתָּה בַּעֲוֹנוֹתֵינוּ חָרְבָה עִירֵנוּ וְנִשְׂרַף בֵּית מִקְדָּשֵׁנוּ, וְאֵין לָנוּ קָרְבָּנוֹת שֶׁיְּכַפְּרוּ בַּעֲדֵנוּ. יְהִי רָצוֹן שֶׁיְּהֵא נֶחְשָׁב דַּם בְּרִית הַזֶּה כְּאִלּוּ בָּנִיתִי מִזְבֵּחַ וְהֶעֱלֵיתִי עָלָיו עוֹלוֹת וּזְבָחִים.

יִהְיוּ לְרָצוֹן אִמְרֵי פִי וְהֶגְיוֹן לִבִּי לְפָנֶיךָ, יהוה צוּרִי וְגֹאֲלִי.[4] וִיהִי נֹעַם אֲדֹנָי אֱלֹהֵינוּ עָלֵינוּ, וּמַעֲשֵׂה יָדֵינוּ כּוֹנְנָה עָלֵינוּ, וּמַעֲשֵׂה יָדֵינוּ כּוֹנְנֵהוּ.[5]

תפלת הסנדק

The following prayer from *Avodas HaKodesh* (Chida) is recited by the *sandak* before the *bris*.

לְשֵׁם יִחוּד קוּדְשָׁא בְּרִיךְ הוּא וּשְׁכִינְתֵּהּ בִּדְחִילוּ וּרְחִימוּ וּרְחִימוּ וּדְחִילוּ לְיַחֵד שֵׁם י״ה בְּו״ה בְּיִחוּדָא שְׁלִים, בְּשֵׁם כָּל יִשְׂרָאֵל.

הִנֵּה אָנֹכִי בָא לִהְיוֹת סַנְדָּק, וְאֶהְיֶה כִּסֵּא וּמִזְבֵּחַ לַעֲשׂוֹת עַל יְרֵכַי הַמִּילָה. יְהִי רָצוֹן מִלְּפָנֶיךָ יהוה אֱלֹהַי וֵאלֹהֵי אֲבוֹתַי שֶׁיִּהְיֶה מִזְבֵּחַ כַּפָּרָה, שֶׁתְּכַפֵּר עַל כָּל חַטֹּאתַי עֲוֹנוֹתַי וּפְשָׁעַי, וּבִפְרָט מַה שֶׁפָּגַמְתִּי בִּירֵכַי וּבְאוֹת בְּרִית קֹדֶשׁ.

וְתַעֲלֶה עָלֵינוּ כְּאִלּוּ כִּוַּנְנוּ בְּכָל הַכַּוָּנוֹת הָרְאוּיוֹת לְכַוֵּן, וּתְמַלֵּא כָּל הַשֵׁמוֹת שֶׁפָּגַמְתִּי בָּהֶם, וּתְהֵא הַמִּילָה חֲשׁוּבָה כִּקְטֹרֶת סַמִּים, כְּדִכְתִיב: גִּבְעַת הָעֲרָלוֹת,[6] וּכְתִיב: גִּבְעַת הַלְּבוֹנָה.[7] וְיִתְקַיֵּם בָּנוּ מִקְרָא שֶׁכָּתוּב: יָשִׂימוּ קְטוֹרָה בְּאַפֶּךָ וְכָלִיל עַל מִזְבְּחֶךָ, בָּרֵךְ יהוה חֵילוֹ וּפֹעַל יָדָיו תִּרְצֶה.[8]

וִיהִי נֹעַם אֲדֹנָי אֱלֹהֵינוּ עָלֵינוּ, וּמַעֲשֵׂה יָדֵינוּ כּוֹנְנָה עָלֵינוּ וּמַעֲשֵׂה יָדֵינוּ כּוֹנְנֵהוּ.[5]

---

(1) *Genesis* 17:10. (2) *Proverbs* 10:25. (3) *Psalms* 65:5. (4) 19:15. (5) 90:17.
(6) *Joshua* 5:3. (7) *Song of Songs* 4:6. (8) *Deuteronomy* 33:10-11.

MOHEL'S PRAYER

The following Kabbalistic prayer from *Zecher David* is recited by the *mohel* before the *bris*. Some *siddurim*, notably *Beis Yaakov* and *Otzar HaTefillos*, have much longer versions.

לְשֵׁם יִחוּד For the sake of the unification of the Holy One, Blessed is He, and His Presence, in fear and love, and love and fear, to unify the Name — yud-kei with vav-kei — in perfect unity, in the name of all Israel.

Behold I have come to circumcise °this child [°If the father serves as *mohel* he substitutes: my son] to fulfill a positive commandment, as it is written: 'This is My covenant which you shall keep between Me and you and your descendants after you: Every male among you shall be circumcised';[1] to enter him into the covenant of our forefather Abraham, and to enter him in the splendid share of the Holy One, Blessed is He, as it is written: 'And the righteous one is the foundation of the world'.[2]

May the Holy One, Blessed is He, find favor with this offering, and may He delight in it. May [the child] merit the ten canopies that the Holy One, Blessed is He, will make for the righteous in the World to Come as it is written: 'Praises to the one You choose and draw near to dwell in Your courts, may we be sated with the goodness of Your House, the holiness of Your Temple'.[3]

But now, because of our sins, our city [Jerusalem] has been destroyed, our Holy Temple consumed, and we have no sacrificial offering to atone on our behalf. May it be favorable [to You] to reckon the blood of this covenant as if I built an altar and brought onto it, burnt-offerings and sacrifices.

May the expressions of my mouth and the thoughts of my heart find favor before You, HASHEM, my Rock and my Redeemer.[4] May the pleasantness of my Lord, our God, be upon us — our handiwork may He establish for us; our handiwork may He establish.[5]

SANDAK'S PRAYER

The following prayer from *Avodas HaKodesh* (Chida) is recited by the *sandak* before the *bris*.

לְשֵׁם יִחוּד For the sake of the unification of the Holy One, Blessed is He, and His Presence, in fear and love, and love and fear, to unify the Name — yud-kei with vav kei — in perfect unity, in the name of all Israel.

Behold I have come to be a sandak. I will be a throne and an altar, so that the circumcision may be performed [with the baby] upon my lap. May it be Your will, HASHEM, my God and the God of my forefathers, that it should be an altar of atonement; that it should atone for all my sins, wicked acts, and rebellious deeds, and specifically that which I may have flawed in my sensual behavior and in the sign of the holy covenant.

And consider it for us, as if we concentrated upon all the intentions which are fit to be concentrated upon. Make whole all the Names that I have flawed [with my sins]. May the circumcision be reckoned as the burning of incense, as it is written: 'the hill of Aralos [foreskins]'[6] and 'the hill of frankincense.'[7] May it be fulfilled for us the verse which states: 'They bring incense before You and burnt-offerings upon Your Altar. May HASHEM bless his possessions and graciously accept the achievements of his hands.'[8]

May the pleasantness of my Lord, our God, be upon us — our handiwork may He establish for us; our handiwork may He establish.[5]

⁂ בְּרִית מִילָה ⁂

The *Kvatterin* (Godmother) brings the baby to the room where the *bris* will take place.
She gives the child to the *Kvatter* (Godfather) who brings the infant to the *bris* area.

When the infant is brought in, the entire assemblage greets him:

בָּרוּךְ הַבָּא!

The *mohel* greets the baby:

בָּרוּךְ הַבָּא הַנִּימוֹל לִשְׁמוֹנָה!

Scriptural verses are usually recited by the *mohel* at this point. Customs vary regarding the
order and number of verses recited. In some congregations, the verses are recited by all.

וַיְדַבֵּר יהוה אֶל מֹשֶׁה לֵּאמֹר. פִּינְחָס בֶּן אֶלְעָזָר בֶּן אַהֲרֹן הַכֹּהֵן
הֵשִׁיב אֶת חֲמָתִי מֵעַל בְּנֵי יִשְׂרָאֵל, בְּקַנְאוֹ אֶת קִנְאָתִי
בְּתוֹכָם, וְלֹא כִלִּיתִי אֶת בְּנֵי יִשְׂרָאֵל בְּקִנְאָתִי. לָכֵן אֱמֹר, הִנְנִי נֹתֵן
לוֹ אֶת בְּרִיתִי שָׁלוֹם.¹

The *mohel* recites:

אָמַר הַקָּדוֹשׁ בָּרוּךְ הוּא לְאַבְרָהָם אָבִינוּ, הִתְהַלֵּךְ לְפָנַי וֶהְיֵה
תָמִים.²

In most congregations in *Eretz Yisrael* the following verses
are recited responsively by the father and the entire assemblage.

שְׁמַע יִשְׂרָאֵל, יהוה אֱלֹהֵינוּ, יהוה אֶחָד.³
יהוה מֶלֶךְ, יהוה מָלָךְ, יהוה יִמְלֹךְ לְעֹלָם וָעֶד.
יהוה מֶלֶךְ, יהוה מָלָךְ, יהוה יִמְלֹךְ לְעֹלָם וָעֶד.
אָנָּא יהוה הוֹשִׁיעָה נָּא.   אָנָּא יהוה הוֹשִׁיעָה נָּא.
אָנָּא יהוה הַצְלִיחָה נָּא.   אָנָּא יהוה הַצְלִיחָה נָּא.⁴

◆§ Recitations Prior to the Circumcision

בָּרוּךְ הַבָּא — *Blessed is the one who has come!* The numerical value of the word הַבָּא is eight. Thus, in addition to its simple meaning, the greeting of בָּרוּךְ הַבָּא homiletically conveys: Blessed is the one who has come to be circumcised on the eighth day (*Daas Zekeinim, Bereishis* 21:4; *Abudraham*). Others see הַבָּא as an acronym for הִנֵּה בָּא אֵלִיָּהוּ, *Here comes Eliyahu* (the angel of the bris, see p. 77). Additionally, הַבָּא is an acronym for הַדְּבֵקִים בַּה׳ אֱלֹהֵיכֶם, [You] *who cling to HASHEM, your God* (Deuteronomy 4:4). This indicates that by virtue of his circumcision the child will come to cleave to God (*Sefer HaMatamim*).

When the mohel says בָּרוּךְ הַבָּא, all assembled should stand in honor of Eliyahu who comes to witness every *bris* (*Aruch HaShulchan* Y.D. 265:14).

וַיְדַבֵּר ה׳ — *HASHEM spoke.* The recitation of these verses is based on the Midrashic opinion that פִּנְחָס, Pinchas [Phineas], the Kohen and Elijah the Prophet are one and the same (See *Yalkut Shimoni, Pinchas* 771; *Zohar, Pinchas* 215a; *Rashi, Bava Metzia* 114b; and *Pirkei d'Rabbi Eliezer*, Ch. 29).

Pinchas, who was a grandson of the High Priest Aaron, risked his life to avenge the desecration of God's name, committed by a prince of the tribe of

❧ CIRCUMCISION ❧

The *Kvaterrin* (Godmother) brings the baby to the room where the *bris* will take place. She gives the child to the *Kvatter* (Godfather) who brings the infant to the *bris* area.

When the infant is brought in, the entire assemblage greets him:

Blessed is the one who has come!

The *mohel* greets the baby:

Blessed is the one who has come to be circumcised on the eighth day!

Scriptural verses are usually recited by the *mohel* at this point. Customs vary regarding the order and number of verses recited. In some congregations, the verses are recited by all.

וַיְדַבֵּר *HASHEM spoke to Moses, saying: Phineas, son of Elazar the son of Aaron the Kohen, withdrew My wrath from upon the Children of Israel when he zealously took up My vengeance among them, so that I did not annihilate the Children of Israel in My vengeance. Therefore say, 'Behold! I give him My covenant of Peace'.*[1]

The *mohel* recites:

אָמַר *The Holy One, Blessed is He, said to Abraham, our forefather, 'Walk before me and be perfect.'*[2]

In most congregations in *Eretz Yisrael* the following verses
are recited responsively by the father and the entire assemblage.

Hear, O Israel: HASHEM is our God, HASHEM, the One and Only.[3]
HASHEM reigns, HASHEM has reigned, HASHEM shall reign for all eternity.
HASHEM reigns, HASHEM has reigned, HASHEM shall reign for all eternity.
O HASHEM, please save [us]. O HASHEM, please save [us].
O HASHEM, please [make us] prosper! O HASHEM, please [make us] prosper![4]

---

(1) *Numbers* 25:10-12. (2) *Genesis* 17:1. (3) *Deuteronomy* 6:4. (4) *Psalms* 118:25.

Simeon with a Midianite princess (See *Numbers* 25:7). In the merit of this zealous act, God bequeathed to Pinchas, 'My covenant of peace' (ibid. 25:13).

Elijah is 'present' at every *bris*, hence these verses that refer to Pinchas/Elijah are appropriate. Others, however, omit these verses contending that the *Arizal* did not include them as part of the *bris* ceremony. *Os Sholom* remarks in a letter (printed in the introduction of *Zocher HaBris*) that at the occasion of a *bris* we desire God's favor and it is therefore not fitting to mention the verse which speaks of His wrath — הֵשִׁיב אֶת חֲמָתִי, *He [Pinchas] withdrew My wrath.*

הִתְהַלֵּךְ לְפָנַי וֶהְיֵה תָמִים — *Walk before Me and be perfect.* The Talmud (*Nedarim* 32a) states that when God said to Abraham, 'Be perfect,' Abraham began to tremble with trepidation. Perhaps God had found an imperfection in him that required correction. However, when God told him that he wished to establish a covenant with him, Abraham's fears were allayed.

[Abraham understood that God's willingness to establish a covenant with him indicated that God was completely satisfied with the way he had lived his life. He was lacking only the physical mark of the covenant. Thus, the *milah* made him perfect.]

Two seats are prepared: one for אֵלִיָּהוּ הַנָּבִיא, *Elijah the Prophet*, and one for the *sandak* as he holds the baby during the circumcision. The baby is first placed upon the כִּסֵּא שֶׁל אֵלִיָּהוּ, *Throne of Eliyahu*, by the *mohel* or one of the prominent guests, and the *mohel* says:

זֶה הַכִּסֵּא שֶׁל אֵלִיָּהוּ הַנָּבִיא, זָכוּר לַטּוֹב.

לִישׁוּעָתְךָ קִוִּיתִי יהוה.[1] שִׂבַּרְתִּי לִישׁוּעָתְךָ יהוה, וּמִצְוֹתֶיךָ עָשִׂיתִי.[2] אֵלִיָּהוּ מַלְאַךְ הַבְּרִית, הִנֵּה שֶׁלְּךָ לְפָנֶיךָ, עֲמוֹד עַל יְמִינִי וְסָמְכֵנִי. שִׂבַּרְתִּי לִישׁוּעָתְךָ יהוה. שָׂשׂ אָנֹכִי עַל אִמְרָתֶךָ, כְּמוֹצֵא שָׁלָל רָב.[3] שָׁלוֹם רָב לְאֹהֲבֵי תוֹרָתֶךָ, וְאֵין לָמוֹ

זֶה הַכִּסֵּא שֶׁל אֵלִיָּהוּ — *This is the Throne of Elijah.* With these words Elijah the prophet is invited to sit on the chair that has been designated for him (*Edus LeYisrael;* see pages 77, 157).

זָכוּר לַטּוֹב — *Who is remembered for the good.* This Talmudic expression of respect and blessing is used sparingly and only for people whose service to the Jewish People is of eternal benefit.

שִׂבַּרְתִּי לִישׁוּעָתְךָ ה' וּמִצְוֹתֶיךָ עָשִׂיתִי — *I hoped for Your salvation, HASHEM, and I performed Your commandments.* *Dover Shalom* interprets this verse as referring to Abraham, who had always hoped that God would grant him salvation by blessing him with a son from his wife Sarah. When Isaac was finally born, Abraham was then able to perform the *mitzvah* of circumcising his own son.

הִנֵּה שֶׁלְּךָ לְפָנֶיךָ — *Behold yours is now before you.* 'Yours' refers to *bris milah* which is Elijah's *mitzvah*, since he zealously decried those who neglected it (*Iyun Tefillah*).

עֲמוֹד עַל יְמִינִי וְסָמְכֵנִי — *Stand at my right and assist me.* This phrase is followed by a repetition of the verse שִׂבַּרְתִּי לִישׁוּעָתְךָ ה', *I hoped for your salvation,* HASHEM, to stress that our prayers are only to God, not to Elijah (*Iyun Tefillah*); for as the Talmud (*Yerushalmi Berachos* ch. 9) teaches, one may not direct his prayers toward the angels. The intent of this prayer is: God, just as You stood at Abraham's right and assisted him to excise his own foreskin

(see *Agudah Bereishis* 19:2), so may You stand at my side, and assist me (*Kores HaBris*).

Alternatively, this phrase is addressed to the father, who, according to *halachah* (*Yoreh Deah* 265:9), must stand alongside the *mohel* and appoint him as his agent to perform circumcision (*Kores HaBris*). According to this interpretation, סָמְכֵנִי means *confer permission upon me.*

שָׂשׂ אָנֹכִי עַל אִמְרָתֶךָ — *I rejoice over Your word.* Since the Psalmist uses the singular, *Your word,* the Talmud (*Shabbos* 130a) interprets the term as a reference to *milah,* the first *mitzvah* given to any Jew. [That is, at the time the *mitzvah* of *milah* was given to Abraham, it was the only *word* (i.e., commandment) of God to the Jews.] The uniqueness of *milah* is that it is a constant emblem and indelible sign of the Jew's status as a servant of God. There are similar *mitzvos,* such as *tefillin, mezuzah* and *tzitzis,* but they can be donned and removed at will. Only the sign of *milah* is inseparable from its bearer. This is cause for special joy (*Rashi,* ibid.).

Thus, when King David entered the bathhouse he exclaimed, 'I am devoid of *mitzvos!*' He was wearing neither *tefillin* nor *tzitzis,* the door of the bathhouse may not be adorned with a *mezuzah* and Torah study is not permitted there. When King David remembered that his body bore the sign of the holy covenant, his mind was put at ease. Upon leaving the bathhouse, he said, לַמְנַצֵּחַ עַל,

Two seats are prepared: one for אֵלִיָּהוּ הַנָּבִיא, Elijah the Prophet, and one for the sandak as he holds the baby during the circumcision. The baby is first placed upon the כִּסֵּא שֶׁל אֵלִיָּהוּ, Throne of Eliyahu, by the mohel or one of the prominent guests, and the mohel says:

זֶה This is the Throne of Elijah the prophet, who is remembered for the good.

לִישׁוּעָתְךָ For Your salvation do I long, HASHEM.[1] I hoped for Your salvation, HASHEM, and I performed Your commandments.[2] Elijah, angel of the covenant, behold yours is now before you; stand at my right and assist me. I hoped for Your salvation, HASHEM. I rejoice over Your word, like one who finds abundant spoils.[3] There is abundant peace for the lovers of Your Torah, and there is no

――――――――――――
(1) Genesis 49:18). (2) Psalms 119:166. (3) 119:162.

הַשְּׁמִינִית, To the One Who grants victory on the eighth... (Psalms 12:1), a reference to milah which is performed on the eighth day of the child's life (Menachos 43b). This then is the meaning of the verse: [When David 'discovered' that he was not devoid of mitzvos, he proclaimed,] 'I rejoice over Your word — milah — like one who discovers abundant spoils' (Maharsha, Shabbos 130a).

The Talmud also notes that since the commandment of circumcision was originally accepted with joy it continues to be performed with joy (Shabbos 130a). This emotion is manifested by the tendering of a festive meal (Rashi, ibid.) and as Tosafos notes, Abraham tendered a great banquet when he circumcised his son.[1]

כְּמוֹצֵא שָׁלָל רָב — Like one who finds abundant spoils. The term finds indicates an effortless act, yet abundant spoils are usually acquired after a battle has been waged. Maharsha (Shabbos 130a) explains that when the circumcised child matures he will realize that as an infant the sign of the covenant was placed on him with no effort on his part; thus, he had indeed 'found' (i.e., effortlessly) a great spoil.

The victorious warrior who finds great spoils experiences a double joy — the spoils of his victory and the rejoicing over the enemy being weakened. With milah, too, there is firstly the spiritual benefit to the child on whom the mitzvah is performed, and at the same time the added value that it debilitates the Evil Inclination, for as Rambam (Moreh 3:49) writes: Circumcision weakens man's excessive sensuality (Meshech Chochmah, Lech Lecha).

לְאֹהֲבֵי תוֹרָתֶךָ — For the lovers of Your Torah. This verse is recited because

1. In the book of Esther, when the Jews were saved from their tormentor, Haman, the Megillah states: לַיְּהוּדִים הָיְתָה אוֹרָה וְשִׂמְחָה וְשָׂשֹׂן וִיקָר, The Jews had light and gladness, and joy and honor (Esther 8:16). The Talmud (Megillah 16b, see Rashi) interprets 'light' as an allusion to the light of Torah; 'gladness' to the celebration of the Festivals; 'joy' to bris milah; and 'honor' to the tefillin.

The question arises as to why Scripture alluded to these four mitzvos rather than mention them openly — The Jews had Torah, Festivals, milah, and tefillin.

R' Shimon Schwab suggests that it was not the act of each mitzvah itself that was restored, for the Jews had been able to perform them in a limited way. What was missing was an appreciation of the light, the gladness, the joy and the honor inherent in the performance of a mitzvah. They performed the mitzvah of milah all along, but without the joy that should accompany it. After their triumph, however, Jews celebrated each bris with the joy it should be accorded.

For this reason the Megillah does not use the word מִילָה, but the word שָׂשֹׂן, joy, as a reference to the way the mitzvah is celebrated, and not the mitzvah itself.

מִכְשׁוֹל.[1] אַשְׁרֵי, תִּבְחַר וּתְקָרֵב, יִשְׁכֹּן חֲצֵרֶיךָ —

All present respond:

— נִשְׂבְּעָה, בְּטוּב בֵּיתֶךָ, קְדֹשׁ הֵיכָלֶךָ.[2]

The father then takes the child from the Throne of Eliyahu [or is given the baby by one of the guests] and places him on the *sandak's* lap.

ACCORDING TO SOME AUTHORITIES THE FATHER SHOULD VERBALLY APPOINT THE *MOHEL* AS HIS AGENT TO PERFORM CIRCUMCISION.

As the *mohel* is preparing to perform the circumcision, both he and the infant's father recite short prayers (some omit the passage in parentheses).

Mohel recites:

הִנְנִי מוּכָן וּמְזֻמָּן לְקַיֵּם מִצְוַת עֲשֵׂה שֶׁצִּוָּנוּ הַבּוֹרֵא יִתְבָּרַךְ לָמוֹל.

Father recites:

הִנְנִי מוּכָן וּמְזֻמָּן לְקַיֵּם מִצְוַת עֲשֵׂה שֶׁצִּוַּנִי הַבּוֹרֵא יִתְבָּרַךְ לָמוּל אֶת בְּנִי.

(לְשֵׁם יִחוּד קוּדְשָׁא בְּרִיךְ הוּא וּשְׁכִינְתֵּהּ, עַל יְדֵי הַהוּא טָמִיר וְנֶעְלָם, בְּשֵׁם כָּל יִשְׂרָאֵל. וִיהִי נֹעַם אֲדֹנָי אֱלֹהֵינוּ עָלֵינוּ, וּמַעֲשֵׂה יָדֵינוּ כּוֹנְנָה עָלֵינוּ, וּמַעֲשֵׂה יָדֵינוּ כּוֹנְנֵהוּ.)[3]

Just before performing the circumcision, the *mohel* recites:

בָּרוּךְ אַתָּה יהוה אֱלֹהֵינוּ מֶלֶךְ הָעוֹלָם, אֲשֶׁר קִדְּשָׁנוּ בְּמִצְוֹתָיו, וְצִוָּנוּ עַל הַמִּילָה. (אָמֵן.—All)

As the *mohel* performs the circumcision, the father recites:

בָּרוּךְ אַתָּה יהוה אֱלֹהֵינוּ מֶלֶךְ הָעוֹלָם, אֲשֶׁר קִדְּשָׁנוּ בְּמִצְוֹתָיו, וְצִוָּנוּ לְהַכְנִיסוֹ בִּבְרִיתוֹ שֶׁל אַבְרָהָם אָבִינוּ. (אָמֵן.—All)

---

(1) *Psalms* 119:165. (2) 65:5. (3) 90:17.

understanding the secrets of Torah is dependent on one's being circumcised (*Kores HaBris*). [See *Teshuvos R' Akiva Eiger* (§42) which notes that the physical removal of the עָרְלָה, foreskin, is a prerequisite for eventually removing the עָרְלָה of the heart (i.e., the Evil Inclination; see pp. 80-81). Only then can one's heart be open to embrace Torah and *mitzvos*. See also *Midrash* regarding Akilas the convert on page 85.]

וְאֵין לָמוֹ מִכְשׁוֹל — *And there is no stumbling block for them.* The Kabbalists suggested that this verse be recited by the *mohel* as a prayer that the procedure go smoothly, without any

complications (*Edus LeYisrael*).

תִּבְחַר — *You choose.* God selected the Jews from among all the nations to be His chosen people. To indicate this He commanded them to bear an insignia — the seal of *bris milah.* It is this mark of identity that betokens our belonging to God. It is for this reason that we recite the verse of 'choosing' at the *bris milah* ceremony (*Iyun Tefillah;* see *Bamidbar Rabbah* 14:10).

Zohar (*Lech Lecha* 94a) states that the ten words in this verse correspond to the ten canopies which will be granted to the righteous in the World to Come (*Darkei Moshe*, Y. D. 265:4).

In general, Ashkenazic custom calls

The Ritual / Order of the Bris [122]

stumbling block for them.[1] *Praiseworthy is the one You choose and draw near to dwell in Your courts —*

All present respond:

— may we be satisfied by the goodness of Your House — Your Holy Temple.[2]

The father then takes the child from the Throne of Eliyahu [or is given the baby by one of the guests] and places him on the sandak's lap.

ACCORDING TO SOME AUTHORITIES THE FATHER SHOULD VERBALLY APPOINT THE *MOHEL* AS HIS AGENT TO PERFORM CIRCUMCISION.

As the *mohel* is preparing to perform the circumcision, both he and the infant's father recite short prayers (some omit the passage in parentheses):

Father recites:	Mohel recites:
הִנְנִי *Behold, I am prepared and ready to perform the positive commandment that the Creator, Blessed is He, has commanded me, to circumcise my son.*	**הִנְנִי** *Behold, I am prepared and ready to perform the positive commandment that the Creator, Blessed is He, has commanded us, to circumcise.*

(For the sake of the unification of the Holy One, Blessed is He, and His Presence, through Him Who is hidden and inscrutable — [I pray] in the name of all Israel. May the pleasantness of my Lord, our God, be upon us — our handiwork may He establish for us; our handiwork may He establish.)[3]

Just before performing the circumcision, the *mohel* recites:

בָּרוּךְ *Blessed are You, HASHEM, our God, King of the universe, Who has sanctified us with His commandments, and has commanded us regarding circumcision.* (All — Amen.)

As the *mohel* performs the circumcision, the father recites:

בָּרוּךְ *Blessed are You, HASHEM, our God, King of the universe, Who has sanctified us with His commandments, and has commanded us to bring him into the covenant of Abraham, our forefather.* (All — Amen.)

for the first half of this verse, אַשְׁרֵי... חֲצֵרֶיךָ, to be recited by the *mohel*, and the remainder נִשְׂבְּעָה... הֵיכָלֶךָ, by all present. According to Sephardic custom (based on *Zohar*, see p. 178) the father says the first half, and the assembled respond with the latter half. *Taz (Y. D.* 265:12), however, says that the widespread custom in his time was for the assemblage to recite the entire verse when the child was brought in. Many communities today follow this practice.

◆§ The Two Milah Blessings

As with most other *mitzvos* the performance of *bris milah* requires the recitation of a blessing prior to its performance. *Milah* however is unique, for unlike other *mitzvos* that require only one blessing, *milah* requires two: עַל הַמִּילָה, *regarding circumcison*; and לְהַכְנִיסוֹ בִּבְרִיתוֹ שֶׁל אַבְרָהָם אָבִינוּ, *to enter him into the covenant of Abraham our forefather.*[1]

1. Various reasons have been suggested for the omission (by Ashkenazic communities outside of *Eretz Yisrael*) of the *Shehecheyanu* blessing — recited upon the performance of certain *mitzvos* and at many festive and joyous occasions — from the *bris* ceremony. Among them are:
— Our joy is incomplete because of the child's discomfort (*Tosafos Eruvin* 40b, s.v. דלמא;

בָּרוּךְ אַתָּה יהוה אֱלֹהֵינוּ מֶלֶךְ הָעוֹלָם, שֶׁהֶחֱיָנוּ וְקִיְּמָנוּ וְהִגִּיעָנוּ
לַזְּמַן הַזֶּה. (אָמֵן.—All)

All present proclaim loudly and joyfully:

כְּשֵׁם שֶׁנִּכְנַס לַבְּרִית, כֵּן יִכָּנֵס לְתוֹרָה וּלְחֻפָּה וּלְמַעֲשִׂים טוֹבִים.

The commentators give various reasons for the two separate blessings. Most of them are compiled by *Beis Yosef* and *Bach* (*Tur, Yoreh Deah* 265). The blessing of the *mohel* is obvious, since it is no different from the blessing performed before the performance of other commandments. Why, however, does the father recite a separate blessing? Among the reasons are:

— The father has a personal obligation for the circumcision of his child; however, the *mohel's* role is of a different nature. While in the father's presence he acts as an agent to fulfill the father's personal obligation for him. But in the father's absence, the *mohel* acts as the representative of the congregation to fulfill its communal obligation to have every baby boy circumcised. Since there are two levels of responsibility, the Sages wished each to have his own blessing (*Hagahos Maimonios*).

— The father has other responsibilities to his child, such as *Pidyon Haben* (if he is a firstborn), teaching him Torah, marrying him off and so on. Consequently the Sages assigned the father a special blessing, symbolic of his personal and continuing responsibility (*Abudraham*).

— The second blessing is one of thanksgiving for the privilege of bringing the newborn infant to the lifelong service of God (*Bach*).

— The two blessings signify that

there are two parts to *milah:* חִיתוּךְ, *excision, and the unique act of* פְּרִיעָה, *uncovering* (*Bach*). Indeed, according to *Tur* (*Yoreh Deah* 265) the *mohel* recites the first blessing before the excision, and the father recites the second blessing before the uncovering.

— The second blessing signifies a unique aspect of *milah*. Unlike physical *mitzvah* acts, which are not incumbent upon minors and certainly not upon infants, the act of *milah* has initiated this infant into the Abrahamitic covenant, with all the holiness and responsibility that this implies (*Aruch HaShulchan, Y.D.* 265:8).

— Others understand the intent of the second blessing לְהַבְנִיסוֹ, *to bring him in,* as the father's expression of joy at his being commanded to present his child for circumcision. According to this opinion, this blessing should be recited even before the *bris* has begun, when the child has been brought to where the *bris* will take place. This is the custom in some Sephardic communities (see *Sefer HaBris* 265:11).

◄§ The Congregation's Response

כְּשֵׁם שֶׁנִּכְנַס לַבְּרִית — *Just as he has entered into the covenant.* The comparison to *bris* has been interpreted in several ways:

— As the child's *bris* is celebrated with great joy, so too his Torah study, marriage and performance of good

see also *Kesubos* 8a; *Beis Yosef, Yoreh Deah* 265);

— *Shehecheyanu* is recited for a *mitzvah* that only occurs from time to time [e.g., lighting the Chanukah *Menorah*] but a *bris* can occur every day (*Rav Sherira Gaon; Tosafos, Sukkah* 46a, s.v. העושה).

This is not to be confused with the *Shehecheyanu* blessing recited on joyous occasions [e.g., acquisition of a new house]. Even though these can happen at any time of the year, the *Shehecheyanu* for personal pleasures has criteria different from those of the *Shehecheyanu* for *mitzvos* (see *Orach Chaim* 225).

All present proclaim loudly and joyfully:

Just as he has entered into the covenant, so may he enter into the [study of] Torah, the marriage canopy, and [the performance of] good deeds.

deeds should be associated with great joy and happiness.

— As the act of *bris milah* is irreversible, and so, once performed, symbolizes that God's covenant is everlasting, so we pray that the child's Torah study, marriage and good deeds should also be everlasting.

— Just as the *bris* has been done in purity of thought and intent, so too the child's Torah study, marriage and good deeds should be done in purity of thought and devotion to ideals.

Our text of the people's response is that which is found in our editions of the Talmud *(Shabbos* 137b): כְּשֵׁם שֶׁנִּכְנַס, *just as he has entered ... so may he enter. Rambam's* text *(Milah* 3:2), however, reads ... כְּשֵׁם שֶׁהִכְנַסְתּוֹ כֵּן תַּכְנִיסֵהוּ, *Just as you have entered him ... so may you enter him,* a direct declaration to the father [and this is indeed the text used at a Sephardic *bris,* see p. 180]. *Taz (Yoreh Deah* 265:1:2) comments that those at the *bris* who can actually see the father say כְּשֵׁם שֶׁהִכְנַסְתּוֹ, *just as you have entered him,* while those who are further back in the crowd and do not see him, make the indirect statement כְּשֵׁם שֶׁנִּכְנַס, *just as he has entered.*

Shach (Yoreh Deah 265:13) explains, however, that כְּשֵׁם שֶׁנִּכְנַס, *just as he has been entered,* is preferred because that includes all situations (even if the father is not present).

לְתוֹרָה וּלְחֻפָּה וּלְמַעֲשִׂים טוֹבִים — *Into the [study of] Torah, the marriage canopy, and [the performance of] good deeds.* The order of these three seems strange

for the performance of good deeds can be done before one marries. A number of interpretations have been offered:

— The Talmud teaches that a father is obligated to circumcise his son, redeem him (if he is firstborn),[1] teach him Torah, arrange his marriage and teach him a trade *(Kiddushin* 29a). It is because of the Talmudic sequence that the prayer has its specific order. Thus, we say to the father, 'Now that you have been fortunate enough to accomplish the first of your obligations (*bris*), may you merit to accomplish the others — teaching your son Torah, bringing him to marriage and teaching him a trade, which is equated with good deeds.' For as the Talmud (ibid.) teaches: Refraining from teaching a child a craft is, in essence, teaching him theft.

— The understanding and knowledge of what constitutes a good deed can only come through the education received by Torah study. It is through reflective Torah scholarship that one gains an insight into what is truly good. Through marriage one learns the art of compassion, concern for others, and the ability to identify with the problems of other people. Thus תּוֹרָה, *Torah,* and חֻפָּה, *marriage,* are prerequisites to carrying out מַעֲשִׂים טוֹבִים, *good deeds.*

— It is relatively easy for a person to be an idealist and do good deeds before he has the responsibilities of marriage and family. However, if one still finds time for good deeds after he already has family responsibilities, that is indeed highly commendable.

1. Redeeming is left out of the prayer, since it is not applicable in the majority of cases. It is required only if: (a) the boy is his mother's first conception; (b) neither grandfather of the child is a *Kohen* or a *Levi;* and (c) the baby was not born by Caesarean section.

After the circumcision, the baby is held by one of the guests, while the following prayers (including giving the name) are recited. The honors of reciting the blessings and of giving the name may be awarded to one person, or two. Similarly, two people may hold the baby, one during the blessing, one for the naming.

A cup of wine is filled and held in the right hand by the man reciting the blessing.

בָּרוּךְ אַתָּה יהוה אֱלֹהֵינוּ מֶלֶךְ הָעוֹלָם, בּוֹרֵא פְּרִי הַגָּפֶן.
(All—אָמֵן.)

בָּרוּךְ אַתָּה יהוה אֱלֹהֵינוּ מֶלֶךְ הָעוֹלָם, אֲשֶׁר קִדַּשׁ יָדִיד מִבֶּטֶן,
וְחֹק בִּשְׁאֵרוֹ שָׂם, וְצֶאֱצָאָיו חָתַם בְּאוֹת בְּרִית קֹדֶשׁ. עַל כֵּן
בִּשְׂכַר זֹאת, אֵל חַי, חֶלְקֵנוּ צוּרֵנוּ, צַוֵּה לְהַצִּיל יְדִידוּת שְׁאֵרֵנוּ
מִשַּׁחַת. לְמַעַן בְּרִיתוֹ אֲשֶׁר שָׂם בִּבְשָׂרֵנוּ. בָּרוּךְ אַתָּה יהוה, כּוֹרֵת
הַבְּרִית.
(All—אָמֵן.)

◆§ Blessings after the Circumcision

בּוֹרֵא פְּרִי הַגָּפֶן — *Who creates the fruit of the vine.* The custom of reciting the post-*milah* blessing over a cup of wine is not mentioned in the Talmud, but is mentioned as a matter of course in the Geonic literature. *Mordechai (Yoma §726)* indicates that it is based upon the Talmudic teaching *(Berachos 35a)*: A song of praise is recited only over wine *(Beis Yosef, Y.D. 265).*

◆§ אֲשֶׁר קִדַּשׁ/Asher Kidash

The text of this blessing is found in the Talmud *(Shabbos 137b)*, with the omission of the word צוּרֵנוּ, *our Rock.* This word is added from *Tosefta (Berachos* Chapter 6).

קִדַּשׁ — *Has sanctified* [alternatively, *prepared,* see *Zocher HaBris*]. This is the reading found in most *siddurim.* R' Yaakov Emden vowelizes קֵדֵשׁ.

יָדִיד — *The beloved one.* There are three opinions as to whom the word יָדִיד, *the beloved one,* refers to. There are Scriptural references to substantiate its being any of the three Patriarchs — Abraham, Isaac or Jacob. The subsequent phrases are variously interpreted, depending on which Patriarch יָדִיד refers to. Thus the commentary will explain this blessing in general, and

then as it applies to each of the three Patriarchs specifically.

וְחֹק — *And the decree.* The commentaries are troubled by the use of the word חֹק, *decree,* with regard to *bris milah,* for חֹק usually refers to a *mitzvah* for which we do not know the reason — such as *shaatnez* [the prohibition against wearing clothes made from a combination of wool and linen], and the Red Cow, which paradoxically purified the defiled but defiled the pure. The term חֹק, *decree,* does not seem to apply to *milah,* for which numerous reasons are suggested: as a perpetual mark of Jewish identity on the Jewish male; to reduce the animal drives in man; as a symbol of perfection on the body; to serve as a reminder to man that one can elevate to holiness even that which can potentially bring one to the abyss of immorality.

Menoras HaMaor (Ner III) writes that *bris milah* is considered a חֹק for we do not know the reason why *milah* was chosen above other *mitzvos* as the sign of the covenant that God made with Abraham. If God had so chosen, He could have made His covenant dependent on the performance of a different *mitzvah,* such as *tefillin.*

Abudraham explains that the reasons for *milah* stated above are Midrashic and Rabbinic in origin. The Torah itself

After the circumcision, the baby is held by one of the guests, while the following prayers (including giving the name) are recited. The honors of reciting the blessings and of giving the name may be awarded to one person, or two. Similarly, two people may hold the baby, one during the blessing, one for the naming.

A cup of wine is filled and held in the right hand by the man reciting the blessing.

בָּרוּךְ *Blessed are You, HASHEM, our God, King of the universe, Who creates the fruit of the vine.* (All—*Amen.*)

בָּרוּךְ *Blessed are You, HASHEM, our God, King of the universe, Who has sanctified the beloved one from the womb and placed the mark of the decree in his flesh, and sealed his offspring with the sign of the holy covenant. Therefore, as reward for this, O Living God, our Portion, our Rock, may You issue the command to rescue the beloved [soul] within our flesh from destruction, for the sake of His covenant that He has placed in our flesh. Blessed are You HASHEM, Who establishes the covenant.*

(All-*Amen.*)

does not state an explicit reason for *milah* as it does for other *mitzvos* such as *succah, matzah,* and *Shabbos.* Hence, it is deemed a חֹק.

וְחֹק בִּשְׁאֵרוֹ שָׂם — *Placed the [mark of the] decree [of circumcision] on his flesh.* A *bris* is unique in that it is the only *mitzvah* that is inseparable from the body of man as opposed to other *mitzvos* such as *tefillin* or *tzitzis* which can be removed (*Maharsha Shabbos* 137b).

[Possibly the use of the combination וְחֹק ... שָׂם, *He placed the decree,* with reference to *milah* has its basis in Scripture: וַיִּכְרֹת יְהוֹשֻׁעַ בְּרִית לָעָם בַּיּוֹם הַהוּא וַיָּשֶׂם לוֹ חֹק, *Joshua made a covenant with the people that day and established the decree (Joshua 24:25).*]

חָתַם — *Sealed.* This word may also mean *signed, concluded,* and is used here to symbolize *milah's* status as Abraham's final act, since he had performed all the Torah's *mitzvos* except for circumcision (*Yoma* 28b).

Just as a loyal servant wears the badge or seal of his master, so also is the circumcision on the body of the Jew a seal of his covenant with God (*Sforno, Bereishis* 17:11).

בְּאוֹת — *With the sign. Milah* was designated as a sign in the verse: וְהָיָה לְאוֹת בְּרִית בֵּינִי וּבֵינֵיכֶם, *and it will be a sign of*

the covenant between Me and you (Genesis 17:11).

In *Song of Songs* (2:7), God says, הִשְׁבַּעְתִּי אֶתְכֶם בְּנוֹת יְרוּשָׁלַיִם בִּצְבָאוֹת..., *I adjure you, O Daughters of Jerusalem, by gazelles...* The Midrash (ibid.) sees the word בִּצְבָאוֹת (literally *by gazelles*) as a contraction of two words: בְּצָבָא, *by the army,* and אוֹת, *sign,* a reference to the Nation of Israel, the army of God, that proudly wears its emblem — the sign of *milah.*

קֹדֶשׁ — *Holy. Bris milah* is referred to as the holy covenant for there is a great measure of holiness that man can attain by bridling his temptations in this area. Indeed, the *bris* is performed on this part of the body to serve as a constant reminder for man to contain and control his sensual desires (*R' Shlomo Garmiza*).

'In every case where regulations are found as a guard against immorality, one also finds sanctity.' It is for this reason that the portion of *Acherei* (*Leviticus* 16), that details ordinances regarding illicit relations, is followed by the dictum, קְדוֹשִׁים תִּהְיוּ, *You shall be holy* (*Vayikra Rabbah Vayikra* 24:6; *Yerushalmi, Yevamos* 2:4; See also *II Kings* 4:9 with *Rashi*).

אֵל חַי — *Living God.* This appellation is borrowed from the verse, לִבִּי וּבְשָׂרִי

וְרַנְּנוּ אֶל אֵל חָי, *My heart and flesh will sing with joy to the living God (Psalms 84:3).* In that verse, בְּשָׂרִי, *my flesh,* refers to the *mitzvah* of *milah,* which is performed upon the flesh of man *(Abudraham).* The body sings to God for being privileged to possess upon itself the sign of the covenant between God and Israel.

חֶלְקֵנוּ צוּרֵנוּ — *Our Portion, our Rock.* These references to God are derived from the verse *(Psalms 73:26)* that uses similar wording in conjunction with the word שְׁאֵר, *flesh,* used earlier in this blessing: כָּלָה שְׁאֵרִי וּלְבָבִי צוּר לְבָבִי וְחֶלְקִי אֱלֹהִים לְעוֹלָם, *Though my flesh and my heart fail, God is the Rock of my heart and my Portion forever (Abudraham).*

לְהַצִּיל ... מִשַּׁחַת — *To rescue ... from destruction.* This is a prayer for the future. We appeal to God that in merit of our performing the *mitzvah* of circumcision which He decreed, we be spared from *Gehinnom (Shach Yoreh Deah 265:5).*

An alternative reading for this word is צִוָּה, *He has decreed.* This is the pronunciation suggested by *R' Hai Gaon* and also indicated by *R' Yaakov Emden* in *Siddur Bais Yaakov.* Those who pronounce it this way use this form so that it should not appear that we do the *mitzvah* of *milah* merely for the sake of reward, which, they contend, is implied in the word צִוָּה, *decree (Zocher HaBris).*

The reading of צִוָּה is in consonance with *Midrash Tanchuma (Lech Lecha, §20)* which states: *Milah* is so dear to God that He swore to Abraham that anyone who is circumcised will not descend to *Gehinnom.* The *Midrash (Genesis 48:8)* further quotes *R' Levi:* In the future, Abraham will sit at the entrance of *Gehinnom* and will not allow any circumcised member of Israel to descend into the abyss *(Baal HaTurim, Genesis 18:1; see also Eruvin 19a).*

לְהַצִּיל יְדִידוּת — *To rescue the beloved* [*soul*]. This refers to man's soul which is his most precious possession *(Taz, Y.D.*

265:5). *Kores HaBris* suggests that יְדִידוּת, *the beloved one,* refers to the Nation of Israel, based on the verse נָתַתִּי אֶת יְדִידוּת נַפְשִׁי בְּכַף אֹיְבֶיהָ, *I have given the beloved of my soul into the hand of the enemy (Jeremiah 12:7).*

מִשַּׁחַת — *From destruction. Kores HaBris* sees שַׁחַת, *destruction,* as a reference to the current Exile, for God told the prophet *Zechariah* that the Jewish nation will merit the Final Redemption in reward for having upheld the commandment of *bris milah* even while in the depths of exile. *You, too, in the merit of your covenantal blood I delivered your bound ones from an abyss devoid of water (see Rashi, Zechariah 9:11).*

לְמַעַן בְּרִיתוֹ אֲשֶׁר שָׂם בִּבְשָׂרֵנוּ — *For the sake of His covenant that He has placed in our flesh.* We ask God to spare us from *Gehinnom* for the sake of His covenant. For it is a disgrace to the King for a servant bearing His emblem to enter into a despicable place *(Etz Yosef).*

כּוֹרֵת הַבְּרִית — *Who establishes the covenant.* This term is similar to וּכָרוֹת עִמּוֹ הַבְּרִית, *And You established with him the covenant (Nechemiah 9:8);* also בַּיּוֹם הַהוּא כָּרַת ה' אֶת אַבְרָם בְּרִית, *On that day HASHEM made a covenant with Abram (Genesis 15:18.)*

Literally, the word כָּרַת means *to cut off,* connoting a separation. Yet, paradoxically, the same word means to establish an agreement and create a bond. *HaKsav VeHaKabbalah (Bereishis 15:18)* reconciles this paradox with the following explanation:

The word בְּרִית, *covenant,* is an extension of the word בָּרִי meaning to choose (as in בְּרֵירָה). When two parties enter into a covenant it is defined by the obligations which the participants have accepted toward each other. The two parties involved have 'cut themselves off' from the rest of mankind with respect to the terms of their mutual agreement. The bond which has been created for them is unique and for them alone.

The covenant that God made with

Abraham bound them together and at the same time separated Abraham and his descendants from the nations of the world. Hence בְּרִיתוֹת בְּרִית, *the cutting of the covenant*. [Additionally, the *bris* indicates the separation from the status of עֲרֵלוּת, *uncircumcised*, which is a euphemism for the nations of the world (see *Rambam, Milah* 3:8).]

יְדִיד/Abraham

The Talmud (*Menachos* 53b) relates that when God was about to destroy the First Temple, Abraham came to plead for his descendants. God exclaimed, מֶה לִידִידִי בְּבֵיתִי, *What is My beloved one doing in My house? (Jeremiah* 11:15). Thus 'beloved one' is a reference to Abraham (*Tosafos, Shabbos* 137b).

קִדֵּשׁ יְדִיד מִבֶּטֶן — *Sanctified the beloved one from the womb.* Even prior to Abraham's birth God had already decided that He would appoint Abraham as a leader for all Jews. *Rabbeinu Tam (Tosafos, Menachos* 53b) interprets the following verse in *Jeremiah* (1:5) as a reference to Abraham: בְּטֶרֶם אֶצָּרְךָ בַבֶּטֶן יְדַעְתִּיךָ ... נָבִיא לַגּוֹיִם נְתַתִּיךָ, *Before I created you, while you were still in the womb, I recognized...that I would appoint you as a prophet.*

וְחֹק בִּשְׁאֵרוֹ שָׂם — *And placed the [mark of the] decree [of circumcision] in his flesh.* God Himself placed the mark of circumcision on Abraham, for the Midrash (*Bereishis Rabbah* 49:2) relates that when Abraham was about to circumcise himself, he became frightened, and God Himself assisted him (*R' Yehudah ben R' Yakar).*

חֹק בִּשְׁאֵרוֹ can also be translated: *an engraving in his close relative.* R' Yosef Chaim Sonnenfeld offered a novel explanation based on this translation. The Torah uses the word שְׁאֵרוֹ, *his close relative,* to refer to one's wife (*Numbers* 27:11; see *Bava Basra* 111b — שְׁאֵרוֹ זוּ אִשְׁתּוֹ). Therefore, the close relation of Abraham referred to in the word שְׁאֵרוֹ is his wife Sarah. Sarah lacked ovaries and therefore could not conceive (*Yevamos* 64b; *Bereishis Rabbah* 47:2). God

therefore fashioned or 'engraved' (חָקַק) an ovary so that she could bear Isaac. Thus, the meaning here is, *God engraved* [i.e., made an ovary] *in his* [Abraham's] *close relative'(Iyun Tefillah).*

וְצֶאֱצָאָיו — *And his offspring.* This refers to all Jews, who descend from Abraham (*Maharsha, Shabbos* 137b). The root of the word is יָצָא, *went out* (*Metzudos, Ibn Ezra,* to *Isaiah* 34:1).

יְדִיד/Isaac

Rashi (Shabbos 137b) is of the opinion that יְדִיד, *the beloved one,* refers to Isaac, for when God addressed Abraham prior to the *Akeidah* (binding on the altar), He said, קַח נָא אֶת בִּנְךָ אֶת יְחִידְךָ, אֲשֶׁר אָהַבְתָּ, *Please take your son, your only one, whom you love... (Genesis* 22:2).

קִדֵּשׁ יְדִיד מִבֶּטֶן — *Sanctified the beloved one from the womb.* Abraham was told to circumcise himself at age ninety-nine (ibid. 17:1), a year before Isaac was born (ibid. 21:5) so that Isaac would be conceived in holiness (*Avudraham).* [This was not the case with Ishmael who was born when Abraham was eighty-six (*Genesis* 16:16).]

מִבֶּטֶן — *From the womb.* Prior to Isaac's birth, God had already told Abraham, וְאֶת בְּרִיתִי אָקִים אֶת יִצְחָק, *I will establish My covenant with Isaac (Genesis* 17:21). The word אָקִים, *establish,* is the acrostic for אֲשֶׁר קִדֵּשׁ יְדִיד מִבֶּטֶן, the first words of this prayer (*Daas Zekeinim,* ibid).

וְחֹק בִּשְׁאֵרוֹ שָׂם — *And placed the [mark of the] decree [of circumcision] in his flesh.* By circumcising his son Isaac, Abraham placed on him the sign of the covenant (*Abudraham).*

Isaac was the first infant to be circumcised when he was eight days old. It is logical then that the blessing at an infant's circumcision should commence by citing Isaac's *bris* on the eighth day, which set a precedent for Jews to follow forever.

Upon reaching the words in bold type, the reader pauses while all present recite them aloud. The reader then repeats them and continues:

‎אֱלֹהֵינוּ‎ ‎וֵאלֹהֵי אֲבוֹתֵינוּ, קַיֵּם אֶת הַיֶּלֶד הַזֶּה לְאָבִיו וּלְאִמּוֹ,‎
‎וְיִקָּרֵא שְׁמוֹ, בְּיִשְׂרָאֵל‎ **בֶּן** (baby's Hebrew name) ‎בֶּן‎ (father's Hebrew

name). ‎יִשְׂמַח הָאָב בְּיוֹצֵא חֲלָצָיו, וְתָגֵל אִמּוֹ בִּפְרִי בִטְנָהּ. כַּכָּתוּב:‎
‎יִשְׂמַח אָבִיךָ וְאִמֶּךָ, וְתָגֵל יוֹלַדְתֶּךָ.[1] וְנֶאֱמַר: וָאֶעֱבֹר עָלַיִךְ וָאֶרְאֵךְ‎
‎מִתְבּוֹסֶסֶת בְּדָמָיִךְ, וָאֹמַר לָךְ בְּדָמַיִךְ חֲיִי, וָאֹמַר לָךְ בְּדָמַיִךְ חֲיִי.[2]‎
‎וְנֶאֱמַר: זָכַר לְעוֹלָם בְּרִיתוֹ, דָּבָר צִוָּה לְאֶלֶף דּוֹר. אֲשֶׁר כָּרַת אֶת‎
‎אַבְרָהָם, וּשְׁבוּעָתוֹ לְיִשְׂחָק. וַיַּעֲמִידֶהָ לְיַעֲקֹב לְחֹק, לְיִשְׂרָאֵל בְּרִית‎
‎עוֹלָם.[3] וְנֶאֱמַר: וַיָּמָל אַבְרָהָם אֶת יִצְחָק בְּנוֹ, בֶּן שְׁמֹנַת יָמִים,‎
‎כַּאֲשֶׁר צִוָּה אֹתוֹ אֱלֹהִים.[4] **הוֹדוּ לַיהוה כִּי טוֹב, כִּי לְעוֹלָם חַסְדּוֹ.**‎
הוֹדוּ לַיהוה כִּי טוֹב, כִּי לְעוֹלָם חַסְדּוֹ.[5] (baby's Hebrew name) ‎זֶה הַקָּטֹן‎
‎גָּדוֹל יִהְיֶה. כְּשֵׁם שֶׁנִּכְנַס לַבְּרִית, כֵּן יִכָּנֵס לַתּוֹרָה, וּלְחֻפָּה,‎
‎וּלְמַעֲשִׂים טוֹבִים.‎

‎וְצֶאֱצָאָיו‎ — *The offspring.* All of Isaac's male descendants were to be circumcised.

‎יְדִיד‎/Jacob

The beloved one refers to Jacob, based on the verse (*Malachi* 1:2), ‎וָאֹהַב‎ ‎אֶת יַעֲקֹב‎, [*God said]...and I loved Jacob* (*Aruch*).

‎קִדֵּשׁ יְדִיד מִבֶּטֶן‎ — *Sanctified the beloved one from the womb.* When Rebecca was carrying Jacob and Esau, God told her, 'Two nations will separate themselves from within you' (*Genesis* 25:23). *Rashi* (ibid.) comments: This one [Jacob] to righteousness, this one [Esau] to wickedness.

Furthermore, the Midrash notes that when Rebecca passed by the Torah-study halls of Shem and Eber, Jacob struggled to come out (*Rashi, Genesis* 25:22). Thus, even before birth, Jacob was destined for righteousness (*Shibbolei HaLeket;* see also *Hosea* 12:4, ‎בַּבֶּטֶן עָקַב אֶת אָחִיו‎, *while still in the*

womb he [Jacob] held on to the heel of his brother).

‎וְחֹק בִּשְׁאֵרוֹ שָׂם‎ — *And placed the [mark of the] decree [of circumcision] in his flesh.* The Midrash states that Jacob was born circumcised (*Avos d'Rabbi Nassan* 2:4). Thus God Himself placed the mark of *bris milah* on Jacob (*Shibbolei HaLeket*).

‎וְצֶאֱצָאָיו חָתַם‎ — *And sealed his offspring.* This refers to the twelve tribes, who, as descendants of Jacob, were *all* obligated to perform *bris milah*, unlike other descendants of Abraham [Ishmael's offspring] and Isaac [Esau's offspring] who were not obligated to perform this *mitzvah* (*Bris Avraham;* see *Daas Zekeinim, Bereishis* 25:25).

Rabbeinu Tam (*Tosafos, Shabbos* 137b) sees this prayer as encompassing all three patriarchs collectively: ‎יְדִיד‎, *the beloved one,* refers to Abraham (see above); ‎וְחֹק בִּשְׁאֵרוֹ שָׂם‎, *and placed the decree in his flesh* — refers to Isaac (see

⊰৹{ GIVING THE NAME }৹⊱

*Upon reaching the words in bold type, the reader pauses while all present recite them aloud.
The reader then repeats them and continues:*

אֱלֹהֵינוּ *Our God and the God of our forefathers, preserve this child for his father and mother, and may his name be called in Israel* (baby's Hebrew name) *son of* (father's Hebrew name). *May his father rejoice in the issue of his loins and may his mother exult in the fruit of her womb, as it is written: 'May your father and mother rejoice and may the one who bore you exult.'[1] And it is said: "Then I passed by you and saw you trampling in your blood,* **and I said to you: 'Because of your blood you shall live!' and I said to you: 'Because of your blood you shall live!'"[2]** *And it is said: 'He remembered His covenant forever; the word of His command for a thousand generations — that He made with Abraham and His vow to Isaac. Then He established it for Jacob as a statute, for Israel as an everlasting statute.'[3] And it is said: 'Abraham circumcised his son Isaac at the age of eight days as God had commanded him.'[4]* **Give thanks to HASHEM for He is good; His kindness endures forever! Give thanks to HASHEM for He is good; His kindness endures forever![5]** *May this infant* (baby's Hebrew name) *become great.* **Just as he has entered the covenant so may he enter into the [study of] Torah, the marriage canopy, and [the performance of] good deeds.**

---

(1) *Proverbs* 23:25. (2) *Ezekiel* 16:6. (3) *Psalms* 105:8-10. (4) *Genesis* 21:4. (5) *Psalms* 118:1

above); רְצֶאֱצָאָיו חָתַם, *and his descendants He marked,* refers to Jacob and the twelve tribes.

⊰৹§ קְרִיאַת הַשֵׁם/Giving the Name

The formula for naming a baby is actually a supplication for the well-being of the infant. This is because he has gone through the traumas of life within the womb, emergence into the world, and the surgical procedure of *bris milah* (Abudraham).

Inasmuch as this prayer contains a request to God for the welfare of the child, it is deemed relevant to the previous *milah* blessing and is not to be considered a הֶפְסֵק, interruption, between the blessing over the wine, previously recited, and the drinking of the wine. For this reason one delays drinking the wine until this prayer has been recited (*Beis Yosef, Y. D.* 265).

There are some who contend that this prayer was found in Tractate *Shabbos* of the Talmud *Yerushalmi.* Although *Rishonim* (early Rabbinic commentators) did have this section of the *Yerushalmi,* today it, along with others in this tractate, is missing. [For a more thorough discussion see *Edus LeYisrael,* p.131.]

[It is interesting to note that this prayer resembles the format of *Shemoneh Esrei.* It begins with שֶׁבַח, *praise:* אֱלֹהֵינוּ וֵאלֹהֵי אֲבוֹתֵינוּ *Our God and the God of our forefathers;* this is followed by בַּקָשָׁה, *request:* קַיֵּם אֶת הַיֶּלֶד, *sustain this child ...;* and then an offering of הוֹדָאָה, *gratitude:* הוֹדוּ לַה' ... כִּי טוֹב, *Give thanks to HASHEM, for He is good.*]

לְאָבִיו וּלְאִמּוֹ — *For his father and mother.* That they alone should raise him, not that he be brought up by others (*Siddur Derech HaChaim*).

וְיִקָּרֵא שְׁמוֹ בְּיִשְׂרָאֵל — *And may his name*

be called in Israel. This expression is from *Ruth* (4:14). There it was a blessing that the women conferred upon Ruth's newborn son, Oved, the implication being that the child should make a 'name' for himself, i.e., 'may he be famous in Israel.'

יִשְׂמַח ... וְתָגֵל — *Rejoice ... exult.* שִׂמְחָה, *rejoicing,* is an enduring happiness; גִּילָה, *exultation,* is a spontaneous burst of joy (*Malbim*). In this verse, the hope is expressed that the child will bring both spontaneous and lasting 'joy' to his parents.

יוֹלַדְתֶּךָ — *The one who bore you.* Kores HaBris offers two homiletic definitions. The Talmud (*Kiddushin* 30b) teaches: שְׁלֹשָׁה שֻׁתָּפִין הֵן בָּאָדָם, הקב"ה וְאָבִיו וְאִמּוֹ, *There are three partners [in the creation] of a human being; God, his father and his mother.* Since the other two partners in the child's creation are explicitly mentioned in this prayer, יוֹלַדְתֶּךָ must refer to God.

Alternatively, he cites the dictum כָּל הַמְלַמֵּד בֶּן חֲבֵירוֹ תּוֹרָה כְּאִלּוּ יוֹלְדוֹ, *He who teaches his friend's child Torah is considered as if he bore him (Sanhedrin* 19b). יוֹלַדְתֶּךָ then refers to the child's future teachers who, hopefully, will take pleasure in him.

Maharsha (*Taanis* 23a) remarks that אָבִיךָ, *your father,* refers to God, our Father in heaven; אִמֶּךָ, *your mother,* is an allusion to the Nation of Israel, and יוֹלַדְתֶּךָ, *those who bore you,* means the actual parents (see also *Yerushalmi Taanis,* 3:10).

יִשְׂמַח ... בְּדָמַיִךְ חֲיִי — *Rejoice ... Because of your blood you shall live.* The parents are encouraged to rejoice at this occasion even though their infant has experienced some discomfort. For even though there was some blood at the *bris,* God has already reassured His nation that because of this blood, they will merit life (*R' David Cohen*).

וָאֶעֱבֹר עָלַיִךְ וָאֶרְאֵךְ :וְנֶאֱמַר — *And it is said: Then I passed by you and saw you.* During the Jews' enslavement in

Egypt, Pharaoh decreed that the Jews would no longer be given straw for the bricks they had to produce (*Exodus* 5:7, 10,16) and so they were forced to spread and search for straw. This random straw was filled with thorns and bristles which the men, women, and children had to trample in order to process clay for the bricks. The thorns and bristles cut into their feet and they became sullied with blood. God passed by and in His mercy assured them that this blood would not be a symbol of their permanent enslavement; to the contrary, in the merit of blood, that of *milah* and the Pesach offering, they would be redeemed, not only from Egypt but from the final exile as well (*Pirkei d'Rabbi Eliezer* Chaps. 29 and 48 — *Radal* §92).

בְּדָמַיִךְ חֲיִי ... בְּדָמַיִךְ חֲיִי — *Because of your blood you shall live ... because of your blood you shall live.* The double reference to blood refers to the two *mitzvos, milah* and the Pesach offering, that God commanded the Jewish people to perform in order to merit redemption from Egypt. An uncircumcised person may not eat from the Pesach offering and so it was necessary for all who had not been circumcised to perform this *mitzvah.* God said, אִם אֵין אַתֶּם נִימוֹלִין אֵין אַתֶּם אוֹכְלִין, *If you are not circumcised then you may not eat* (see *Shemos Rabbah* 19:5, also 17:3 and 15:12).

Alternatively, this phrase is repeated twice to indicate the two redemptions, the one from Egypt and the final future one (*Pirkei d'Rabbi Eliezer* Chap. 29). Furthermore, the repetition alludes to the first two stages of *bris milah*: חִיתּוּךְ, *excision,* and פְּרִיעָה, *revealing* (*R' Yaakov Emden;* see page 99). It also signifies that one who is circumcised will merit goodness, both in this world and in the world to come (*Abudraham*).

◆§ Wine for the Child

חֲיִי — *You shall live.* A drop of wine is given to the child by the *mohel*[1] at the

---

1. It is customary for the *mohel* to form the Divine name שַׁדַּי, *the Almighty,* with his fingers

pronouncement of the word חַיֵי, *you shall live*, thereby indicating that the wine is given in happiness.

[The popular idea that wine is give to the infant to dull his senses and lull him to sleep has no basis in truth.] The infant is given wine to taste because just as the one who recites the blessing is required to taste of the wine, so is the one for whom the blessing is recited (*Machzor Vitri*). It is much like the bride and groom who are given a taste of the wine at their wedding ceremony (*Kores HaBris*).

R' Yehudah Ben Yakar states that the custom is based on the Midrash: When the Jews were circumcised in Egypt, Moses performed the first part of the bris — (חִיתוּךְ, *excision*); Aaron the second part — (פְּרִיעָה, *revealing*); after which Joshua gave the circumcised males wine to drink [i.e., from the cup over which the blessings were recited] (*Midrash Bamidbar* 11:13; *Maharzu*, see also *Shemos Rabbah* 19:5).

When Rabbi Akiva made a feast for his son, with every drink of wine that he served, he said, חַמְרָא וְחַיֵי לְפוּם רַבָּנָן הַמְרָא וְחַיֵי לְפוּם רַבָּנָן וְתַלְמִידֵיהֶן, *Wine and life to the lips of the rabbis; wine and life to the lips of the rabbis and their disciples* (*Shabbos* 67b). Thus the wish חַיֵי, *you shall live*, is accompanied by the taste of wine (*Bris Avraham*)

דָּבָר צִוָּה לְאֶלֶף דּוֹר — *The word of His command for a thousand generations* (*Psalms* 105:8). There are two Midrashic references to this phrase with regard to *milah* and it is presumably for this reason that these verses were included in the *bris milah* ceremonial prayers.

— God intended to instruct the world regarding the covenant of circumcision a thousand generations after Creation. However, He saw that the world was depraved with sin and so, to elevate man, He made His covenant with

Abraham after only twenty generations (*Koheles Rabbah* 1:15, *Maharzu*, see also *Bereishis Rabbah* 28:4).

— *Tanchuma* (*Lech Lecha*, 11), citing the same phrase, holds an opposite opinion. Not the depravity of mankind, but rather the outstanding characteristics of Abraham persuaded God to pre-empt all the generations he was waiting for and instead make His covenant with Abraham only twenty generations after Creation. This view is based on the verse: *He has hidden salvation [and reserved it] for the upright, as a shield to those who walk with integrity* (*Proverbs* 2:7).

Thus, the meaning of our phrase is: *The word [the covenant of milah] that was [to be] commanded [at the point of history] after a thousand generations was made with Abraham.*

דָּבָר — *The word.* Etz Yosef (to *Tanchuma*, ibid.) notes that King David's choice of the term דָּבָר, *word*, is a reference to *milah*, for it alludes to the phrase: זֶה הַדָּבָר אֲשֶׁר מָל יְהוֹשֻׁעַ, *This is the reason [lit. word] why Joshua circumcised* (*Joshua* 5:4). Rashi writes that Joshua convinced the Jews to become circumcised with these words of reasoning. He told them, 'Do you think you can inherit the land of Israel if you are uncircumcised? Did not God tell Abraham (*Genesis* 17, 8:9): *And I will give to you ... the land of Canaan ... you shall keep My covenant?*'

Ibn Ezra is of the opinion that the expression *a thousand generations* is not meant literally; rather it signifies eternity (*Deuteronomy* 7:9).

The law which God laid down will be applicable even to generations a thousand times removed from the generation which originally received the Torah (*R' Hirsch, Psalms* ibid.).

וּשְׁבוּעָתוֹ לְיִשְׂחָק — *And his vow to Isaac.* The vow made to Abraham at the Akeidah (*Genesis* 22:16-18) which

as he gives the infant from the wine (*Bais Yosef, Y.D.* 265).

This can be done in various ways. One way is by spreading the last three fingers to form the שׁ; bending the index finger to form the ד; and considering the thumb as the letter י (*Migdal Oz, Nachal* 10:6).

The one who recited the blessings drinks some wine.
It is also customary for the baby's mother to drink from the wine.

The *mohel* then blesses the child. [Some include the bracketed phrase.]

מִי שֶׁבֵּרַךְ אֲבוֹתֵינוּ אַבְרָהָם יִצְחָק וְיַעֲקֹב, הוּא יְבָרֵךְ אֶת הַיֶּלֶד

בֶּן (baby's Hebrew name) הַנִּימוֹל רַךְ, (father's Hebrew name)

וְיִשְׁלַח לוֹ [וּלְאִמּוֹ (baby's mother's Hebrew name) בַּת (her father's Hebrew name)]

רְפוּאָה שְׁלֵמָה, בַּעֲבוּר שֶׁנִּכְנַס לַבְּרִית. וּכְשֵׁם שֶׁנִּכְנַס לַבְּרִית כֵּן
יִכָּנֵס לַתּוֹרָה, וּלְחֻפָּה, וּלְמַעֲשִׂים טוֹבִים. וְנֹאמַר: אָמֵן.

summarized all previous promises made to him was made for the sake of Isaac [and his offspring] and not for Ishmael nor for the sons of Keturah [Abraham's concubine] (*Rashi, I Chronicles* 16:16).

Isaac's name is here spelled יִשְׂחָק although it is usually spelled יִצְחָק. At the Covenant between the Parts, God told Abraham that the Jews would be strangers in a foreign land for four hundred years (*Genesis* 15:13). Later, God mercifully reduced the years of bondage to two hundred and ten by reckoning the four hundred years not from Jacob's descent to Egypt, but from Isaac's birth. Numerically, the difference between the ש (300) in יִשְׂחָק and the צ (90) in יִצְחָק is 210. Thus, the very name יִשְׂחָק/יִצְחָק, which in either spelling means *he shall laugh*, alludes to the Jews' joy that the years of bondage were reduced. And because the reckoning of the four hundred years began with Isaac's birth, the difference in years is alluded to in the spelling of his name (*Chazah Zion*).

Shlah notes that יִשְׂחָק is a contraction of שׁ חק, *there exists a statute*. The statute alluded to is that of circumcision.

R' Hirsch (Psalms 105:10) writes that the name יִצְחָק, *Isaac* [lit. *he will laugh*], implies that though it seems laughable for rational men today to have trust in the ancient promise of the future that God made to Abraham, it is precisely those who never lost confidence in God's promise who will laugh in the end. This promise has been partially fulfilled already by the fact that we have survived and persevered in contradiction to the natural order of things, and even though this partial fulfillment may not yet justify צְחוֹק, *unsuppressed laughter*, nevertheless שְׂחוֹק, *a joyous and confident smile*, may well be upon our lips even now.

לְיַעֲקֹב לְחֹק לְיִשְׂרָאֵל ... — *For Jacob as a statute, for Israel* ... Once God established His covenant with Jacob, after having done so already with both Abraham and Isaac, it was like an engraving (חָק) etched into the souls of Israel forever (*R' David Cohen*).[1]

וַיָּמָל אַבְרָהָם אֶת יִצְחָק בְּנוֹ — *Abraham circumcised his son Isaac.* Abraham

---

1. A *Midrash Pliah* (puzzling and wondrous Midrash) states: Esau said to Jacob, 'I will go with you to *Gan Eden* [Paradise] or you come with me to *Gehinnom.*' To this Jacob replied, 'I liked it and you abhorred it.'

This baffling Midrash is interpreted by *Koreis HaBris* in the following manner: Esau, as wicked people are wont to do, saw himself as an equal to his righteous brother Jacob. He felt that he was as worthy of *Gan Eden* as Jacob was, and that, conversely, if he was not to be admitted to *Gan Eden*, then neither should Jacob, but both should be sent to *Gehinnom.*

To this Jacob replied that the merit of *bris milah* saves one from *Gehinnom* [for as the Midrash states, Abraham sits at the entrance to *Gehinnom* and does not allow any circumcised person to enter] (see p. 128).

Thus Jacob, who was circumcised and loved the *mitzvah*, would not be allowed to enter *Gehinnom*, whereas Esau who despised *milah* had no saving grace (see *Daas Zekeinim*, *Bereishis* 25:25 who says that Esau refused to be circumcised; see also p. 89).

The one who recited the blessings drinks some wine.
It is also customary for the baby's mother to drink from the wine.
The *mohel* then blesses the child. [Some include the bracketed phrase.]

מִי שֶׁבֵּרַךְ *He Who blessed our forefathers Abraham, Isaac, and Jacob,
may He bless the tender infant who has been circumcised,*
(baby's Hebrew name) *son of* (father's Hebrew name) *and send him* [*and his mother*
(Hebrew name) *daughter of* (her father's Hebrew name)] *a complete recovery,
because he has entered the covenant. Just as he has entered the covenant, so
may he enter into the* [*study of*] *Torah, the marriage canopy, and* [*the
performance of*] *good deeds. And let us say Amen.*

himself circumcised the child, not an agent. No doubt it distressed Abraham to inflict pain upon the child for whom he had waited so long. However, because a deed is more meritorious when it is performed personally than when it is done through an agent, Abraham himself performed the *mitzvah* (*Ksav Sofer*).

הוֹדוּ לַה' — *Give thanks to HASHEM.* Based on a custom of the *Arizal*, this verse is recited twice by the guests, and then twice again by the one reciting the prayer. Some of the reasons for its inclusion in the *bris* prayers are:

— The Talmud (*Sotah* 12a) interprets the verse, [*When Moses was born*] *she* [Yocheved] *saw that he* [Moses] *was good* (*Exodus* 2:2), as an indication that Moses *was born circumcised.* (In this context the word טוֹב, *good,* symbolizes perfection.) Thus, we thank God that the child is now טוֹב (i.e., *perfect*) and hence ready and worthy to enter into the practice of *mitzvos* (*HaManhig*).

— We thank God that the child has been circumcised, for now he will be spared from *Gehinnom* (*Abudraham*).

— The Talmud (*Berachos* 54a) states that there are four who are required to give thanks to God, among whom is one who had been imprisoned and subsequently released. In the same vein, thanks must be offered for the child who had been confined for nine months in his mother's womb (*Maharil*).

— The assembled express their gratitude to God for giving them the opportunity to participate in a *mitzvah*

which the Talmud (*Nedarim* 32a) states is equal to all other *mitzvos* combined (see p. 89; *R' Yaakov HaGozer*).

The verse is repeated twice, for when one has a son he is required to recite the blessing of הַטוֹב וְהַמֵּטִיב, *Who is good and does good* (*Brachos* 59b). The repetition of הוֹדוּ corresponds to the dual mention of 'good' in the blessing. Others maintain that the first הוֹדוּ is for the הַטוֹב וְהַמֵּטִיב blessing, while the second is for the child's release from 'confinement' in the womb.

זֶה הַקָּטָן גָּדוֹל יִהְיֶה — *May this infant become great.* This prayer is modeled after the blessing that God gave Abraham, וְאַבְרָהָם הָיוֹ יִהְיֶה לְגוֹי גָּדוֹל, *Abraham is surely to become a great nation* (*Genesis* 18:18; *Zichron Bris LaRishonim*). Some *mohelim* place their hands on the head of the infant when saying the words זֶה הַקָּטָן, *this infant,* and then raise their hands high when saying גָּדוֹל יִהְיֶה, *become great.*

Some of the wine is given to the mother to drink, for drinking from the cup over which a *mitzvah* blessing has been recited is itself considered a blessing. By drinking from this wine, the mother will be blessed with a healthy recuperation from childbirth (*Orchas Chaim; HaManhig*).

⊷§ מִי שֶׁבֵּרַךְ/**Mohel's Blessing**

Although it is customary when reciting prayers for the sick to use the name of the patient and the name of his mother, here the father's name is used. Assumedly this is because being

In many communities, the *mohel* and father then recite the following prayer:

רִבּוֹנוֹ שֶׁל עוֹלָם, יְהִי רָצוֹן מִלְּפָנֶיךָ, שֶׁיְּהֵא זֶה חָשׁוּב וּמְרֻצֶּה וּמְקֻבָּל לְפָנֶיךָ, כְּאִלּוּ הִקְרַבְתִּיהוּ לִפְנֵי כִסֵּא כְבוֹדֶךָ. וְאַתָּה, בְּרַחֲמֶיךָ הָרַבִּים, שְׁלַח עַל יְדֵי מַלְאָכֶיךָ הַקְּדוֹשִׁים נְשָׁמָה קְדוֹשָׁה וּטְהוֹרָה

Mohel says:		*Father* says:
(fathers' Hebrew name) בֶּן (baby's Hebrew name) לְ		(baby's Hebrew name) לִבְנִי

הַנִּמּוֹל עַתָּה לְשִׁמְךָ הַגָּדוֹל. שֶׁיִּהְיֶה לִבּוֹ פָּתְוּחַ כְּפִתְחוֹ שֶׁל אוּלָם, בְּתוֹרָתְךָ הַקְּדוֹשָׁה, לִלְמֹד וּלְלַמֵּד, לִשְׁמֹר וְלַעֲשׂוֹת. וְתֵן לוֹ אֲרִיכוּת יָמִים וְשָׁנִים, חַיִּים שֶׁל יִרְאַת חֵטְא, חַיִּים שֶׁל עְשֶׁר וְכָבוֹד, חַיִּים שֶׁתְּמַלֵּא מִשְׁאֲלוֹת לִבּוֹ לְטוֹבָה. [The father continues — וְזַכֵּנִי לְגַדְּלוֹ לַתּוֹרָה וּלְחֻפָּה וּלְמַעֲשִׂים טוֹבִים, וְלִרְאוֹת מִמֶּנּוּ בָנִים וּבְנֵי בָנִים עוֹסְקִים בַּתּוֹרָה וּבְמִצְוֹת, וּתְקַבֵּל תְּפִלָּתוֹ בְּקֶרֶב תְּפִלַּת כָּל יִשְׂרָאֵל, וְיִהְיוּ לְרָצוֹן אִמְרֵי פִי וְהֶגְיוֹן לִבִּי לְפָנֶיךָ, יהוה צוּרִי וְגֹאֲלִי.] אָמֵן, כֵּן יְהִי רָצוֹן.

All present recite עָלֵינוּ.

עָלֵינוּ לְשַׁבֵּחַ לַאֲדוֹן הַכֹּל, לָתֵת גְּדֻלָּה לְיוֹצֵר בְּרֵאשִׁית, שֶׁלֹּא עָשָׂנוּ כְּגוֹיֵי הָאֲרָצוֹת, וְלֹא שָׂמָנוּ כְּמִשְׁפְּחוֹת הָאֲדָמָה. שֶׁלֹּא שָׂם חֶלְקֵנוּ כָּהֶם, וְגוֹרָלֵנוּ כְּכָל הֲמוֹנָם. (שֶׁהֵם מִשְׁתַּחֲוִים לְהֶבֶל וָרִיק, וּמִתְפַּלְּלִים אֶל אֵל לֹא יוֹשִׁיעַ.) וַאֲנַחְנוּ כּוֹרְעִים וּמִשְׁתַּחֲוִים וּמוֹדִים, לִפְנֵי מֶלֶךְ מַלְכֵי הַמְּלָכִים הַקָּדוֹשׁ בָּרוּךְ הוּא. שֶׁהוּא נוֹטֶה שָׁמַיִם וְיֹסֵד אָרֶץ, וּמוֹשַׁב יְקָרוֹ בַּשָּׁמַיִם מִמַּעַל, וּשְׁכִינַת עֻזּוֹ בְּגָבְהֵי מְרוֹמִים. הוּא אֱלֹהֵינוּ, אֵין עוֹד. אֱמֶת מַלְכֵּנוּ, אֶפֶס זוּלָתוֹ, כַּכָּתוּב בְּתוֹרָתוֹ: וְיָדַעְתָּ הַיּוֹם וַהֲשֵׁבֹתָ אֶל לְבָבֶךָ, כִּי יהוה הוּא הָאֱלֹהִים בַּשָּׁמַיִם מִמַּעַל וְעַל הָאָרֶץ מִתָּחַת, אֵין עוֹד.

וְעַל כֵּן נְקַוֶּה לְּךָ יהוה אֱלֹהֵינוּ לִרְאוֹת מְהֵרָה בְּתִפְאֶרֶת עֻזֶּךָ, לְהַעֲבִיר גִּלּוּלִים מִן הָאָרֶץ, וְהָאֱלִילִים כָּרוֹת יִכָּרֵתוּן, לְתַקֵּן עוֹלָם בְּמַלְכוּת שַׁדַּי. וְכָל בְּנֵי בָשָׂר יִקְרְאוּ בִשְׁמֶךָ, לְהַפְנוֹת אֵלֶיךָ כָּל רִשְׁעֵי אָרֶץ. יַכִּירוּ וְיֵדְעוּ כָּל יוֹשְׁבֵי תֵבֵל, כִּי לְךָ תִּכְרַע כָּל בֶּרֶךְ, תִּשָּׁבַע כָּל לָשׁוֹן. לְפָנֶיךָ יהוה אֱלֹהֵינוּ יִכְרְעוּ וְיִפֹּלוּ, וְלִכְבוֹד שִׁמְךָ יְקָר יִתֵּנוּ. וִיקַבְּלוּ כֻלָּם אֶת עֹל מַלְכוּתֶךָ, וְתִמְלֹךְ עֲלֵיהֶם מְהֵרָה לְעוֹלָם וָעֶד. כִּי הַמַּלְכוּת שֶׁלְּךָ הִיא וּלְעוֹלְמֵי עַד תִּמְלוֹךְ בְּכָבוֹד, כַּכָּתוּב בְּתוֹרָתֶךָ: יהוה יִמְלֹךְ לְעֹלָם וָעֶד. וְנֶאֱמַר: וְהָיָה יהוה לְמֶלֶךְ עַל כָּל הָאָרֶץ, בַּיּוֹם הַהוּא יִהְיֶה יהוה אֶחָד וּשְׁמוֹ אֶחָד.

circumcised is not an illness. Rather the intent of the prayer is that the child not become ill as a result of the surgery of the *bris* (*Shulchan Aruch HaRav, Seder HaMilah,* Additions — vol. 6, note 10).

ולאמו — *And his mother.* The addition of the prayer for the mother is based on the prayer — תְּשַׁתְּלַח אֲסוּתָא, *Send*

healing — that appears in *Siddur Rav Amram Gaon*. In this supplication prayers are offered for both the mother and child. [As noted above regarding the infant, the mother is blessed using her father's name, because childbirth is not considered an illness. However, if the delivery was by Caesarean section, or if serious complications are present,

In many communities, the *mohel* and father then recite the following prayer:

רִבּוֹנוֹ שֶׁל עוֹלָם *Master of the universe, may it be Your will that he be worthy,*
favored, and acceptable before You as if I had offered him before
the throne of Your glory, and may You, in Your abundant mercy, send through
Your holy angels a holy and pure soul to

Father says:	Mohel says:
my son, (baby's Hebrew name)	*(baby's Hebrew name) son of (father's Hebrew name)*

who has now been circumcised for the sake of Your Great Name. May his heart be
as open to Your holy Torah as the entrance of the Temple, to learn and to teach, to
observe and perform. Give him long days and years, a life of fear of sin, a life of
wealth and honor, a life in which You fulfill all the wishes of his heart for good.
[The father continues — Grant me the merit to raise him to the study of Torah, to the
marriage canopy, and to the performance of good deeds; to see from him children
and grandchildren engaged in Torah and mitzvos. Accept his prayers among the
prayers of all Israel. May the expressions of my mouth, and the thoughts of
my heart find favor before You, HASHEM, my Strength and my Redeemer.]
Amen — may such be Your will.

All present recite *Aleinu.*

עָלֵינוּ *It is our duty to praise the Master of all, to ascribe greatness to the Molder of*
primeval creation, for He has not made us like the nations of the lands and
has not emplaced us like the families of earth; for He has not assigned our portion
like theirs nor our lot like all their multitudes. (For they bow to vanity and
emptiness and pray to a god which helps not.) But we bend our knees, bow, and
acknowledge our thanks before the King who reigns over kings, the Holy One,
Blessed is He. He stretches out heaven and establishes earth's foundation, the seat of
His homage is in the heavens above and His powerful Presence is in the loftiest
heights. He is our God and there is none other. True is our God, there is nothing
beside Him, as it is written in His Torah: 'You are to know this day and take to your
heart that HASHEM is the only God — in heaven above and on the earth below —
there is none other.'

וְעַל כֵּן *And therefore we put our hope in You, HASHEM our God, that we may soon*
see Your mighty splendor, to remove detestable idolatry from the earth,
and false gods will be utterly cut off, to perfect the universe through the Almighty's
sovereignty. Then all humanity will call upon Your Name, to turn all the earth's
wicked toward You. All the world's inhabitants will recognize and know that to
You every knee should bend, every tongue should swear. Before You, HASHEM, our
God, they will bend every knee and cast themselves down and to the glory of Your
Name they will render homage, and they will all accept upon themselves the yoke of
Your kingship that You may reign over them soon and eternally. For the kingdom is
Yours and You will reign for all eternity in glory as it is written in Your Torah:
HASHEM shall reign for all eternity. And it is said: HASHEM will be King over all the
world — on that day HASHEM will be One and His Name will be One.

present, her mother's name should be used.]

עָלֵינוּ/Aleinu

A number of reasons have been suggested for the custom of reciting the *Aleinu* prayer at the conclusion of the *bris* ceremony.

— *Aleinu* contains the phrase: *For He has not made us like the nations of the lands.* Having been circumcised, the child is now distinctly set apart from his male counterparts in the nations of the world (*Levush*).

— *Aleinu* ends with the declaration of God's eternal sovereignty over the

סְעוּדַת הַבְּרִית

A festive meal is served in honor of the circumcision.
It is customary to sing the following liturgical poem at this meal.

יוֹם לְיַבָּשָׁה נֶהֶפְכוּ מְצוּלִים,   שִׁירָה חֲדָשָׁה שִׁבְּחוּ גְאוּלִים.

הִטְבַּעְתָּ בְּתַרְמִית   רַגְלֵי בַת עֲנָמִית,   וּפַעֲמֵי שׁוּלַמִּית
יָפוּ בַנְּעָלִים.   שִׁירָה חֲדָשָׁה שִׁבְּחוּ גְאוּלִים.

וְכָל רוֹאֵי יְשׁוּרוּן,   בְּבֵית הוֹדִי יְשׁוֹרְרוּן,   אֵין כָּאֵל יְשׁוּרוּן,
וְאוֹיְבֵינוּ פְלִילִים.   שִׁירָה חֲדָשָׁה שִׁבְּחוּ גְאוּלִים.

דְּגָלֵי כֵן תָּרִים,   עַל הַנִּשְׁאָרִים,   וּתְלַקֵּט נִפְזָרִים,
כִּמְלַקֵּט שִׁבֳּלִים.   שִׁירָה חֲדָשָׁה שִׁבְּחוּ גְאוּלִים.

הַבָּאִים עִמָּךְ,   בִּבְרִית חוֹתָמָךְ,   וּמִבֶּטֶן לְשִׁמָךְ,
הֵמָּה נְמוֹלִים.   שִׁירָה חֲדָשָׁה שִׁבְּחוּ גְאוּלִים.

universe: ה׳ יִמְלֹךְ לְעֹלָם וָעֶד, HASHEM *shall reign forever and ever.* This verse (*Exodus* 15:18) is taken from the end of שִׁירַת הַיָּם, *the Song of the Sea,* where the Jews pronounced these words for the first time. It was because of the Jews' adherence to the precept of *milah* that they merited the miraculous splitting of the sea, which inspired them to utter this song (see pp. 112-114) Thus, *Aleinu* is recited at the conclusion of the *bris* (R' David Cohen).

יוֹם לְיַבָּשָׁה/Yom LeYabashah

The author of this *piyut* [liturgical poem], R' Yehudah HaLevi is best known for his classic philosophical work *HaKuzari.* He was a master poet and liturgist in both Hebrew and Arabic (see *The Rishonim,* Artscroll History Series, p. 71). An acrostic of the author's name — יְהוּדָה הַלֵּוִי — is formed by the first letter of each stanza.

יוֹם — *The day.* In many congregations, *Yom LeYabashah* is recited on the seventh day of Pesach, prior to the *Shemoneh Esrei* of the *Shacharis* service.[1] That was the day of God's

miraculous splitting of the Sea of Reeds, and the Jews' triumphant march across the dry sea floor, which is the theme of this liturgy. It is recited at the *bris* meal because of its reference to *bris milah* in the fifth and seventh stanzas. Additionally, *Yalkut Shimoni* (*Yirmiyah,* §321) notes that God said, 'Because the Jews had themselves circumcised [when they left Egypt] they merited that I split the Sea for them.'

Pri Megadim (Mishbetzos Zahav, O.C. 584:7, 590:6) writes that only on the seventh day of Passover does the liturgy begin יוֹם לְיַבָּשָׁה, *the 'day' the depths.* At other times such as at a *bris* the proper reading would be יָם לְיַבָּשָׁה, *From sea to dry land.*

שִׁירָה חֲדָשָׁה — *A new song.* The Song of the Sea is called 'a new song,' for it was inspired by a new level of *Ruach HaKodesh* (Divine Inspiration) attained by that generation at the splitting of the Sea (*Zocher HaBris*).

בְּתַרְמִית — *Because of [their] fraud.* The translation follows the use of this word in *Jeremiah* 8:5 (see *Rashash, Temurah* 24b; R' Eliyahu Cohen). Others, based

1. Some recite it in the *Shacharis* service of the Sabbath of *Parashas Beshalach,* the Torah portion that describes the Jews' crossing of the Sea. Others include it in the *Shacharis* service whenever a *bris* occurs on the Sabbath or a Festival.

A festive meal is served in honor of the circumcision.
It is customary to sing the following liturgical poem at this meal.

יוֹם לְיַבָּשָׁה *The day the depths turned to dry land,*
With a new song the redeemed ones gave praise.

ה *You sank because of fraud, the cavalcade of the Anamite's daughter,*
while the footsteps of the perfectly faithful were beautiful in shoes.
With a new song the redeemed ones gave praise.

ו *All who will see Jeshurun will sing in my home of splendor:*
'There is none like the God of Jeshurun,'
even our enemies will so judge.
With a new song the redeemed ones gave praise.

ד *So shall You raise my banners over the survivors,*
and gather the dispersed like one who gathers ears of grain.
With a new song the redeemed ones gave praise.

ה *Those who accompany You with the covenant of Your seal,*
from the womb they are circumcised, for Your Name's sake.
With a new song the redeemed ones gave praise.

---

on *Judges* 9:31, translate בְתָרְמִית, *with wisdom.* Hence, *You sank [the Egyptians] through Your wisdom (Arugas HaBosem).*

עֲנָמִית — *Anamite.* Anamim was a son of Mitzraim, the progenitor of Egypt (*Genesis* 10:13).

וּפַעֲמֵי שׁוּלַמִּית יָפוּ בַּנְּעָלִים — *The footsteps of the perfectly faithful were beautiful in shoes.* This is a reference to *Song of Songs* 7:1 where the nation of Israel is allegorically called שׁוּלַמִּית, *perfect one.* The verse following it reads, מַה יָּפוּ פְעָמַיִךְ בַּנְּעָלִים, *How lovely are your footsteps in shoes,* that is, as the Jewish nation passed through the dry sea bed (see *Isaiah* 11:15; *Zocher HaBris*). The Talmud (*Sotah* 49b) says that this phrase refers to the festival pilgrimages to the temple in Jerusalem (see *Chagigah* 3a).

יְשׁוּרוּן — *Jeshurun.* This name indicates the Jewish nation in its state of righteousness (see *Deuteronomy* 32:15). Homiletically, the word יְשׁוּרוּן is a contraction of יָשָׁר וְנָאֶה, *honest and beautiful.* Moreover, the numerical

equivalents of יְשׁוּרוּן and of יָשָׁר וְנָאֶה are identical, 572 (*Arugas HaBosem*).

בְּבֵית הוֹדִי — *In my home of splendor.* In *Lamentations* 1:13, the prophet mourns כָּל הַיּוֹם דָּוָה, *all the day [Jerusalem] is in misery.* When the Messiah will come, the misery will change to splendor. An allusion to this is that the letters of the word דָּוָה, *misery,* when reversed, spell הוֹד, *splendor* (*Zocher HaBris*).

וְאוֹיְבֵינוּ פְלִילִים — *Even our enemies will so judge.* From *Deuteronomy* 32:31; *Ohr HaChaim* explains that even the nations will admit that there is none like the God of Israel. An alternate translation is, *Our enemies, who today are our judges, will sing...* (*Arugas HaBosem*)

דְּגָלַי כֵּן תָּרִים — *So shall You raise my banners.* From *Isaiah* 62:10. Just as our banners were raised in the desert following our redemption from Egypt, so shall our banner be raised in our final redemption (*Zocher HaBris*).

כִּמְלַקֵּט שִׁבֳּלִים — *Like one who gathers ears of grain.* The farmer who is harvesting is primarily interested in

הַרְאֵה אוֹתוֹתָם, לְכָל רוֹאֵי אוֹתָם, וְעַל כַּנְפֵי כְסוּתָם,
יַעֲשׂוּ גְדִילִים. שִׁירָה חֲדָשָׁה שִׁבְּחוּ גְאוּלִים.

לְמִי זֹאת נֶרְשֶׁמֶת, הַכֶּר נָא דְבַר אֱמֶת, לְמִי הַחוֹתֶמֶת,
וּלְמִי הַפְּתִילִים. שִׁירָה חֲדָשָׁה שִׁבְּחוּ גְאוּלִים.

וְשׁוּב שֵׁנִית לְקַדְּשָׁהּ, וְאַל תּוֹסִיף לְגָרְשָׁהּ, וְהַעֲלֵה אוֹר שִׁמְשָׁהּ,
וְנָסוּ הַצְּלָלִים. שִׁירָה חֲדָשָׁה שִׁבְּחוּ גְאוּלִים.

יְדִידִים רוֹמְמוּךָ, בְּשִׁירָה קִדְּמוּךָ, מִי כָמֹכָה,
יהוה בָּאֵלִים. שִׁירָה חֲדָשָׁה שִׁבְּחוּ גְאוּלִים.

בִּגְלַל אָבוֹת תּוֹשִׁיעַ בָּנִים, וְתָבִיא גְאוּלָה לִבְנֵי בְנֵיהֶם.

﴾ ברכת המזון ﴿

שִׁיר הַמַּעֲלוֹת, בְּשׁוּב יהוה אֶת שִׁיבַת צִיּוֹן, הָיִינוּ כְּחֹלְמִים. אָז יִמָּלֵא
שְׂחוֹק פִּינוּ וּלְשׁוֹנֵנוּ רִנָּה, אָז יֹאמְרוּ בַגּוֹיִם, הִגְדִּיל יהוה
לַעֲשׂוֹת עִם אֵלֶּה. הִגְדִּיל יהוה לַעֲשׂוֹת עִמָּנוּ, הָיִינוּ שְׂמֵחִים. שׁוּבָה יהוה אֶת
שְׁבִיתֵנוּ, כַּאֲפִיקִים בַּנֶּגֶב. הַזֹּרְעִים בְּדִמְעָה בְּרִנָּה יִקְצֹרוּ. הָלוֹךְ יֵלֵךְ וּבָכֹה נֹשֵׂא
מֶשֶׁךְ הַזָּרַע, בֹּא יָבֹא בְרִנָּה, נֹשֵׂא אֲלֻמֹּתָיו.

gathering produce and will rarely stoop to collect the insignificant ears of corn. Our prayer expresses the hope that at the ingathering of the exiles God will include even the undeserving among us (*Zocher HaBris*)

וּמִבֶּטֶן ... הֵמָּה נִמּוֹלִים — *From the womb ... they are circumcised.* Jews are circumcised only days after birth, as opposed to the descendants of Ishmael who circumcise at age thirteen (*R' David Cohen*).

אוֹתוֹתָם — *Their signs.* This refers to *tefillin,* which are called אוֹת, *a sign* (see *Exodus* 13:16). In *Deuteronomy* 28:10, the Torah states, *And all the people of the earth shall see that the Name of HASHEM is called upon you and they will fear you.* The Talmud (*Menachos* 35b) says that this refers to those who will see the Jews wearing *tefillin* of the head (*Mateh Levi*).

גְדִילִים — *Fringes,* i.e., *tzitzis.* The eight strands of the *tzitzis* symbolize the eight

days that elapsed from the time the Jews in Egypt brought their Pesach offering [which was considered the beginning of their redemption] until they sang the Song at the Sea (*Rashi* to *Numbers* 15:41 with *Sifsei Chachamim;* see also *R' Bachya* ibid.).

הַחוֹתֶמֶת — *The seal.* This is a reference to the seal of circumcision. The *paytan* (poet) uses a play on the verse in *Genesis* 38:25 where the terms חוֹתֶמֶת and פְּתִילִים refer to Judah's signet and wrap.

הַפְּתִילִים — *The threads.* The Talmud (*Menachos* 44a) relates an incident where the wearing of *tzitzis* deterred a man from an act of sexual immorality, which our Sages commonly refer to as פְּגִימַת הַבְּרִית, *a blemish of the covenant.* Perhaps *tzitzis* and *bris* are mentioned here, for both are protections against immorality.

לְקַדְּשָׁהּ — *To betroth her.* A reference to *Hosea* 2:21, *And I will betroth you to*

ה Display their signs to all who see them,
and on the corners of their garments they shall make fringes.
With a new song the redeemed ones gave praise.

ל For whom are these marked? Recognize, please, this truth.
For whom is the seal? And for whom are the threads?
With a new song the redeemed ones gave praise.

ו Once again to betroth her, and to drive her out no more.
Let the light of her sun rise, and let the shadows flee.
With a new song the redeemed ones gave praise.

י The beloved ones exalt You, and with song they come to greet You,
Who is like You, HASHEM, among the mighty ones.
With a new song the redeemed ones gave praise.

In the merit of the ancestors save their offspring,
and bring redemption to their children's children.

⊱ GRACE AFTER MEALS ⊰

שִׁיר הַמַּעֲלוֹת *A song of ascents. When HASHEM will return the captivity of Zion,*
we will be like dreamers. Then our mouth will be filled with
laughter and our tongue with glad song. Then they will declare among the nations,
'HASHEM has done greatly with these.' HASHEM has done greatly with us, we were
gladdened. O HASHEM — return our captivity like springs in the desert. Those who
tearfully sow will reap in glad song. He who bears the measure of seeds walks along
weeping, but will return in exultation, a bearer of his sheaves.

Me forever. The metaphor of husband and wife is often used in both Scripture and Midrash to illustrate the unique relationship between God and His people. The *betrothing* in the verse cited refers to the renewal of this closeness which will occur with the future redemption.

לְגָרְשָׁהּ — *To drive her out* [lit. *to divorce her*]. A metaphor for Israel in a state of Exile.

אוֹר שִׁמְשָׁהּ — *The light of her sun.* The light of redemption (see *Isaiah* 60:20; *Psalms* 89:37; and commentary below p. 158).

הַצְּלָלִים — *The shadows.* A metaphor for trials and tribulations (see *Song of Songs* 2:17; *Mateh Levi*).

מִי כָמֹכָה ה' בָּאֵלִים — *Who is like You, HASHEM, among the mighty ones.* By splitting the Sea of Reeds and showing

His total mastery over nature, God made it unmistakably clear that no power above or below can match Him. From *Exodus* 15:11, with the words בָּאֵלִים and ה' reversed to preserve the rhyme scheme.

בִּגְלַל אָבוֹת תּוֹשִׁיעַ בָּנִים — *In the merit of the ancestors save their offspring.* [These words are probably not part of the original poem, but were added for the times this prayer is recited before the *Shemoneh Esrei* (see comment to יוֹם above). This is in consonance with the rule that the words immediately preceding בָּרוּךְ אַתָּה ה', *Blessed are You HASHEM,* at the end of any blessing must be similar in meaning to the words that follow בָּרוּךְ אַתָּה ה'. Hence a phrase that contained the concept of redemption וְתָבִיא גְאוּלָה, *and brings redemption,* was inserted to parallel the phrase גָּאַל יִשְׂרָאֵל, [*the One*] *Who redeems Israel,* which follows בָּרוּךְ אַתָּה ה'.]

The *zimun* is recited by the leader with a cup of wine in hand.
[If a *minyan* is not present, the words in brackets are deleted.]

Leader—רַבּוֹתַי נְבָרֵךְ.

Others—יְהִי שֵׁם יהוה מְבֹרָךְ מֵעַתָּה וְעַד עוֹלָם.

Leader—יְהִי שֵׁם יהוה מְבֹרָךְ מֵעַתָּה וְעַד עוֹלָם.

נוֹדֶה לְשִׁמְךָ בְּתוֹךְ אֱמוּנַי,   בְּרוּכִים אַתֶּם לַיהוה.

Others—נוֹדֶה לְשִׁמְךָ בְּתוֹךְ אֱמוּנַי,   בְּרוּכִים אַתֶּם לַיהוה.

Leader—בִּרְשׁוּת אֵל אָיוֹם וְנוֹרָא,   מִשְׂגָּב לְעִתּוֹת בַּצָּרָה,

אֵל נֶאְזָר בִּגְבוּרָה,   אַדִּיר בַּמָּרוֹם יהוה.

Others—נוֹדֶה לְשִׁמְךָ בְּתוֹךְ אֱמוּנַי,   בְּרוּכִים אַתֶּם לַיהוה.

Leader—בִּרְשׁוּת הַתּוֹרָה הַקְּדוֹשָׁה,   טְהוֹרָה הִיא וְגַם פְּרוּשָׁה,

צִוָּה לָנוּ מוֹרָשָׁה,   מֹשֶׁה עֶבֶד יהוה.

Others—נוֹדֶה לְשִׁמְךָ בְּתוֹךְ אֱמוּנַי,   בְּרוּכִים אַתֶּם לַיהוה.

Leader—בִּרְשׁוּת הַכֹּהֲנִים הַלְוִיִּם   אֶקְרָא לֵאלֹהֵי הָעִבְרִיִּים,

אֲהוֹדֶנּוּ בְּכָל אִיִּים,   אֲבָרְכָה אֶת יהוה.

Others—נוֹדֶה לְשִׁמְךָ בְּתוֹךְ אֱמוּנַי,   בְּרוּכִים אַתֶּם לַיהוה.

Leader—בִּרְשׁוּת מָרָנָן וְרַבָּנָן וְרַבּוֹתַי,   אֶפְתְּחָה בְּשִׁיר פִּי וּשְׂפָתַי,

וְתֹאמַרְנָה עַצְמוֹתַי,   בָּרוּךְ הַבָּא בְּשֵׁם יהוה.

Others—נוֹדֶה לְשִׁמְךָ בְּתוֹךְ אֱמוּנַי,   בְּרוּכִים אַתֶּם לַיהוה.

Leader—בִּרְשׁוּת מָרָנָן וְרַבָּנָן וְרַבּוֹתַי, נְבָרֵךְ [אֱלֹהֵינוּ]שֶׁאָכַלְנוּ מִשֶּׁלּוֹ.

Others—בָּרוּךְ [אֱלֹהֵינוּ] שֶׁאָכַלְנוּ מִשֶּׁלּוֹ, וּבְטוּבוֹ חָיִינוּ.

Leader—בָּרוּךְ [אֱלֹהֵינוּ] שֶׁאָכַלְנוּ מִשֶּׁלּוֹ, וּבְטוּבוֹ חָיִינוּ.

All—בָּרוּךְ הוּא וּבָרוּךְ שְׁמוֹ.

נוֹדֶה לְשִׁמְךָ/Zimun ⊷§

There are indications that this song was recited following *all* festive meals by Polish Jews. With the passage of time, it was discontinued except at circumcisions [possibly because circumcisions, as the Sages teach (*Shabbos* 130a), have always been celebrated with particular joy].

אֱמוּנַי — *My faithful.* The one who leads the group in *Bircas HaMazon* refers to his companions as *faithful,* i.e., people whose faith is in God.

בִּרְשׁוּת אֵל אָיוֹם — *With permission of the Almighty.* Because God's Divine Presence is at every *bris,* it is proper to acknowledge His Presence by asking His permission, as it were, to recite the Grace after the Meal (*Sefer HaBris* 265:192).

מוֹרָשָׁה — *Heritage.* The Torah is the *heritage* of Israel. As such we are not free to neglect it or to cede it to any

The *zimun* is recited by the leader with a cup of wine in hand.
[If a *minyan* is not present, the words in brackets are deleted.]

Leader— *Gentlemen, let us bless.*

Others— *Blessed be the Name of* HASHEM *from this time and forever!*

Leader— *Blessed be the Name of* HASHEM *from this time and forever!*
Let us give thanks to Your Name among my faithful;
blessed are you to HASHEM.

Others— *We give thanks to Your Name among my faithful;*
blessed are you to HASHEM.

Leader— *With permission of the Almighty — revered and awesome,*
the Stronghold in times of distress,
the Almighty girded with strength, the Mighty on high — HASHEM.

Others— *We give thanks to Your Name among my faithful;*
blessed are you to HASHEM.

Leader— *With permission of the holy Torah, it is pure and explicit,*
commanded to us as a heritage, by Moses, the servant of HASHEM.

Others— *We give thanks to Your Name among my faithful;*
blessed are you to HASHEM.

Leader— *With permission of the Kohanim, the Levites,*
I will call upon the God of the Hebrews,
I will thank Him throughout all the islands, I will bless HASHEM.

Others— *We give thanks to Your Name among my faithful;*
blessed are you to HASHEM.

Leader— *With permission of the rabbis, teachers and assemblage,*
I open in song my mouth and lips,
and every part of my being shall proclaim,
'Blessed is the one who comes in the Name of HASHEM.'

Others— *We give thanks to Your Name among my faithful;*
blessed are you to HASHEM.

Leader— *With permission of the rabbis, teachers and assemblage,*
let us bless [our God,] He of Whose we have eaten.

Others— *Blessed be [our God,] He of Whose we have eaten*
and through Whose goodness we live.

Leader— *Blessed be [our God,] He of Whose we have eaten*
and through Whose goodness we live.

All— *Blessed is He and Blessed is His Name.*

---

other nation.

עֶבֶד ה' — *Servant* [lit. *slave*] *of* HASHEM. A slave is totally the property of his master. He has no personality or initiative of his own. Moses is honored with this title because he was completely devoted to God.

הַכֹּהֲנִים הַלְוִיִם — *The Kohanim, the Levites.* All *Kohanim* come from the tribe of Levi, therefore the meaning here

is, the *Kohanim* [who are] *Levites* (*Magen Avraham*, O.C. 201:4). Others, however, read הַכֹּהֲנִים וְהַלְוִיִם, *the Kohanim and the Levites.*

אִיִּים — *Islands.* The expression *islands* is used to indicate that the praise of God will be so universal that even the isolated inhabitants of far-flung islands will praise Him (*see Isaiah* 42:10 and *Malbim* there).

בָּרוּךְ אַתָּה יהוה אֱלֹהֵינוּ מֶלֶךְ הָעוֹלָם, הַזָּן אֶת הָעוֹלָם כֻּלּוֹ, בְּטוּבוֹ, בְּחֵן בְּחֶסֶד וּבְרַחֲמִים, הוּא נוֹתֵן לֶחֶם לְכָל בָּשָׂר, כִּי לְעוֹלָם חַסְדּוֹ. וּבְטוּבוֹ הַגָּדוֹל, תָּמִיד לֹא חָסַר לָנוּ, וְאַל יֶחְסַר לָנוּ מָזוֹן לְעוֹלָם וָעֶד. בַּעֲבוּר שְׁמוֹ הַגָּדוֹל, כִּי הוּא אֵל זָן וּמְפַרְנֵס לַכֹּל, וּמֵטִיב לַכֹּל, וּמֵכִין מָזוֹן לְכָל בְּרִיּוֹתָיו אֲשֶׁר בָּרָא. כָּאָמוּר: פּוֹתֵחַ אֶת יָדֶךָ, וּמַשְׂבִּיעַ לְכָל חַי רָצוֹן. —Leader בָּרוּךְ אַתָּה יהוה, הַזָּן אֶת הַכֹּל. (אָמֵן.—Others)

נוֹדֶה לְךָ יהוה אֱלֹהֵינוּ, עַל שֶׁהִנְחַלְתָּ לַאֲבוֹתֵינוּ אֶרֶץ חֶמְדָּה טוֹבָה וּרְחָבָה. וְעַל שֶׁהוֹצֵאתָנוּ יהוה אֱלֹהֵינוּ מֵאֶרֶץ מִצְרַיִם, וּפְדִיתָנוּ מִבֵּית עֲבָדִים, וְעַל בְּרִיתְךָ שֶׁחָתַמְתָּ בִּבְשָׂרֵנוּ, וְעַל תּוֹרָתְךָ שֶׁלִּמַּדְתָּנוּ, וְעַל חֻקֶּיךָ שֶׁהוֹדַעְתָּנוּ, וְעַל חַיִּים חֵן וָחֶסֶד שֶׁחוֹנַנְתָּנוּ, וְעַל אֲכִילַת מָזוֹן שָׁאַתָּה זָן וּמְפַרְנֵס אוֹתָנוּ תָּמִיד, בְּכָל יוֹם וּבְכָל עֵת וּבְכָל שָׁעָה.

On Chanukah and Purim:

וְעַל הַנִּסִּים וְעַל הַפֻּרְקָן וְעַל הַגְּבוּרוֹת וְעַל הַתְּשׁוּעוֹת וְעַל הַמִּלְחָמוֹת שֶׁעָשִׂיתָ לַאֲבוֹתֵינוּ בַּיָּמִים הָהֵם בַּזְּמַן הַזֶּה.

On Purim:	On Chanukah:

On Chanukah:

בִּימֵי מַתִּתְיָהוּ בֶּן יוֹחָנָן כֹּהֵן גָּדוֹל חַשְׁמוֹנָאִי וּבָנָיו, כְּשֶׁעָמְדָה מַלְכוּת יָוָן הָרְשָׁעָה עַל עַמְּךָ יִשְׂרָאֵל, לְהַשְׁכִּיחָם תּוֹרָתֶךָ, וּלְהַעֲבִירָם מֵחֻקֵּי רְצוֹנֶךָ. וְאַתָּה בְּרַחֲמֶיךָ הָרַבִּים, עָמַדְתָּ לָהֶם בְּעֵת צָרָתָם, רַבְתָּ אֶת רִיבָם, דַּנְתָּ אֶת דִּינָם, נָקַמְתָּ אֶת נִקְמָתָם. מָסַרְתָּ גִּבּוֹרִים בְּיַד חַלָּשִׁים, וְרַבִּים בְּיַד מְעַטִּים, וּטְמֵאִים בְּיַד טְהוֹרִים, וּרְשָׁעִים בְּיַד צַדִּיקִים, וְזֵדִים בְּיַד עוֹסְקֵי תוֹרָתֶךָ. וּלְךָ עָשִׂיתָ שֵׁם גָּדוֹל וְקָדוֹשׁ בְּעוֹלָמֶךָ, וּלְעַמְּךָ יִשְׂרָאֵל עָשִׂיתָ תְּשׁוּעָה גְדוֹלָה וּפֻרְקָן כְּהַיּוֹם הַזֶּה. וְאַחַר כֵּן בָּאוּ בָנֶיךָ לִדְבִיר בֵּיתֶךָ, וּפִנּוּ אֶת הֵיכָלֶךָ, וְטִהֲרוּ אֶת מִקְדָּשֶׁךָ, וְהִדְלִיקוּ נֵרוֹת בְּחַצְרוֹת קָדְשֶׁךָ, וְקָבְעוּ שְׁמוֹנַת יְמֵי חֲנֻכָּה אֵלּוּ, לְהוֹדוֹת וּלְהַלֵּל לְשִׁמְךָ הַגָּדוֹל.

On Purim:

בִּימֵי מָרְדְּכַי וְאֶסְתֵּר בְּשׁוּשַׁן הַבִּירָה, כְּשֶׁעָמַד עֲלֵיהֶם הָמָן הָרָשָׁע, בִּקֵּשׁ לְהַשְׁמִיד לַהֲרֹג וּלְאַבֵּד אֶת כָּל הַיְּהוּדִים, מִנַּעַר וְעַד זָקֵן, טַף וְנָשִׁים בְּיוֹם אֶחָד, בִּשְׁלוֹשָׁה עָשָׂר לְחֹדֶשׁ שְׁנֵים עָשָׂר, הוּא חֹדֶשׁ אֲדָר, וּשְׁלָלָם לָבוֹז. וְאַתָּה בְּרַחֲמֶיךָ הָרַבִּים הֵפַרְתָּ אֶת עֲצָתוֹ, וְקִלְקַלְתָּ אֶת מַחֲשַׁבְתּוֹ, וַהֲשֵׁבוֹתָ לּוֹ גְּמוּלוֹ בְרֹאשׁוֹ, וְתָלוּ אוֹתוֹ וְאֶת בָּנָיו עַל הָעֵץ.

וְעַל הַכֹּל יהוה אֱלֹהֵינוּ אֲנַחְנוּ מוֹדִים לָךְ, וּמְבָרְכִים אוֹתָךְ, יִתְבָּרַךְ שִׁמְךָ בְּפִי כָּל חַי תָּמִיד לְעוֹלָם וָעֶד.°°

כַּכָּתוּב, וְאָכַלְתָּ וְשָׂבָעְתָּ, וּבֵרַכְתָּ אֶת יהוה אֱלֹהֶיךָ, עַל הָאָרֶץ

°° In some German communities, the liturgical poem *Bris Olam* (p. 160) is recited at this point.

בָּרוּךְ Blessed are You, HASHEM, our God, King of the universe, Who nourishes the entire world, in His goodness — with grace, with kindness, and with mercy. He gives nourishment to all flesh, for His kindness is eternal. And through His great goodness, we have never lacked, and may we never lack, nourishment, for all eternity. For the sake of His Great Name, because He is God Who nourishes and sustains all, and benefits all, and He prepares food for all of His creatures which He has created. As it is said: 'You open Your hand, and satisfy the desire of every living thing.' Leader— Blessed are You, HASHEM, Who nourishes all.

(Others— Amen.)

נוֹדֶה We thank You, HASHEM, our God, because You have given to our forefathers as a heritage a desirable, good and spacious land; because You removed us, HASHEM, our God, from the land of Egypt and You redeemed us from the house of bondage; for Your covenant which You sealed in our flesh; for Your Torah which You taught us and for Your statutes which You made known to us; for life, grace, and lovingkindness which You granted us; and for the provision of food with which You nourish and sustain us constantly, in every day, in every season, and in every hour.

On Chanukah and Purim:

וְעַל And for the miracles, and for the salvation, and for the mighty deeds, and for the victories, and for the battles which You performed for our forefathers in those days, at this time.

On Chanukah:

בִּימֵי In the days of Mattisyahu, the son of Yochanan, the High Priest, the Hasmonean, and his sons — when the wicked Greek kingdom rose up against Your people Israel to make them forget Your Torah and compel them to stray from the statutes of Your Will — You in Your great mercy stood up for them in the time of their distress. You took up their grievance, judged their claim, and avenged their wrong. You delivered the strong into the hands of the weak, the many into the hands of the few, the impure into the hands of the pure, the wicked into the hands of the righteous, and the wanton into the hands of the diligent students of Your Torah. For Yourself You made a great and holy Name in Your world, and for Your people Israel You worked a great victory and salvation as this very day. Thereafter, Your children came to the Holy of Holies of Your House, cleansed Your Temple, purified the site of Your Holiness and kindled lights in the Courtyards of Your Sanctuary; and they established these eight days of Chanukah to express thanks and praise to Your great Name.

On Purim:

בִּימֵי In the days of Mordechai and Esther, in Shushan, the capital, when Haman, the wicked, rose up against them and sought to destroy, to slay, and to exterminate all the Jews, young and old, infants and women, on the same day, on the thirteenth of the twelfth month which is the month of Adar, and to plunder their possessions. But You, in Your abundant mercy, nullified his counsel and frustrated his intention and caused his design to return upon his own head and they hanged him and his sons on the gallows.

וְעַל הַכֹּל For all, HASHEM, our God, we thank You and bless You. May Your Name be blessed by the mouth of all the living, continuously for all eternity.°° As it is written: 'And you shall eat and you shall be satisfied and you shall bless HASHEM, your God, for the good land

°° In some German communities, the liturgical poem Bris Olam (p. 160) is recited at this point.

הַטּוֹבָה אֲשֶׁר נָתַן לָךְ. Leader—בָּרוּךְ אַתָּה יהוה, עַל הָאָרֶץ וְעַל
הַמָּזוֹן. (אָמֵן—Others)

רַחֵם נָא יהוה אֱלֹהֵינוּ עַל יִשְׂרָאֵל עַמֶּךָ, וְעַל יְרוּשָׁלַיִם עִירֶךָ,
וְעַל צִיּוֹן מִשְׁכַּן כְּבוֹדֶךָ, וְעַל מַלְכוּת בֵּית דָּוִד מְשִׁיחֶךָ, וְעַל
הַבַּיִת הַגָּדוֹל וְהַקָּדוֹשׁ שֶׁנִּקְרָא שִׁמְךָ עָלָיו. אֱלֹהֵינוּ אָבִינוּ רְעֵנוּ
זוּנֵנוּ פַּרְנְסֵנוּ וְכַלְכְּלֵנוּ וְהַרְוִיחֵנוּ, וְהַרְוַח לָנוּ יהוה אֱלֹהֵינוּ מְהֵרָה
מִכָּל צָרוֹתֵינוּ. וְנָא אַל תַּצְרִיכֵנוּ יהוה אֱלֹהֵינוּ, לֹא לִידֵי מַתְּנַת
בָּשָׂר וָדָם, וְלֹא לִידֵי הַלְוָאָתָם, כִּי אִם לְיָדְךָ הַמְּלֵאָה הַפְּתוּחָה
הַקְּדוֹשָׁה וְהָרְחָבָה, שֶׁלֹּא נֵבוֹשׁ וְלֹא נִכָּלֵם לְעוֹלָם וָעֶד.

On the Sabbath:

רְצֵה וְהַחֲלִיצֵנוּ יהוה אֱלֹהֵינוּ בְּמִצְוֹתֶיךָ, וּבְמִצְוַת יוֹם הַשְּׁבִיעִי הַשַּׁבָּת הַגָּדוֹל
וְהַקָּדוֹשׁ הַזֶּה, כִּי יוֹם זֶה גָּדוֹל וְקָדוֹשׁ הוּא לְפָנֶיךָ, לִשְׁבָּת בּוֹ וְלָנוּחַ בּוֹ
בְּאַהֲבָה כְּמִצְוַת רְצוֹנֶךָ, וּבִרְצוֹנְךָ הָנִיחַ לָנוּ יהוה אֱלֹהֵינוּ, שֶׁלֹּא תְהֵא צָרָה וְיָגוֹן
וַאֲנָחָה בְּיוֹם מְנוּחָתֵנוּ, וְהַרְאֵנוּ יהוה אֱלֹהֵינוּ בְּנֶחָמַת צִיּוֹן עִירֶךָ, וּבְבִנְיַן יְרוּשָׁלַיִם
עִיר קָדְשֶׁךָ, כִּי אַתָּה הוּא בַּעַל הַיְשׁוּעוֹת וּבַעַל הַנֶּחָמוֹת.

On Rosh Chodesh and Festivals add:

אֱלֹהֵינוּ וֵאלֹהֵי אֲבוֹתֵינוּ, יַעֲלֶה, וְיָבֹא, וְיַגִּיעַ, וְיֵרָאֶה, וְיֵרָצֶה, וְיִשָּׁמַע, וְיִפָּקֵד,
וְיִזָּכֵר זִכְרוֹנֵנוּ וּפִקְדוֹנֵנוּ, וְזִכְרוֹן אֲבוֹתֵינוּ, וְזִכְרוֹן מָשִׁיחַ בֶּן דָּוִד עַבְדֶּךָ,
וְזִכְרוֹן יְרוּשָׁלַיִם עִיר קָדְשֶׁךָ, וְזִכְרוֹן כָּל עַמְּךָ בֵּית יִשְׂרָאֵל לְפָנֶיךָ, לִפְלֵיטָה לְטוֹבָה
לְחֵן וּלְחֶסֶד וּלְרַחֲמִים, לְחַיִּים וּלְשָׁלוֹם בְּיוֹם

On Rosh Hashanah	On Shavuos	On Pesach	On Rosh Chodesh
רֹאשׁ הַחֹדֶשׁ	חַג הַשָּׁבֻעוֹת	חַג הַמַּצּוֹת	הַזִּכָּרוֹן

On Shemini Atzeres/Simchas Torah	On Succos
שְׁמִינִי עֲצֶרֶת הַחַג	חַג הַסֻּכּוֹת

הַזֶּה. זָכְרֵנוּ יהוה אֱלֹהֵינוּ בּוֹ לְטוֹבָה, וּפָקְדֵנוּ בּוֹ לִבְרָכָה, וְהוֹשִׁיעֵנוּ בּוֹ לְחַיִּים
טוֹבִים. וּבִדְבַר יְשׁוּעָה וְרַחֲמִים, חוּס וְחָנֵּנוּ וְרַחֵם עָלֵינוּ וְהוֹשִׁיעֵנוּ, כִּי אֵלֶיךָ עֵינֵינוּ,
כִּי אֵל מֶלֶךְ חַנּוּן וְרַחוּם אָתָּה.

Leader—**וּבְנֵה** יְרוּשָׁלַיִם עִיר הַקֹּדֶשׁ בִּמְהֵרָה בְיָמֵינוּ. בָּרוּךְ אַתָּה
יהוה, בּוֹנֵה בְרַחֲמָיו יְרוּשָׁלָיִם. אָמֵן. (אָמֵן—Others)

בָּרוּךְ אַתָּה יהוה אֱלֹהֵינוּ מֶלֶךְ הָעוֹלָם, הָאֵל אָבִינוּ מַלְכֵּנוּ
אַדִּירֵנוּ בּוֹרְאֵנוּ גּוֹאֲלֵנוּ יוֹצְרֵנוּ קְדוֹשֵׁנוּ קְדוֹשׁ יַעֲקֹב, רוֹעֵנוּ
רוֹעֵה יִשְׂרָאֵל, הַמֶּלֶךְ הַטּוֹב וְהַמֵּטִיב לַכֹּל, שֶׁבְּכָל יוֹם וָיוֹם הוּא
הֵטִיב, הוּא מֵטִיב, הוּא יֵיטִיב לָנוּ. הוּא גְמָלָנוּ הוּא גוֹמְלֵנוּ הוּא
יִגְמְלֵנוּ לָעַד, לְחֵן וּלְחֶסֶד וּלְרַחֲמִים וּלְרֶוַח הַצָּלָה וְהַצְלָחָה, בְּרָכָה
וִישׁוּעָה נֶחָמָה פַּרְנָסָה וְכַלְכָּלָה Leader—וְרַחֲמִים וְחַיִּים וְשָׁלוֹם וְכָל
טוֹב, וּמִכָּל טוּב לְעוֹלָם אַל יְחַסְּרֵנוּ. (אָמֵן—Others)

The Ritual / Bircas HaMazon [146]

which He gave you.' Leader— *Blessed are You, HASHEM, for the land and for the nourishment.* (Others— *Amen.*)

רַחֵם *Have mercy, please, HASHEM, our God, on Israel Your people; on Jerusalem, Your city, on Zion, the resting place of Your Glory; on the monarchy of the House of David, Your anointed; and on the great and holy House upon which Your Name is called. Our God, our Father — tend us, nourish us, sustain us, support us, relieve us; HASHEM, our God, grant us speedy relief from all our troubles. Please, make us not needful — HASHEM, our God — of the gifts of human hands nor of their loans, but only of Your Hand that is full, open, holy, and generous, that we not feel inner shame nor be humiliated for ever and ever.*

On the Sabbath:

רְצֵה *May it please You, HASHEM, our God — give us rest through Your commandments and through the commandment of the seventh day, this great and holy Sabbath. For this day is great and holy before You to rest on it and be content on it in love, as ordained by Your will. May it be Your will, HASHEM, our God, that there be no distress, grief, or lament on this day of our contentment. And show us, HASHEM, our God, the consolation of Zion, Your city, and the rebuilding of Jerusalem, City of Your holiness, for You are the Master of salvations and Master of consolations.*

On Rosh Chodesh and Festivals:

אֱלֹהֵינוּ *Our God and God of our forefathers, may there rise, come, reach, be noted, be favored, be heard, be considered, and be remembered — the remembrance and consideration of ourselves; the remembrance of our forefathers; the remembrance of Messiah, son of David, Your servant; the remembrance of Jerusalem, the City of Your Holiness; the remembrance of Your entire people the Family of Israel — before You for deliverance, for goodness, for grace, for kindness, and for compassion, for life, and for peace on this day of*

On Rosh Chodesh	On Pesach	On Shavuos
Rosh Chodesh.	*the Festival of Matzos.*	*the Shavuos Festival.*
On Rosh Hashanah	On Succos	On Shemini Atzeres/Simchas Torah
Remembrance.	*the Succos Festival.*	*the Shemini Atzeres Festival.*

Remember us on it, HASHEM, our God, for goodness; consider us on it for blessing; and help us on it for good life. In the matter of salvation and compassion, pity, be gracious and compassionate with us and help us, for our eyes are turned to You, because You are God, the gracious, and compassionate King.

וּבְנֵה Leader—*Rebuild Jerusalem, the Holy City, soon in our days. Blessed are You, HASHEM, Who rebuilds Jerusalem in His mercy. Amen.* (Others— *Amen.*)

בָּרוּךְ *Blessed are You, HASHEM, our God, King of the Universe, the Almighty, our Father, our King, our Sovereign, our Creator, our Redeemer, our Maker, our Holy One, Holy One of Jacob, our Shepherd, the Shepherd of Israel, the King Who is good and Who does good for all. For every single day He did good, He does good, and He will do good to us. He was bountiful with us, He is bountiful with us, and He will forever be bountiful with us — with grace and with kindness and with mercy, with relief, salvation, success, blessing, help, consolation, sustenance, support,* Leader— *mercy, life, peace, and all good; and of all good things may He never deprive us.* (Others— *Amen.*)

הָרַחֲמָן הוּא יִמְלוֹךְ עָלֵינוּ לְעוֹלָם וָעֶד. הָרַחֲמָן הוּא יִתְבָּרַךְ בַּשָּׁמַיִם וּבָאָרֶץ. הָרַחֲמָן הוּא יִשְׁתַּבַּח לְדוֹר דּוֹרִים, וְיִתְפָּאַר בָּנוּ לָעַד וּלְנֵצַח נְצָחִים, וְיִתְהַדַּר בָּנוּ לָעַד וּלְעוֹלְמֵי עוֹלָמִים. הָרַחֲמָן הוּא יְפַרְנְסֵנוּ בְּכָבוֹד. הָרַחֲמָן הוּא יִשְׁבּוֹר עֻלֵּנוּ מֵעַל צַוָּארֵנוּ, וְהוּא יוֹלִיכֵנוּ קוֹמְמִיּוּת לְאַרְצֵנוּ. הָרַחֲמָן הוּא יִשְׁלַח לָנוּ בְּרָכָה מְרֻבָּה בַּבַּיִת הַזֶּה, וְעַל שֻׁלְחָן זֶה שֶׁאָכַלְנוּ עָלָיו. הָרַחֲמָן הוּא יִשְׁלַח לָנוּ אֶת אֵלִיָּהוּ הַנָּבִיא זָכוּר לַטּוֹב, וִיבַשֶּׂר לָנוּ בְּשׂוֹרוֹת טוֹבוֹת יְשׁוּעוֹת וְנֶחָמוֹת.

At this point some German communities recite the הָרַחֲמָן prayers found on p. 166.

Guests recite the following (children at their parents' table include the words in parentheses):	Those eating at their own table recite (including the words in parentheses that apply):
הָרַחֲמָן הוּא יְבָרֵךְ אֶת (אָבִי מוֹרִי) בַּעַל הַבַּיִת הַזֶּה, וְאֶת (אִמִּי מוֹרָתִי) בַּעֲלַת הַבַּיִת הַזֶּה, אוֹתָם וְאֶת בֵּיתָם וְאֶת זַרְעָם וְאֶת כָּל אֲשֶׁר לָהֶם.	הָרַחֲמָן הוּא יְבָרֵךְ אוֹתִי (וְאֶת אִשְׁתִּי/ בַּעֲלִי. וְאֶת זַרְעִי) וְאֶת כָּל אֲשֶׁר לִי.

אוֹתָנוּ וְאֶת כָּל אֲשֶׁר לָנוּ, כְּמוֹ שֶׁנִּתְבָּרְכוּ אֲבוֹתֵינוּ אַבְרָהָם יִצְחָק וְיַעֲקֹב בַּכֹּל מִכֹּל כֹּל, כֵּן יְבָרֵךְ אוֹתָנוּ כֻּלָּנוּ יַחַד בִּבְרָכָה שְׁלֵמָה, וְנֹאמַר, אָמֵן.

בַּמָּרוֹם יְלַמְּדוּ עֲלֵיהֶם וְעָלֵינוּ זְכוּת, שֶׁתְּהֵא לְמִשְׁמֶרֶת שָׁלוֹם. וְנִשָּׂא בְרָכָה מֵאֵת יהוה, וּצְדָקָה מֵאֱלֹהֵי יִשְׁעֵנוּ, וְנִמְצָא חֵן וְשֵׂכֶל טוֹב בְּעֵינֵי אֱלֹהִים וְאָדָם.

The following six prayers are recited aloud by either the leader of *Bircas HaMazon* or by other guests designated for this honor.

Someone other than the father should recite the following stanza.

הָרַחֲמָן הוּא יְבָרֵךְ אֲבִי הַיֶּלֶד וְאִמּוֹ,

וְיִזְכּוּ לְגַדְּלוֹ וּלְחַנְּכוֹ וּלְחַכְּמוֹ,

מִיּוֹם הַשְּׁמִינִי וָהָלְאָה יֵרָצֶה דָמוֹ,

וִיהִי יהוה אֱלֹהָיו עִמּוֹ.

(אָמֵן. —All)

◆§ Harachaman Prayers

The six stanzas of the following *piyut* [liturgical poem] were authored by *R' Avraham ben Yitzchak HaKohen*, who lived in the twelfth century. His name —

אַבְרָהָם כֹּהֵן צֶדֶק — is formed by the acrostic of the verses (after the introductory phrase). He also composed a special liturgy for the *Shacharis* service of a Sabbath on which a *bris* is performed. That prayer is signed with

הָרַחֲמָן *The compassionate One! May He reign over us forever. The compassionate One! May He be blessed in heaven and on earth. The compassionate One! May He be praised throughout all generations, may He be glorified through us forever to the ultimate ends, and be honored through us forever and for all eternity. The compassionate One! May He sustain us in honor. The compassionate One! May He break the yoke of oppression from our necks and guide us erect to our Land. The compassionate One! May he send us abundant blessing to this house and upon this table at which we have eaten. The compassionate One! May He send us Elijah, the Prophet — he is remembered for good — to proclaim to us good tidings, salvations, and consolations.*

At this point some German communities recite the הָרַחֲמָן prayers found on page 166.

Those eating at their own table recite (including the words in parentheses that apply):	Guests recite the following (children at their parents' table include the words in parentheses):
The compassionate One! May He bless me (my wife/husband and my children) and all that is mine.	*The compassionate One! May He bless (my father, my teacher) the master of this house, and (my mother, my teacher) lady of this house, them, their house, their family, and all that is theirs.*

Ours and all that is ours — just as our forefathers Abraham, Isaac, and Jacob were blessed in everything, from everything, with everything. So may He bless us all together with a perfect blessing. And let us say: Amen!

בַּמָרוֹם *On high, may merit be pleaded upon them and upon us, for a safeguard of peace. May we receive a blessing from HASHEM and just kindness from the God of our salvation, and find favor and good understanding in the eyes of God and man.*

The following six prayers are recited aloud by either the leader of *Bircas HaMazon* or by other guests designated for this honor.

Someone other than the father should recite the following stanza.

הָרַחֲמָן *The compassionate One! May He bless the father of the child and his mother;*

and may they merit to raise him, to educate him, and to make him wise, from the eighth day onward may his blood be accepted, and may HASHEM, his God, be with him. (All— *Amen.*)

---

the acrostic, אַבְרָהָם בַּר יִצְחָק הַכֹּהֵן
The stanzas allude to many verses, people and events in Scripture. By referring to a wide range of topics running the gamut from the building of the Second Temple, the Temple sacrifices, the pilgrimage festivals, the Messiah, and to the outstanding personalities associated with *bris milah*, Abraham, Moses and Elijah, the author

underscores the magnitude of this *mitzvah*.

These prayers were recited by most of European Jewry; however the German community west of the Elbe river, including the cities of Frankfurt, Mainz, and the communities on the Rhine River, inserted other *piyutim* in the *Bircas HaMazon* (see p. 160 and 166).

The commentary is drawn primarily

from *Kores HaBris*, *Zocher HaBris*, *Bris Avraham*, *Mateh Yehudah* and *Otzer HaTefillos*.

The הָרַחֲמָן prayers are recited either by the leader of *Bircas HaMazon* or by other participants designated for this purpose. In some communities, it is customary to honor six guests, each reciting one stanza. In any case, since the first, second and fourth stanzas contain specific blessings for the father, *sandak* and *mohel* respectively, it is unseemly that any of them should recite the particular stanza in which his role is mentioned.

In this vein *Maaseh Rokeach* describes how *Rambam* [Maimonides] was angered at a groom who recited *Sheva Berachos* (the seven special blessings in honor of the newlyweds) in what seemed ostentatious self-glorification *(Kores HaBris)*.

◂§ Blessing the Parents

אֲבִי הַיֶּלֶד — *The father of the child.* The father is the first one mentioned in these blessings because the important *mitzvah* of circumcising the child is his. The laws of *milah (Yoreh Deah* 260:1) begin: It is a positive commandment incumbent upon the father to circumcise his son and this mitzvah is greater than any other positive commandment.

It has been suggested that the word אָב, *father,* is spelled with the first two letters of the *aleph-beis,* as an allusion to the father's responsibility to teach his son the Torah, which is written in the holy letters of the *aleph-beis.*

לְגַדְּלוֹ וּלְחַנְּכוֹ וּלְחַכְּמוֹ — *To raise him, to educate him, and to make him wise.* Commentators equate this threefold blessing with the threefold blessing recited after the blessings over the circumcision: כְּשֵׁם שֶׁנִּכְנַס לַבְּרִית, כֵּן יִכָּנֵס לְתוֹרָה וּלְחֻפָּה וּלְמַעֲשִׂים טוֹבִים, *Just as the*

child has entered into the covenant, so may he enter into [the study of] Torah, marriage, and [the performance of] good deeds.

Kores HaBris, concerned that the order of both blessings be identical, equates 'Torah' with 'to raise him,' citing *Pesachim* 113a: Among those who inherit the World to Come is he who *raises* his sons to study Torah.

He matches 'to educate him,' with 'marriage,' and cites the Talmud *(Kiddushin* 30a) that discusses the age at which parents should encourage their son to marry, keeping in mind that every child is unique. In this context the Talmud (ibid.) cites the verse, חֲנוֹךְ לַנַּעַר עַל פִּי דַרְכּוֹ, *Educate a child according to his individual abilities (Proverbs* 22:6). 'To make him wise' is seen as being similar to 'good deeds,' which refers to doing *mitzvos.* King David wrote, מֵאֹיְבַי תְּחַכְּמֵנִי מִצְוֹתֶךָ, *Your commandments make me wiser than my enemies (Psalms* 119:98). The wisdom of God's *mitzvos* provides a Jew who performs them with the arsenal needed to overcome his greatest enemies — his evil inclination and raging desires *(Malbim* ibid.).

Zocher HaBris also sees similarities between the two sets of threefold blessings but he does not interpret them to be in the same corresponding order. 'To raise him' corresponds to 'marriage,' for the time to raise and instill ethics and character in a child is before he is married.

'To educate him' parallels 'good deeds,' to educate and train even a young child in the performance of *mitzvos.*

'To make him wise' alludes to 'Torah,' to teach a child the world's greatest wisdom — the Torah.[1]

מִיּוֹם הַשְּׁמִינִי וָהָלְאָה — *From the eighth day onward.* This phrase is borrowed

---

1. R' Yehoshua Leib Diskin, too, ponders the order of this threefold blessing. He says that לְגַדְּלוֹ, *to raise him,* is derived from גָּדוֹל, *adult,* implying the age of *bar-mitzvah* when a child becomes personally responsible for his religious obligations. Yet, there is much teaching and training to be done long before a boy reaches the age of *bar-mitzvah.* Perhaps, then, וּלְחַנְּכוֹ, *to educate him,* should really precede לְגַדְּלוֹ?

R' Diskin perceptively comments that to raise a pre-schooler or even a grade-school child is relatively easy compared to the rearing of a teen-ager. Therefore, we pray that God bless the

from *Leviticus* (22:27), where God tells Moses with regard to animal offerings: וּמִיּוֹם הַשְּׁמִינִי וָהָלְאָה יֵרָצֶה לְקָרְבַּן אִשֶּׁה לַה׳, *and from the eighth day [following birth] onward, shall it be acceptable to be brought near as an offering... (Mateh Yehudah).* The simile relating a circumcised child to an offering is significant, for *Zohar* writes that the act of *bris milah* is the consummate offering (*Shelach* 164a, see also *Zohar Beshalach* 66b, *Pikudei* 255b).

R' Bachya (*Bereishis* 17:13) notes numerous similarities between *bris milah* and an offering. He concludes by noting that the power of the *bris* is even greater than that of an offering in the Temple, for one who brings an offering has merely given of his money, while through circumcision one actually gives of himself.

Additionally *milah* is referred to as an offering in two instances in Scripture. In Jonah (1:16) it details how, *the men (on the ship with Jonah) feared HASHEM greatly and they offered sacrifice...* *Pirkei d'R' Eliezer* explains that they had themselves circumcised as the first step of their conversion to Judaism.

Another Midrash (*Shemos Rabbah* 19:5) interprets, כֹּרְתֵי בְרִיתִי עֲלֵי זָבַח, *those that have made a covenant with Me by sacrifice (Psalms* 50:5), as a reference to the covenant of circumcision.

יֵרָצֶה דָמוֹ — *May his blood be accepted.* Some explain דָמוֹ, *his blood*, as referring to the father's, i.e., the blood of his own *bris* as an infant. For, in reality, the child now being circumcised has not been asked if he is for or against being circumcised. His parents have it

performed because of *their* commitment to *mitzvos*. Only when this same child will become a father and have his own son circumcised, will it becomes obvious that he is pleased that his parents had him circumcised. Hence, it is at his son's *bris* that it becomes obvious that the father retroactively approves of his own *bris*. It is then that he is perceived as having performed the *mitzvah* of his own *bris* and we pray that *his blood be [retroactively] accepted* (Belzer Rebbe, cited in *Taamei HaMinhagim* 913 §11).

וִיהִי ה׳ אֱלֹהָיו עִמּוֹ — *And may HASHEM, his God, be with him.* This phrase is adapted from two Scriptural passages that contain slightly different wording. It was the charge that Cyrus, King of Persia, gave to the Jews when he granted them the right to build the Second Temple. In *Ezra* (1:3), Cyrus's words are recorded as, יְהִי אֱלֹהָיו עִמּוֹ, *may his God be with him*, while in *II Chronicles* (36:23) he says, ה׳ אֱלֹהָיו עִמּוֹ, *HASHEM, his God, be with him.* Here, the *paytan* has combined the two phrases.

The similarity between the Hebrew words בָּנִים, *children*, and בֹּנִים, *builders*, is not coincidental.[1] In Judaism, building begins with the family. The molding of a child's character and his performance of one *mitzvah* and then another, is the foundation that is laid to build his total personality. With the performance of *bris milah*, the parents have revealed the blueprint of their plan for the child's life. They, as the architects and builders, are blessed, as were the builders of the Temple long ago, '*May HASHEM, his God, be with him [the child]*' as they implement their noble plans.

parents with the good fortune to successfully teach and guide their child even after he has reached a certain level of maturity and independence. Thus, the blessing is this: even after לְגַדְּלוֹ, i.e., bringing him to religious responsibility, may they still be able to teach and train him.

1. This message is of such importance that four different tractates of the Talmud — *Berachos, Nazir, Yevamos,* and *Kreisos* — close with the dictum: אַל תִּקְרֵי בָּנַיִךְ אֶלָּא בֹּנָיִךְ, *read not your children, but your builders.* This dictum has been rendered homiletically: Do not refer to your offspring merely as *children,* but rather as builders. [Interestingly, the names of these four tractates — ברכות נזיר יבמות כריתות — form the acrostic, בָּנַיִךְ.]

Someone other than the *sandak* should recite the following stanza.

הָרַחֲמָן הוּא יְבָרֵךְ בַּעַל בְּרִית הַמִּילָה,
אֲשֶׁר שָׂשׂ לַעֲשׂוֹת צֶדֶק בְּגִילָה,
וִישַׁלֵּם פָּעֳלוֹ וּמַשְׂכֻּרְתּוֹ כְּפוּלָה,
וְיִתְּנֵהוּ לְמַעְלָה לְמָעְלָה.   (אָמֵן. —All)

הָרַחֲמָן הוּא יְבָרֵךְ רַךְ הַנִּמּוֹל לִשְׁמוֹנָה,
וְיִהְיוּ יָדָיו וְלִבּוֹ לְאֵל אֱמוּנָה,

❧ Blessing The Sandak

בַּעַל בְּרִית הַמִּילָה — *The master of the circumcision covenant.* This refers to the *sandak*, the one who holds the child during the *bris*. The title is not merely honorary, but carries halachic significance as well (see p. 103).

[The *sandak* is actually one of three who bear the title בַּעַל בְּרִית, the other two are the father of the child and the *mohel* (see *O.C.* 559:8). The father has already received his blessing in the preceding stanzas, and the *mohel* receives his in the fourth. The *sandak's* role is considered more prominent than the *mohel's* since the *sandak* is compared to the *Kohen* who performed the incense-burning in the Temple (see p. 65). It is for this reason that the *sandak* has priority to the *mohel* with regard to being called to the Torah reading (*Rama Y.D.* 265:11).]

Another interpretation of this stanza understands בַּעַל בְּרִית as an allusion to Abraham (see below, s.v. Abraham)

אֲשֶׁר שָׂשׂ — *Who rejoiced.* This particular term of joy, שָׂשׂוֹן, is used in some Biblical verses with reference to *bris milah*. Rashi (*Shabbos* 130a) comments that the *mitzvah* of *milah* is a constant source of rejoicing for a Jew because it is inseparable from him, unlike other *mitzvos* (such as *tefillin* or *tzitzis*) that can be removed from his person. [See the interpretations of *Psalms* 119:162 on page 120, and of *Esther* 8:16 on page 121.]

צֶדֶק — *Righteousness.* The word also connotes *charity.* In certain communities it was customary for the *sandak* to generously underwrite the expenses of the *bris* and give the child a handsome gift (*Zocher HaBris*).

וִישַׁלֵּם פָּעֳלוֹ וּמַשְׂכֻּרְתּוֹ כְּפוּלָה — *May his deed be rewarded and his recompense doubled.* The choice of words is based on Boaz's blessing to Ruth, יְשַׁלֵּם ה', פָּעֳלֵךְ וּתְהִי מַשְׂכֻּרְתֵּךְ שְׁלֵמָה, *May HASHEM reward your deeds, and may your recompense be full* (Ruth 2:12). Just as Boaz blessed Ruth, who through her conversion to Judaism had come under the protection of the Divine Presence, so too, the *sandak* is blessed for having brought the newborn infant under the protection of the Divine Presence through circumcision (*Kores HaBris*).

The reference to double recompense refers to the two aspects of the *sandak's* role: his actual assistance in holding the child for the *mohel* as he performs the *bris*; and his spiritual role which is compared to the *Kohen* who performs the incense-burning at the Altar (*Chasam Sofer, Responsum O.C.* 158-159).

Alternatively, the 'doubled recompense' is for his participation in the *mitzvah* of *bris milah*, and for the joy with which he carries it out (*Dover Sholom*).

Zocher HaBris notes that the *sandak* is destined for riches (see p. 78-79). The recompense is therefore doubled, in this world as monetary wealth, and in the

Someone other than the *sandak* should recite the following stanza.

הָרַחֲמָן *The compassionate One! May He bless the master of the circumcision covenant,*
who rejoiced to perform righteousness with delight,
may his deed be rewarded and his recompense doubled,
and may He place him ever higher.   *(All— Amen.)*

הָרַחֲמָן *The compassionate One! May He bless the tender one circumcised on the eighth day*
and may his hands and heart be faithful to God,

World to Come as reward for the *mitzvah*.

לְמַעְלָה לְמָעְלָה — *Ever higher*. A phrase indicating great achievement, taken from *Deuteronomy* 28:43.

◆§ Abraham

בַּעַל בְּרִית הַמִּילָה — *Master of the circumcision covenant*. Some commentaries understand this term as referring to Abraham, whose circumcision, which was the first, set a precedent for Jews to follow for all generations. Indeed, in the *milah* blessing, the circumcision rite is referred to as בְּרִיתוֹ שֶׁל אַבְרָהָם אָבִינוּ, *the covenant of our forefather Abraham*. In this view the entire stanza takes on a different meaning. We shall therefore reinterpret the entire stanza in light of this view.

לַעֲשׂוֹת צֶדֶק — *To perform righteousness*. In *Genesis* 18:19, God says that He loves Abraham because he will instruct his offspring to act righteously. The Talmud (*Makkos* 24a) remarks that the verse הֹלֵךְ צְדָקוֹת, *He who walks with righteousness (Isaiah* 33:15), refers to our father Abraham. Interestingly, the Talmud (*Kesubos* 8b) describes those who perform acts of kindness as people who cling to the covenant of Abraham.

בְּגִילָה — *With delight*. A reference to Abraham's delight as it is described in the Sabbath *Minchah* prayer, אַבְרָהָם יָגֵל, *Abraham will delight*. The Midrash understands the verse in *Proverbs* (23:23), *Delight, delight, you father of the righteous*, as referring to the delight

that Abraham had experienced when God told him that Isaac, and not his servant Eliezer, would be his heir (*Etz Yosef*).

וּמַשְׂכֻּרְתּוֹ כְּפוּלָה — *And his recompense doubled*. A reference to *Genesis* 15:1, שְׂכָרְךָ הַרְבֵּה מְאֹד, *your recompense will be very great*, by which God assured Abraham that he would have a son by Sarah.

◆§ Blessing the Baby

רַךְ — *Tender one*. Jacob used this adjective to describe his own children: כִּי הַיְלָדִים רַכִּים, *the children are tender* (*Genesis* 33:13) . This form is used only for young children, thus if the person being circumcised is older than thirteen, the word is omitted (*Kores HaBris*).

הַנִּמּוֹל לִשְׁמוֹנָה — *Circumcised on the eighth day*. For a child who is circumcised after the eighth day, some texts read instead הַנִּמּוֹל בִּנְכוֹנָה, *who has been circumcised properly* (*Eidus LeYisrael*). Others read הַנִּמּוֹל בְּכַוָּנָה, *who has been circumcised with proper intent*.

וְיִהְיוּ יָדָיו וְלִבּוֹ לָאֵל אֱמוּנָה — *And may his hands and heart be faithful to God*. A poetic allusion to *Exodus* 17:12 that details the war between the Jews and Amalek. *And so his [Moses'] hands* [which he raised in prayer] *remained faithful.*

His hands and his heart refer to actions and intentions, both of which must be directed towards God. It is not

וְיִזְכֶּה לִרְאוֹת פְּנֵי הַשְּׁכִינָה,

שָׁלוֹשׁ פְּעָמִים בַּשָּׁנָה.

(אָמֵן. —All)

Someone other than the *mohel* should recite the following stanza.

הָרַחֲמָן הוּא יְבָרֵךְ הַמָּל בְּשַׂר הָעָרְלָה,

וּפָרַע וּמָצַץ דְּמֵי הַמִּילָה,

אִישׁ הַיָּרֵא וְרַךְ הַלֵּבָב עֲבוֹדָתוֹ פְּסוּלָה,

אִם שְׁלָשׁ אֵלֶּה לֹא יַעֲשֶׂה לָהּ.

(אָמֵן. —All)

enough to be merely a Jew at heart — sincerity is incomplete if not followed by action, hence the prayer that the child be complete in his devotion to God (*Zocher HaBris*).

Interestingly, *Ramban* (ibid.) notes that the word אֱמוּנָה, *trust* or *faith*, is used to describe that which endures through a בְּרִית, *covenant*. [See *Nechemiah* 10:1, כֹּרְתִים אֱמָנָה, *those who establish a trust*.]

וְיִזְכֶּה לִרְאוֹת פְּנֵי הַשְּׁכִינָה — *And may he merit to perceive the Divine Presence.* Before Abraham was circumcised he was unable to stand when perceiving the Divine Presence in prophecy. For this reason it says, prior to the circumcision: *Abraham fell upon his face and God spoke with him* (*Rashi* and *Sifsei Chachamim; Genesis* 17:3). However, after his circumcision, Abraham was able to remain standing when God communicated with him (see *Genesis* 18:22; *Zocher HaBris*).

לִרְאוֹת — *To perceive.* Some versions read לֵירָאוֹת, *to be perceived*, by the Divine Presence, as in *Deuteronomy* 16:16.

שָׁלוֹשׁ פְּעָמִים בַּשָּׁנָה — *Three times a year.* This is a reference to the שָׁלֹשׁ רְגָלִים, *three pilgrimage Festivals* — Pesach, Shavuos and Succos, — when every Jewish male is commanded to appear at the Holy Temple (see *Exodus* 23:17; *Deuteronomy* 16:16). In light of the fact that one who is uncircumcised is excluded from the pilgrimage commandment (see *Chagigah* 4b), we pray that this child who has now been

circumcised will merit being able to fulfill this joyous *mitzvah* (*Kores HaBris*).

⌑§ Blessing the Mohel

הַמָּל בְּשַׂר הָעָרְלָה — *The one who circumcised the flesh of the foreskin.* The עָרְלָה, *foreskin*, is the skin which covers the glans prior to circumcision (see p. 80). The phrase is similar to *Genesis* (17:11) where God detailed the circumcision procedure to Abraham, וּנְמַלְתֶּם אֵת בְּשַׂר עָרְלַתְכֶם, *And you shall circumcise the flesh of your foreskin.*

דְּמֵי הַמִּילָה — *The bloods of circumcision.* The first 'blood' is from חִתּוּךְ, *the excision of the outer skin*; the second blood is from פְּרִיעָה, *the revealing* of the glans by uncovering the mucous membrane, the inner tissue-thin layer of skin that covers the glans (see p.99; see *Sforno, Shemos* 4:26).

There are some who are of the opinion that the מְצִיצָה, *drawing of blood*, is done twice, hence the usage of the plural דְּמֵי, *bloods*.

אִישׁ הַיָּרֵא וְרַךְ הַלֵּבָב — *The man who is fearful and fainthearted.* This phrase is derived from *Deuteronomy* 20:8 which describes the quality of the Jewish soldier. *Rashi* comments that according to R' Akiva, it refers to one who is frightened by the hostilities of war and according to R' Yose HaGelili, to one who is afraid that his sinfulness will make him undeserving of God's help. Here the liturgist indicates that a *mohel* who is afraid of the sight of blood and apprehensive at the sound of a baby's

The Ritual / Bircas HaMazon [154]

and may he merit to perceive the Divine Presence,
three times a year.   (All— Amen.)

Someone other than the *mohel* should recite the following stanza.

הָרַחֲמָן *The compassionate One! May He bless the one who circumcised*
the flesh of the foreskin,
and revealed and drew the bloods of circumcision.
The man who is fearful and fainthearted, his service is invalid—
if he did not perform these three acts upon it.   (All— Amen.)

cry, will not be able to perform the *bris* properly (*Mateh Yehudah*).

אִם שְׁלָשׁ אֵלֶּה לֹא יַעֲשֶׂה לָהּ — *If he did not perform these three acts upon it.* A similar expression is found in *Exodus* 21:11 discussing the three obligations of a man to his wife. Here it refers to the three parts of the *bris* procedure: חִתּוּךְ, *excision;* פְּרִיעָה, *revealing;* and מְצִיצָה, *drawing (see p. 99).*

An alternative reading is וְאִם ... 'And' if he did not perform; i.e., if he is fearful and fainthearted, and as a result did not perform these three parts of the circumcision, then his service is invalid. *Zocher HaBris* cites a different version of this stich which conveys the same meaning but from a positive viewpoint: אִישׁ הַזָּהִיר וְהַזָּרִיז עֲבוֹדָתוֹ מְעוּלָּה אִם שְׁלָשׁ אֵלֶּה יַעֲשֶׂה לָהּ, *The diligent and efficient man's service is most eminent, if he has performed these three acts.*

⇜§ Supplication for the Messiah

The final two verses vary significantly from the first four. Whereas the first four conferred blessings upon the principal participants of the circumcision ceremony, the final two are supplications for the Final Redemption which will be heralded by Elijah the Prophet and brought about by the Messiah.

The order of these two stanzas is perplexing. The first is a prayer for the arrival of the Messiah, whose appearance will signal an end to the long exile; the second is a request for the reappearance of Elijah the Prophet. However, it will be Elijah who will appear first and announce the imminent arrival of the Messiah.[1]

Perhaps the *paytan's* order can be understood in the following context. The Talmud (*Sukkah* 52a) says that there will actually be two different Messiahs, the first preparing the way for the second. The first will descend from the tribe of Joseph and will do battle against the foreign kingdoms who in the End of Days will wage war on Jerusalem. This Messiah will ultimately be killed in battle. *R' Hai Gaon* (cited by *Otzar HaGeonim, Sanhedrin* 97a) says that only after this Messiah's death will Elijah appear and herald the arrival of the Davidic Messiah who will bring with him peace and salvation.

[Thus, the *paytan's* order is: First, a supplication for the Messiah from the House of Joseph; then a supplication for Elijah the Prophet. This is followed by the resumption of the conventional *Bircas HaMazon* which prays directly for the advent of the Davidic Messiah, who will follow the coming of Elijah.]

1. *Pesikta Rabbasi* (36:4) states: When God will redeem the Jews, Elijah will appear three days before the arrival of the Messiah. He will stand on the mountains of Israel ... his voice will be heard from one end of the world to the other ... [he will announce that] peace has come to the world. [See *Malachi* 3:23 and *Rashi, Eruvin* 43b, s.v. לפני.]

Moreover, in the blessing following the *Haftarah* reading, we recite an indication of the future order of events; שַׂמְּחֵנוּ בְּאֵלִיָּהוּ הַנָּבִיא עַבְדֶּךָ וּבְמַלְכוּת בֵּית דָּוִד מְשִׁיחֶךָ, *Gladden us with Elijah the Prophet, Your servant, and with the kingdom of Your Messiah from the House of David.*

הָרַחֲמָן הוּא יִשְׁלַח לָנוּ מְשִׁיחוֹ הוֹלֵךְ תָּמִים,
בִּזְכוּת חֲתַן לַמּוּלוֹת דָּמִים,
לְבַשֵּׂר בְּשׂוֹרוֹת טוֹבוֹת וְנִחוּמִים,
לְעַם אֶחָד מְפֻזָּר וּמְפֹרָד בֵּין הָעַמִּים. (All— אָמֵן.)

הָרַחֲמָן הוּא יִשְׁלַח לָנוּ כֹּהֵן צֶדֶק אֲשֶׁר לֻקַח לְעֵילוֹם,

מְשִׁיחוֹ — *His anointed.* In Zechariah 9:9-11, reference is made to the Jewish nation meriting the Final Redemption through the arrival of the Messiah because of their adherence to *bris milah:* הִנֵּה מַלְכֵּךְ יָבוֹא ... גַּם אַתְּ בְּדַם בְּרִיתֵךְ שִׁלַּחְתִּי אֲסִירַיִךְ, *Behold your king will come ... and you, because of the blood of your covenant, I will release your captives* (see *Ibn Ezra* and *Radak* ibid.).

הוֹלֵךְ תָּמִים — *Who goes with perfection.* The Messiah's level of spiritual perfection will be equal to that of the Patriarchs (see *Yalkut Shimoni, Yeshayah* 52).

תָּמִים — *Perfection.* This quality is mentioned here for it was through circumcision that Abraham achieved perfection. God prefaced the command regarding *bris milah* be telling Abraham; הִתְהַלֵּךְ לְפָנַי וֶהְיֵה תָמִים, *Go before Me and become perfect (Genesis 17:1; Zocher HaBris).*

חֲתַן — *Groom.* In Hebrew the word חֲתַן, *groom,* is used to refer to any honored person. In our context it refers to either the father who has fulfilled the obligation to have his child circumcised (*Kores HaBris*), or to the child himself. An alternative reading (*Siddur Beis Yaakov*) is חֲתָנַי, *grooms,* and presumably refers to both.

חֲתַן לַמּוּלוֹת דָּמִים — *The groom of the bloods of circumcisions.* This is an allusion to an incident that occurred when Moses with his family returned from Midian to Egypt. Moses had refrained from circumcising his new-

born son [Eliezer (see *R' Chananel, Yoma* 85b)], inasmuch as the recuperation from the circumcision, coupled with the journey God had commanded him to embark upon immediately, would have endangered the child's health.

At one point during their travels, they stopped at an inn, where Moses had his first opportunity to circumcise his son. However, he first occupied himself with his family's accommodations and for this, God sought to slay him (*Nedarim* 32a). An angel, appearing in the guise of a snake, threatened to devour Moses (see *Rashi; Exodus* 4:26). Zipporah, Moses's wife, understood the implication of the danger and quickly circumcised her son with a stone flint and thereby saved her husband. She then said, 'חֲתַן דָּמִים לַמּוּלֹת, (*You are) a bridegroom of the blood of circumcision,'* i.e., it is through you that a lesson has been learned conveying the importance of *milah* not only for our son Eliezer, but for all sons in the generations to come (*R' Hirsch*).

Additionally, at the very end of the bondage in Egypt, God informed Moses that for the Jews to merit redemption, they would have to be circumcised and then eat from the Pesach offering (*Shemos Rabbah* 19:5). Moses proceeded to have all the Jewish males circumcised.

The theme of this phrase, then, is that just as *bris milah*, which was carried out in Egypt through Moses,[1] brought about our nation's initial redemption, so too, should our observance of this

1. *Ohr HaChaim (Genesis 49:11)* cites *Zohar*, which says that just as Moses redeemed us in the past, so too will he redeem us in the future. This is alluded to in the lyrical phrase מַה שֶׁהָיָה הוּא שֶׁיִּהְיֶה, *That which was, will be (Ecclesiastes 1:9), the acrostic of the words* מַה שֶׁהָיָה הוּא,

הָרַחֲמָן *The compassionate One! May He send us His anointed who goes with perfection,*
in the merit of the groom of the bloods of circumcision,
to proclaim good tidings and consolations to the one nation,
scattered and separated among the nations. (All— *Amen.*)

הָרַחֲמָן *The compassionate One! May He send us the righteous Kohen who was taken to concealment,*

---

mitzvah make us worthy of our final redemption.

לְבַשֵּׂר בְּשׂוֹרוֹת טוֹבוֹת וְנֶחוּמִים — *To proclaim good tidings and consolations,* i.e., regarding the final redemption. It is Elijah, not the Messiah who will herald 'the good tidings and consolations' of the final redemption. Yet, this heralding is referred to here in the supplication for the Messiah, while only in the next stanza is reference made to Elijah. Perhaps then the phrase must be understood in the broad sense. The tide of events surrounding the Messiah will speak for themselves. The awesome events of that era will, by virtue of their uniqueness, proclaim the forthcoming salvation of the Jews.

לְעָם אֶחָד מְפֻזָּר וּמְפֹרָד בֵּין הָעַמִּים — *To the one nation, scattered and separated among the nations.* This expression is based on the derisive slur made by Haman (*Esther* 3:8). Although Haman did not intend it as such, his caustic comment is actually a tribute to the Jews in the Diaspora [otherwise the *paytan* would not choose this description]. Even though Jews are 'scattered' among the gentiles throughout the world, disconnected by geography and language, by virtue of their observance of *mitzvos* and specifically the *mitzvah* of *milah*, they still maintain a separateness from the nations that harbor them.

This separateness was alluded to early in Jewish history. When Rebecca was pregnant with Jacob and Esau, she was informed by God, שְׁנֵי לְאֻמִּים מִמֵּעַיִךְ יִפָּרֵדוּ, *two nations will separate themselves from your innards* (*Genesis* 25:23). While still in her womb the twins already represented two distinct ways of life (see *Rashi*, ibid.). The Midrash (*Bereishis Rabbah* 63:6) asserts that their separateness, was obvious immediately at birth, for Jacob was born circumcised Thus, the word פֵּירוּד, *separation*, symbolizes circumcision (*Kores HaBris*).

[See also p. 89 and 134 regarding Jacob's acceptance and Esau's rejection of *bris milah*. Also *Sanhedrin* 59b, *Yerushalmi Nedarim* 3:8, and *Rambam Hilchos Melachim* 10:7.]

◁§ Supplication for Elijah

כֹּהֵן צֶדֶק — *Righteous Kohen.* This is a reference to Elijah the Prophet, for Elijah and Pinchas the *Kohen* are one and the same (*Zohar, Pinchas* 215a, *Rashi, Bava Metzia* 114b — and see p. 77).

Kores HaBris asserts that every *Kohen* is called כֹּהֵן צֶדֶק, *righteous Kohen*,[1] based on the verse: כֹּהֲנֶיךָ יִלְבְּשׁוּ צֶדֶק, *Your Priests shall don righteousness* (*Psalms* 132:9). It was through the Temple service of the *Kohen* that a penitent merited atonement and was thereafter considered

---

forms the name מֹשֶׁה, Moses. *Ohr HaChaim* explains the *Zohar's* words by saying that the soul of Moses embodied within it the souls of the entire congregation; the Messiah will have this very same uniqueness.

1. Most people with the family name Katz are *Kohanim*. They usually spell their family name in Hebrew, כַּ"ץ, an acrostic for כֹּהֵן צֶדֶק. Those with the name Katz who are not *Kohanim* usually spell their family names קַץ, or קָאץ, using the letter ק instead of כ.

עַד הוּכַן כִּסְאוֹ כַּשֶּׁמֶשׁ וְיָהֲלוֹם,
וַיֵּלֶט פָּנָיו בְּאַדַּרְתּוֹ וַיִּגְלוֹם,
בְּרִיתִי הָיְתָה אִתּוֹ הַחַיִּים וְהַשָּׁלוֹם.
(אָמֵן.) —All

On the Sabbath:

הָרַחֲמָן הוּא יַנְחִילֵנוּ יוֹם שֶׁכֻּלּוֹ שַׁבָּת וּמְנוּחָה לְחַיֵּי הָעוֹלָמִים.

On Rosh Chodesh:

הָרַחֲמָן הוּא יְחַדֵּשׁ עָלֵינוּ אֶת הַחֹדֶשׁ הַזֶּה לְטוֹבָה וְלִבְרָכָה.

On Festivals:

הָרַחֲמָן הוּא יַנְחִילֵנוּ יוֹם שֶׁכֻּלּוֹ טוֹב.

On Rosh Hashanah:

הָרַחֲמָן הוּא יְחַדֵּשׁ עָלֵינוּ אֶת הַשָּׁנָה הַזֹּאת לְטוֹבָה וְלִבְרָכָה.

On Succos:

הָרַחֲמָן הוּא יָקִים לָנוּ אֶת סֻכַּת דָּוִיד הַנֹּפֶלֶת.

On Chanukah or Purim, if וְעַל הַנִּסִּים was not recited in its proper place, add:

הָרַחֲמָן הוּא יַעֲשֶׂה לָנוּ נִסִּים וְנִפְלָאוֹת

כַּאֲשֶׁר עָשָׂה לַאֲבוֹתֵינוּ בַּיָּמִים הָהֵם בַּזְּמַן הַזֶּה.

Continue with בִּימֵי מַתִּתְיָהוּ or בִּימֵי מָרְדְּכַי, p. 144, then go on from this point.

righteous. Thus, the *Kohen's* function was to bring about a state of צֶדֶק, *righteousness* (see *Metzudos*, ibid.).

Yerushalmi (*Yoma* 7:3) notes the relationship of priesthood to *bris milah* by explaining that the eight priestly vestments worn by the *Kohen Gadol* (High Priest) parallel the *mitzvah* of *milah* which is performed on the eighth day of the child's life. (See essay on significance of eight, p. 52.)

לֻקַּח לְעִילוּם — *Taken to concealment.* Elijah did not die; rather he was swept up to heaven while still alive and thereby concealed from humanity (see *II Kings* 2:8). As noted above, he will reappear prior to the coming of the Messiah (*Mateh Moshe*).

עַד הוּכַן כִּסְאוֹ — *Until his throne is established.* This refers to the Throne of Elijah that is prepared at every *bris*[1] (see p. 77 for origin of this custom).

Alternatively, כִּסְאוֹ, *his throne*, refers to that of the Messiah, of which it is said: וְכִסְאוֹ כַשֶּׁמֶשׁ נֶגְדִּי, *And his throne shall be like the sun before Me* (Psalms 89:37). The sun symbolizes the permanence of the Messianic reign (*Kli Yakar*, *Exodus* 17:12).

Additionally the throne can also be referring to the Throne of God which will become complete and established only after Amalek is erased from the world in the time of the Final Redemption (see *Rashi*, *Exodus* 17:16).

וְיָהֲלוֹם — *And diamond.* This refers to

1. Skeptics once asked *R' Yom Tov Lipmann Milhausen*, author of *Sefer HaNitzachon*, 'How can Elijah appear at every circumcision when there is so often more than one circumcision taking place at the same time?' He referred them to *Sanhedrin* 39a which discusses the fact that the Divine Presence is at every assemblage of ten Jewish males, although many such gatherings may occur simultaneously. The Talmud explains that if the sun can cast its glow over a multitude of places at once, then it is certainly possible for the Divine Presence to do the same. So too, said *R' Yom Tov Lipmann*, the spiritual presence of Elijah the Prophet is a glow that can shine simultaneously in many places the world over (*Edus LeYisrael*).

until his throne is established, bright as sun and diamond,
he who covered his face with his cloak and enwrapped himself,
My covenant was with him, for life and peace.   (All— *Amen.*)

one of the precious stones that appeared on the *Choshen* (breastplate) of the *Kohen Gadol*. [Some identify it with the diamond, while others say it is a bluish-green stone, midway between emerald and aquamarine in color (see *The Living Torah*, by R' Aryeh Kaplan, *Exodus* 28:18).]

Diamond is a metaphor for the spiritual brilliance of the Messianic reign. The last four letters of the word יַהֲלֹם form the word הַלֹם [*Halom*] which the Talmud (*Zevachim* 102a) understands as a reference to kingship (see *II Samuel* 7:18; *Kores HaBris*).

וַיָּלֶט פָּנָיו בְּאַדַּרְתּוֹ וַיֵּצֵא — *He who covered his face with his cloak and enwrapped himself.* When Elijah fled from the death threat of Ahab and Jezebel, he hid in a cave where God came to him. As Elijah heard the קוֹל דְּמָמָה דַקָּה, *small, still voice* of God, indicating that His glory was passing over him, he covered his face with his cloak (*I Kings* 19:12-13).

The cloak was unique and distinctive for it was worn only by prophets (*Metzudos* ibid.; see also *II Kings* 2:8).

הַחַיִּים וְהַשָּׁלוֹם — *For life and peace.* A quote from *Malachi* 2:5, where mention is made of the blessings for peace and long life that were conferred upon Pinchas (see above, commentary to כֹּהֵן צֶדֶק) for retaliating against the sinners of his generation (see *Numbers* 25:12).

שָׁלוֹם — *Peace.* The liturgist concludes these prayers with the word *peace.* The final mishnah in the Talmud (*Uktzin* 3;12) concludes: לֹא מָצָא הקב״ה כְּלִי מַחֲזִיק בְּרָכָה לְיִשְׂרָאֵל אֶלָּא הַשָּׁלוֹם, שֶׁנֶּאֱמַר ה׳ עֹז לְעַמּוֹ יִתֵּן ה׳ יְבָרֵךְ אֶת עַמּוֹ בַשָּׁלוֹם, *The Holy One, Blessed is He, found no vessel which could contain blessing for Israel except peace, as it said, 'HASHEM will give might to His people, HASHEM will bless his people with peace' (Psalms* 29:11). Thus, it is with this hope that we conclude some of our most basic and most important prayers: *Shemoneh Esrei, Bircas Kohanim* (the Priestly Blessing), and *Bircas HaMazon* (Grace After Meals) with a plea for peace.

May this blessing be fulfilled, speedily and in our days.

הָרַחֲמָן הוּא יְזַכֵּנוּ לִימוֹת הַמָּשִׁיחַ וּלְחַיֵּי הָעוֹלָם הַבָּא(נַצְלִיחַ).

מַגְדִּל‎ —On weekdays   מִגְדּוֹל‎ —On the Sabbath, Festivals and Rosh Chodesh

יְשׁוּעוֹת מַלְכּוֹ (יַרְוְיחַ) וְעֹשֶׂה חֶסֶד לִמְשִׁיחוֹ (נָשִׂיחַ) לְדָוִד וּלְזַרְעוֹ (בִּרְכָה לְהָנִיחַ) עַד עוֹלָם. עֹשֶׂה שָׁלוֹם בִּמְרוֹמָיו, הוּא יַעֲשֶׂה שָׁלוֹם עָלֵינוּ וְעַל כָּל יִשְׂרָאֵל. וְאִמְרוּ, אָמֵן.

יְראוּ אֶת יהוה קְדֹשָׁיו, כִּי אֵין מַחְסוֹר לִירֵאָיו. כְּפִירִים רָשׁוּ וְרָעֵבוּ, וְדֹרְשֵׁי יהוה לֹא יַחְסְרוּ כָל טוֹב. הוֹדוּ לַיהוה כִּי טוֹב, כִּי לְעוֹלָם חַסְדּוֹ. פּוֹתֵחַ אֶת יָדֶךָ, וּמַשְׂבִּיעַ לְכָל חַי רָצוֹן. בָּרוּךְ הַגֶּבֶר אֲשֶׁר יִבְטַח בַּיהוה, וְהָיָה יהוה מִבְטַחוֹ. נַעַר הָיִיתִי גַם זָקַנְתִּי, וְלֹא רָאִיתִי צַדִּיק נֶעֱזָב, וְזַרְעוֹ מְבַקֶּשׁ לָחֶם. יהוה עֹז לְעַמּוֹ יִתֵּן, יהוה יְבָרֵךְ אֶת עַמּוֹ בַשָּׁלוֹם.

❊⦑ בְּרִית עוֹלָם ⦒❊

This liturgical poem is recited by the German community in the *Bircas Hamazon* prior to the word כַּכָּתוּב, *'as it is written'* in the paragraph beginning with וְעַל הַכֹּל, *'for all …'*

אֱלֹהִים צִוִּיתָ לִידִידְךָ בְּחִירֶךָ,

אֶת בְּרִיתִי תִשְׁמֹר חֹק בִּשְׁאֵרֶךָ,   בְּרִית עוֹלָם.

אַתָּה תִכְרֹת לְיוֹצְרֶךָ,   וְלִקְדוֹשׁ יִשְׂרָאֵל כִּי פֵאֲרֶךָ.¹

פַּאֲרֶךָ לוֹ בְּאֵלֹנֵי מַמְרֵא בְּהֵרָאֲךָ,

פְּקוֹדְךָ בְּיוֹם כִּפּוּר בַּעֲשׂתוֹ בְּמוֹרָאֲךָ,   בְּרִית עוֹלָם.

פְּצָתָ מִמַּחַץ מַכּוֹתֶיךָ אֶרְפָּאֲךָ,   כִּי אֲנִי יהוה רֹפְאֶךָ.²

❧ בְּרִית עוֹלָם / Eternal Covenant

In German-Jewish communities it is customary to recite the *piyut* [liturgical poem] בְּרִית עוֹלָם, *Bris Olam* [lit. *Eternal Covenant*], as part of the *Bircas HaMazon*. Upon reaching the words תָּמִיד לְעוֹלָם וָעֶד, *continuously for all eternity*, in the paragraph that begins וְעַל הַכֹּל, *for all*, the one leading *Bircas HaMazon* recites the *piyut*. The assembled guests either recite the entire *piyut* along with the leader, or, at least, recite the first word of each stanza, and the phrase בְּרִית עוֹלָם, *Eternal covenant*, each time it appears.

Bris Olam is recited at this particular point — in בִּרְכַּת הָאָרֶץ, *the blessing for the Land* — for the Talmud (*Berachos* 48b) notes that it is obligatory to mention the *mitzvah* of *milah* in this blessing. This is appropriate because God promised Abraham that He would give him the Land of Israel in the merit of his performance of *milah* (*Rashi* ibid.; see also *Genesis* 17:8).

Sefer Bris Avraham notes that one of God's priorities when the Jews entered Israel was His command to Joshua to have the Jews circumcised (*Joshua* 5:2). Furthermore, the Jews were not exiled from their homeland until they became negligent in their practice of *milah* (*Isaiah* 24:5-6).

הָרַחֲמָן *The compassionate One! May He make us worthy of the days of Messiah and the life of the World to Come.*

On weekdays:	On the Sabbath, Festivals and Rosh Chodesh:
He Who makes great	*He Who is a tower*
the salvations of His king	*of salvations to His king*

and does kindness for His anointed, to David and to his descendants forever. He Who makes peace in His heights, may He make peace upon us and upon all Israel. Now respond: Amen!

יְראוּ *Fear HASHEM, you — His holy ones — for there is no deprivation for His reverent ones. Young lions may want and hunger, but those who seek HASHEM will not lack any good. Give thanks to God for He is good; His kindness endures forever. You open Your hand and satisfy the desire of every living thing. Blessed is the man who trusts in HASHEM, then HASHEM will be his security. I was a youth and also have aged, and I have not seen a righteous man forsaken, with his children begging for bread. HASHEM will give might to His people; HASHEM will bless His people with peace.*

⊰❈{ BRIS OLAM / ETERNAL COVENANT }❈⊱

This liturgical poem is recited by the German community in the *Bircas Hamazon prior to the words* כַּכָּתוּב, *'as it is written' in the paragraph beginning with* וְעַל הַכֹּל, *'for all ...'*

אֱלֹהִים *O God! You commanded Your beloved, Your chosen,*
    'Observe My covenant, the decree shall be on your flesh.'

Eternal Covenant.

'Circumcise for the sake of your Creator,
Who is Israel's sanctified One, your crowning glory.'[1]

Your crowning glory you revealed to him [Abraham] in the Plains of Mamrei,
Your glory You revealed perform [his bris] in awe on Yom Kippur.

Eternal Covenant.

You said, 'I will heal you from your wounds, For I am HASHEM your Healer.'[2]

---

(1) *Isaiah* 55:5; 60:9. (2) *Exodus* 15:26.

The *piyut* — written by *Rabbi Ephraim ben Yaakov* (1133-1198), chief judge of the rabbinical court of Bonn, Germany — contains thirteen stanzas, alluding to the thirteen times that the word בְּרִית appears in the circumcision commandment to Abraham (see *Genesis* ch. 17). Each stanza contains four rhyming stiches, the first three beginning with the same letter. The thirteen letters of the respective stanzas form the acronym אֶפְרַיִם מֵעִיר בּוֹנָא, *Ephraim from the city Bonn*. The fourth stich is a Scriptural verse. Additionally, the last word of each stanza is the first word of the next.

The allusions to circumcision and the laws described in this *piyut* are all discussed elsewhere in this volume. We have followed the version that appears in *Seder Avodas Yisrael*, other *siddurim* have some minor variations in wording or vowelization.

לִידִידְךָ בְּחִירְךָ — *Your beloved, Your chosen.* Abraham is referred of as יְדִידִי, *My beloved* (*Jeremiah* 11:15; see *Menachos* 53b); and אֲשֶׁר בָּחַרְתָּ, *You have chosen* (*Nechemiah* 9:7).

בְּאֵלֹנֵי מַמְרֵא — *In the plains of Mamrei.*

רְפָאֵךְ בְּחַסְדֵּךְ מֵאֲבָרֵיךְ מוֹדִיעִים הַדָּמִים,

רֶשֶׁם הִתְהַלֵּךְ לְפָנַי וֶהְיֵה תָמִים,³ בְּרִית עוֹלָם.

רָאִיתִי נִקּוּפֵךְ כְּדַם עוֹלָה וּשְׁלָמִים, לְמַעַן יִיטַב לָךְ וְהַאֲרַכְתָּ יָמִים.⁴

יָמִים מִבְּרִית בְּהִתְעַצֵּל אַב הַחֲכָמִים,

יְעוּדָתוֹ אָז אָמְרָה חֲתַן דָּמִים,⁵ בְּרִית עוֹלָם.

יָהּ זֵכֶר לִסְגֻלָּה מֵעַמִּים, הַפְלֵה חֲסָדֶיךָ מוֹשִׁיעַ מִמִּתְקוֹמְמִים.⁶

מִמִּתְקוֹמְמִים אֱסֹף נִדָּחֶיךָ וְאֶצְבּוֹר,

מֵעֵת אַרְאֵךְ מִתְבּוֹסֶסֶת בְּדָמַיִךְ כָּאֵבָר,⁷ בְּרִית עוֹלָם.

מֹטוֹת עֻלֵּךְ אֶשְׁבֹּר,⁸ וַאֲנִי בְדַם בְּרִיתֵךְ שִׁלַּחְתִּי אֲסִירַיִךְ מִבּוֹר.⁹

מִבּוֹר אַב הֲמוֹן בְּצֵאתוֹ,

מִכְּבוֹדֵךְ נֶעֱזַר וְכָרוֹת עִמּוֹ בְּרִיתוֹ, בְּרִית עוֹלָם.

מְנוּחָה דוֹחָה, וּקְצִיצַת בַּהֲרַתּוֹ, בַּיּוֹם הַשְּׁמִינִי יִמּוֹל בְּשַׂר עָרְלָתוֹ.¹⁰

עָרְלָתוֹ וַדַּאי, וְלֹא סָפֵק הַיּוֹם אוֹ אֶתְמוֹל,

עָלֶיהָ דּוֹחִין שַׁבָּת, וְלֹא עַל מַכְשִׁירֵי סַכִּינָא לְהַמּוֹל, בְּרִית עוֹלָם.

עֲשֵׂה מִילָה וּפְרִיעָה וּמְצִיצָה שׁוֹב מֹל,¹¹ וְאִשָּׁה מָלָה וְלֹא גוֹי, הַמָּל יִמּוֹל.

---

(3) *Genesis* 17:1. (4) *Deuteronomy* 22:7. (5) *Exodus* 4:25. (6) *Psalms* 17:7. (7) *Ezekiel* 16:6. (8) *Leviticus* 26:13. (9) *Zechariah* 9:11. (10) *Leviticus* 12:3. (11) *Joshua* 5:2.

It was Mamrei who gave Abraham encouraging advice about performing his *bris* publicly so that others would be inspired to do likewise. Thus Mamrei merited that God visited Abraham in his land (see *Daas Zekeinim, Bereishis* 18:1).

בְּיוֹם כִּפּוּר — *On Yom Kippur*. This coincides with the view of *Pirkei d'R' Eliezer* (chap. 29) that Abraham circumcised himself on Yom Kippur (see also *R' Bachya, Bereishis* 17:13). This is deduced from the similar expression, בְּעֶצֶם הַיּוֹם הַזֶּה, *on that very day*, that appears both with regard to Abraham's performance of *bris milah* (*Genesis* 17:26) and with regard to Yom Kippur (*Leviticus* 23:28).

There are divergent views, however, that Abraham circumcised himself on Pesach (see *Tosafos, Rosh Hoshanah* 11a, s.v. אלא).

בְּחַסְרֵךְ מֵאֲבָרֵיךְ — *When you are missing from your limbs*. Normally when a part of the body is missing it indicates an imperfection, yet the removal of the foreskin from the body for the purpose of *milah* signifies perfection, for the Torah calls this status perfect — *Go before Me and become perfect* (*Genesis* 17:1).

מוֹדִיעִים הַדָּמִים — *Is evidenced by your bloods*. Here the *paytan* plays on a legal phrase. The Talmud (*Bava Basra* 77b) states: הַדָּמִים מוֹדִיעִים, *the amount of money in a transaction* [usually] *indicates* [the value of the items involved]. Since the word דָּמִים can mean both *money* and *blood*, the *paytan* uses the expression to refer to *milah* (*R' David Cohen*).

מִבּוֹר — *From the pit*. Abraham was held in captivity for ten years by Nimrod [or, according to some, by Terach, Abraham's father] because Abraham destroyed Nimrod's idols (*Bava Basra* 91a).

Your healing, when you are missing from your limbs, is evidenced by your bloods,
For it is inscribed [in the Torah], 'Go before Me and be perfect.'³   Eternal Covenant.
I considered your wound like the blood of burnt and peace offerings,
'To do good for you, and to grant you long days.'⁴

For the father of the wise [Moses] deferred the bris [of his son],
Then his wife said to him, 'You are the bridegroom of bloods.'⁵   Eternal Covenant.
O God, recall the most precious among the nations,
Make wondrous Your kindness, He who saves [them] from enemies.⁶

'From [your] enemies, I will gather your displaced ones,
[As I did] from the time I saw you trampling in your blood as I passed you.⁷
                                                                    Eternal Covenant.
The rods of your yoke will I break,⁸ [And in the merit] of
        the blood of your covenant, will I deliver your bound ones from the pit.'⁹

From the pit the father of nations [Abraham] went free,
Your honor assisted him, and established with him his covenant. Eternal Covenant.
Tranquility [of the Sabbath] and [the prohibition against] excising his white spot,
        are set aside.
[For it is written] 'On the eighth day you shall circumcise the flesh of his foreskin.'¹⁰

His foreskin that is a certainty [today], not doubtful whether today or yesterday,
For this the Sabbath is set aside, but not for honing the knife to circumcise.
                                                                    Eternal Covenant.
Perform circumcision; revealing and drawing
        [fulfill the command] 'Circumcise again.'¹¹
A woman may circumcise but a gentile may not,
        for only the circumcised may circumcise [others].

וְכָרוֹת עִמּוֹ בְּרִיתוֹ — And established with him his covenant. Based on Nechemiah 9:8. Abraham feared doing the bris by himself so God assisted him and did it עִמּוֹ, with him (Bereishis Rabbah, 49:2).

מְנוּחָה דוֹחָה — Tranquillity [of the Sabbath] is set aside. Non-emergency surgery is forbidden on the Sabbath. Nevertheless, bris, a surgical procedure, may be performed on the Sabbath.

בַּהֶרֶת — His white spot. It is forbidden by Torah law to remove a white spot that appears on one's body if it is judged by a Kohen to be the affliction called tzaraas (Leviticus chap. 13). If, however, this tzaraas is on the foreskin, it may be removed in the act of milah.

מַכְשִׁירֵי סַכִּינָא — Honing the knife. Any preparations that can be done before the Sabbath may not be done on the Sabbath (Shabbos 130a). Thus, although for the milah itself — which could not have been done before the Sabbath — the Sabbath laws are set aside, these laws are not set aside for the production or sharpening of the knife, for these could have been done on Friday.

שוב מל — Circumcise again. God said to Joshua, 'Return and circumcise the children of Israel a second time' (Joshua 5:2), implying the necessity of the second act of the bris, פְּרִיעָה, revealing. Abraham was commanded on the first part of the bris, חִיתוּךְ, excision.

וְאִשָּׁה מָלָה וְלֹא גוֹי, הַמָּל יִמוֹל — A woman

יָמוֹל בַּיּוֹם וְלֹא בַלַּיְלָה אֲפִילוּ סָפֵק יֶשְׁנָה,

יְחֻבַּב מִצְוָה אַף כִּי בְּעֵירֹם הִנֵּה הֵנָּה,   בְּרִית עוֹלָם.

יָשֵׁן וְעֵר לָבוּשׁ וְעֵרֹם עֵת נִזְכְּרֶנָּה,   יִמָּלֵא שְׂחוֹק פִּינוּ וּלְשׁוֹנֵנוּ רִנָּה.[12]

רִנָּה כְּנִפְצַח בִּלְמְנַצֵּחַ עַל הַשְּׁמִינִית[13] תְּהִלָּתֶךָ,

רָחַשׁ לִבִּי דָבָר טוֹב, שָׂשׂ אָנֹכִי עַל אִמְרָתֶךָ,[14]   בְּרִית עוֹלָם.

רַחֲמִים תְּעוֹרֵר לַעֲדָתֶךָ,   לַיהוה הַיְשׁוּעָה עַל עַמְּךָ בִרְכָתֶךָ.[15]

בִּרְכָתְךָ תִּתֵּן לַחֲבִיבִים בָּנִים,

בְּתִתְּךָ לִי גֻּלֹּת מַיִם יְשׁוּעָה מִמַּעְיָנִים,   בְּרִית עוֹלָם.

בְּשִׂמְחָה שְׁלֵמָה יִשְׂמְחוּ יוֹנֶיךָ בַּחְתּוּנִים,   דְּשֵׁנִים וְרַעֲנַנִּים.[16]

וְרַעֲנַנִּים כִּשְׁתִלֵי זֵיתִים וּלְאַרְצָם יָקְווּ,

וְאוֹיְבֶיךָ חָרֹב יֶחֱרָבוּ,[17]   בְּרִית עוֹלָם.

וְעַד לְבָנֶיךָ וְיָעִידוּ בָאיִם וִיחַוּוּ,

כָּל הַגּוֹיִם כְּאַיִן נֶגְדּוֹ מֵאֶפֶס וָתֹהוּ נֶחְשָׁבוּ.[18]

נֶחְשָׁבוּ כַּבְּהֵמָה נִטְמוּ בְּעֵינֵיכֶם,[19]

נְתוּנִים תַּחַת כַּפּוֹת רַגְלֵיכֶם,[20]   בְּרִית עוֹלָם.

נְטוּלֵי פֶקֶס עֲבוּר אַתֶּם וּבְנֵיכֶם,

וְלָקַחְתִּי אֶתְכֶם מִן הַגּוֹיִם, וְקִבַּצְתִּי אֶתְכֶם.[21]

---

may circumcise but a gentile may not, for only the circumcised may circumcise [others]. In discussing the Scriptural source for the invalidness of circumcision performed by a gentile, the Talmud (*Avodah Zarah* 27a with *Rashi*) states two views: Rav derives this rule from the verse, וְאַתָּה אֶת בְּרִיתִי תִשְׁמֹר, אַתָּה וְזַרְעֲךָ אַחֲרֶיךָ, *And you shall keep My covenant, you and your descendants after you* (Genesis 17:9); while R' Yochanan bases this law on the verse, הִמּוֹל יִמּוֹל, literally, *circumcise shall you circumcise* (ibid. v. 13), which may be interpreted הַמָּל יִמּוֹל, *the circumcised shall circumcise*. The Talmud then differentiates between these two sources. According to the first verse, women are also excluded from performing circumcision, for the covenant was only given to men [זֹאת בְּרִיתִי ... הִמּוֹל לָכֶם כָּל זָכָר, *This is My covenant ... circumcise every male among you* (ibid. v. 19)]. However, according to the

second opinion the verse only prohibits those lacking circumcision, but a woman is considered as if she were circumcised.

The early halachic authorities did not agree on this matter, e.g., *Tosafos* (*Avodah Zarah* 27a, s.v. אשה לאו) maintains that the first view prevails and a woman may not circumcise; yet the same *Tosafos* cites *Halachos Gedolos* that a woman may. R' Ephraim of Bonn, author of the present *piyut*, subscribed to the latter view. However, in actual practice today, the *halachah* follows the decision of *Rama* (Y.D. 264:1) which states: Some hold that a woman may not circumcise, and this is our custom, to seek out a man.

בְּעֵירֹם — *Even in nakedness.* See pages 120-121 regarding King David who, when in the bathhouse — where the *tallis* and *tefillin* are not worn, and where a *mezuzah* is not placed on the

Circumcise by day and not by night, or even twilight.
Show love for the mitzvah, for even in nakedness, it is there.   *Eternal Covenant.*
Asleep or awake, clothed or unclothed, when we remember it,
Our mouths are filled with laughter, our tongues with song.[12]

With song we burst forth Your praise,
  'To the one who grants victory — regarding the eighth.'[13]
My heart whispers a wonderful thing, "I rejoice in Your word.'[14] *Eternal Covenant.*
May your compassion be aroused for Your flock,
[As it is written] 'Salvation is Hashem's, upon Your people is Your blessing,'[15]

Your blessing bestow on Your beloved children,
As You give me springs of water from the wells of salvation.   *Eternal Covenant.*
In total joy may Your doves rejoice in marriage, fresh and vigorous.[16]

Vigorous as olive saplings, may they be gathered unto their homeland,
With your enemies being annihilated.[17]   *Eternal Covenant.*
Prepare for your children the time when testimony will be borne in the Isles
     and they will say,
'The nations are naught compared to Him,
     like emptiness and void they are considered.[18]

They are considered as animals, restricted in Your eyes.[19]
They are placed under the tread of Your feet.[20]   *Eternal Covenant.*
'Because of you and your sons whose foreskin has been taken,
I will take you from the nations and I will gather you.[21]

---

(12) *Psalms* 126:2. (13) 12:1. (14) 119:162. (15) 3:9. (16) 92:15. (17) *Isaiah* 60:12.
(18) 40:17. (19) *Job* 18:30 (20) *Malachi* 3:21. (21) *Ezekiel* 36:24.

door — complained that he was naked of *mitzvos.* Upon realizing that the *mitzvah* of *milah* was always with him, however, David rejoiced.

גְּלֹות מַיִם — *Springs of water* This expression appears in *Joshua* 15:19. The word גְּלֹות is cognate with גַּלְגַּל, *a wheel.* These streams are so called because they roll across the fields *(Bris Avraham)* or because the springs are usually round *(Metzudos).*

Springs of water is a euphemism for the secrets of Torah, and are revealed only to great Torah scholars (see *Temurah* 16a). Additionally, Torah is compared to water because it is the lifeline of the Jewish people. Moreover, just as water cannot remain atop the high mountains but descends and rolls downward, so too, the Torah cannot

have a sustained existence with those who are haughty *(Taanis* 7a).

יֹונָיִךְ — *Your doves.* The comparison of the Jewish nation to doves is found often in *Song of Songs (e.g.,* 1:15, 2:14). It is the nature of doves to constantly glance back towards their nest, just as the Jew always glances back to God, his source of rejuvenation. The Midrash *(Shir HaShirim Rabbah* 1:15:2) notes that just as from the time a dove recognizes her mate she never changes him for another, so Israel never exchanges the Holy One, Blessed is He, for another, once they have learned to know Him. Additionally, just as a dove is outstanding in appearance, so too are the Jews because of *milah* (see also *Berachos* 53b and *Shabbos* 130a).

נְטוּלֵי פֶקֶס — *Whose* [lit. *blossom*] *foreskin has been taken.* פֶקֶס is the

אֶתְכֶם לְבַבְכֶם אָמוֹל מֵעָרְלַתְכֶם,

בְּרִית עוֹלָם.

וְאֶת רוּחִי אֶתֵּן בְּקִרְבְּכֶם,22

אָכוֹל וְשָׂבוֹעַ וְהַלַּלְתֶּם23 עַל אַרְצְכֶם, אֲשֶׁר נָתַן יהוה לָכֶם.

Bircas HaMazon continues with כַּכָּתוּב, *As it is written* (p. 144), until יְשׁוּעוֹת וְנֶחָמוֹת,
Salvation and consolation (p. 148). The one leading *Bircas Hamazon* then recites aloud:

הָרַחֲמָן הוּא אֲשֶׁר חָנַן אֶת הַיֶּלֶד הַזֶּה לְאָבִיו וּלְאִמּוֹ,

הוּא יָגֵן עָלָיו מִמְּרוֹמוֹ,

וּבְשָׁלוֹם יָבֹא עַל מְקוֹמוֹ, וִיהִי אֱלֹהָיו עִמּוֹ,

וּכְאֶפְרַיִם וְכִמְנַשֶּׁה לְשׁוּמוֹ, וְיִקָּרֵא בְיִשְׂרָאֵל שְׁמוֹ.

הָרַחֲמָן הוּא פָקֹד יִפְקְדֵהוּ בְּרַחֲמִים, לַהֲבִינוּ בְּדַת חֲכָמִים,

וִיבַלֶּה בְּטוֹב יָמִים, וּשְׁנוֹתָיו בַּנְּעִימִים,

יַעַבְדּוּהוּ עַמִּים, וְיִשְׁתַּחֲווּ לוֹ לְאֻמִּים.

הָרַחֲמָן הוּא רַבּוֹת שָׁנִים יְחַיֵּהוּ, צֶדֶק לְרַגְלָיו יְקָרָאֵהוּ,

וְנֶחָמַת צִיּוֹן יַרְאֵהוּ, וְאֶת עַמּוֹ לְשָׁלוֹם יְבָרְכֵהוּ,

וִיעוֹרֵר חֲסָדָיו לְרַחֲמֵהוּ, כִּי חָפֵץ חֶסֶד הוּא.

הָרַחֲמָן הוּא יְבָרֵךְ אֶת הֶחָתָן הַזֶּה וּבַעַל בְּרִיתוֹ,

יְשַׂמַּח אָבִיו וְתָגֵל יוֹלַדְתּוֹ,

וְיִתְבָּרְכוּ הַמְּסֻבִּין בִּסְעוּדָתוֹ, וְכֵן יִזְכּוּ שֶׁיִּשְׂמְחוּ בַּחֲתֻנָּתוֹ,

בְּנֵי בָנִים לְהַרְאוֹתוֹ, וְיֵשׁ תִּקְוָה לְאַחֲרִיתוֹ.

הָרַחֲמָן הוּא מְהֵרָה יִזְכּוֹר זֹאת מִצְוָתוֹ, בָּהּ יִפְדֶּה אֲיֻמָּתוֹ,

רַחֲמִים יְעוֹרֵר לַעֲדָתוֹ, קְהָלָיו יְקַבֵּץ בְּחֶמְלָתוֹ,

בְּהַרְאוֹתוֹ אֶת עֹשֶׁר כְּבוֹד מַלְכוּתוֹ, וְאֶת יְקַר תִּפְאֶרֶת גְּדֻלָּתוֹ.

הָרַחֲמָן הוּא יְבָרֵךְ אֶת הֶחָתָן הַזֶּה וּבַעַל בְּרִיתוֹ, וְאֶת אָבִיו וְאֶת אִמּוֹ, וְאֶת
רַבּוֹתֵינוּ וְאֶת אָחֵינוּ הַיּוֹשְׁבִים פֹּה, כְּמוֹ שֶׁנִּתְבָּרְכוּ אֲבוֹתֵינוּ אַבְרָהָם
יִצְחָק וְיַעֲקֹב בַּכֹּל מִכֹּל כֹּל, כֵּן יְבָרֵךְ אוֹתָנוּ כֻּלָּנוּ יַחַד בִּבְרָכָה שְׁלֵמָה, וְנֹאמַר
אָמֵן.

Bircas HaMazon continues with בַּמָּרוֹם, *On High* (p. 148).

uppermost part of such vegetables as cucumbers or gourds. The blossom comes off when the fruit becomes ripe and this expression is used as a euphemism for removing the foreskin (see *Bava Metzia* 88b)

לְבַבְכֶם אָמוֹל מֵעָרְלַתְכֶם — *I will remove the Evil Inclination from* [lit. *I will circumcise*] *your hearts.* Ramban (Deuteronomy 30:6) explains this circumcision as follows: In Messianic times the 'foreskin of the heart' which drives man to follow his physical

cravings will be excised and man's nature will become wholly good. Then the gift of freedom of choice between good and evil, which God granted man in order that he might earn his just reward, will be removed. The new spirit in man will insure that he will want nothing more than to walk in the ways of God. Man will be absorbed with love for God (*R' S.R. Hirsch*).

אָכוֹל וְשָׂבוֹעַ — *Eat, be satiated.* This verse parallels the theme of the next passage

I will remove the Evil Inclination from your hearts,
I will imbue you with My spirit.'[22]   Eternal Covenant.
Eat, be satiated and sing praise[23] about your Land, That HASHEM has given you.

Bircas HaMazon continues with כַּכָּתוּב, As it is written (p. 144), until יְשׁוּעוֹת וְנֶחָמוֹת,
Salvation and consolation (p. 148). The one leading Bircas Hamazon then recites aloud:

הָרַחֲמָן The Compassionate One who has granted this child
        to his father and mother
    May He protect him, from His heavenly abode.
In peace may [this child] reach his [desired] destination,
    May His God be with him.
May he make him like Ephraim and Menashe,
    And may his name be great in Israel.

The compasssionate One, may he always remember him in [His] mercy,
    Give him understanding in the law of wisdom [the Torah],
May he spend his days in goodness, And his years in pleasantness
May nations serve him, And countries be subservient to him.

The compassionate One, may He cause him to live many years,
    Righteousness should stand by him,
May he see the consolation of Zion, May his nation bless him in peace,
May his kindness awaken His compassion, For He seeks kindness.

The compassionate One, may He bless this groom [the child]
    and the master of the bris [the sandak],
    May his father be happy and the one that bore him [his mother] rejoice,
May the assembled guests at his [festive] meal be blessed,
    May they merit to rejoice at his wedding;
May he see his grandchildren, May there be promise to his destiny.

The compassionate One, may He speedily remember this [milah] His mitzvah.
    In its merit may He redeem His awe-filled [nation],
May he arouse compassion for His flock,
    May he gather his congregation in his mercy
As he shows them the wealth of His glorious kingdom,
    And the honor of his splendrous greatness,

הָרַחֲמָן The compassionate One, may He bless this groom [the child] and the
        master of the bris [the sandak], and his father and his mother, and our
teachers and our brethren sitting here, just as our forefathers Abraham, Isaac, and
Jacob were Blessed in everything, from everything, with everything. So may He
bless us all together with a perfect blessing. And let us say: Amen!

Bircas HaMazon continues with בַּמָּרוֹם, On High (p. 148).

---

(22) 36:27. (23) Joel 2:26.

in Bircas HaMazon: כַּכָּתוּב וְאָכַלְתָּ וְשָׂבָעְתָ,   הָרַחֲמָן — The compassionate One. The
As it is written, 'And you shall eat, and   acrostic of these six stanzas spells
you shall be satiated ... '   Ephraim bar Yaakov (see p. 161).

רוח אליהו
Ruach Eliyahu

•Sephardic Customs and Ritual

❖{ CUSTOMS AMONG SEPHARDIC JEWRY }❖

The laws of *milah* are the same for all Jews, (see p. 92). Customs however, vary between countries and communities; a sampling of Sephardic customs is presented below. These customs have been culled from various sources and personal experiences of the author. A very helpful source was Rabbi H. C. Dobrinsky's *Selected Laws and Customs of Sephardic Jewry*.

❧ Prior To the Brit

❧ In most communities, on the night before the *brit*, the men of the family and their friends gather to recite portions of *Zohar* related to *milah*. The gathering itself is called *Zohar* or *Brit Yitzchak* [Covenant of Isaac]. Cakes and various sweets are served and the *Chacham* [Rabbi] delivers a Torah lecture. Some celebrate this evening instead of the *Shalom Zachar* that Ashkenazic Jews celebrate on the Friday night following the birth (see pp. 73, 94). Moroccan Jews celebrate both the *Shalom Zachar* and *Zohar*.

• Many hang Kabbalistic charts on the walls and door of the child's room as a protection against מַזִיקִין, *evil spirits* [Satan and his cohort]. These signs bear many protective Biblical quotations. Some also place the *milah* knife under the pillow of the child as an added protection. [Both of these custom are also practiced in some Ashkenazic circles.]

❧ Day of Brit

❧ At Syrian circumcisions a large tiered tray is filled with flowers and candles. Guests place contributions on the tray and, following the *brit*, the tray is sold to the highest bidder. The money bid, along with that on the tray is then donated to charity. Some use this "money of blessing" to begin a new financial endeavor (e.g., to start a business, to buy a home), as an omen for success.

• At Persian circumcisions, a large tray of apples is placed on a table and young couples are encouraged to partake. Assumedly this custom is based on the Midrash that when Pharaoh ordered the midwives to kill all newborn Jewish males, the Jewish women hid in the apple orchards. There, Heavenly emissaries assisted them with the birth and subsequent care of the baby. This is alluded to in the verse, תַּחַת הַתַּפּוּחַ עוֹרַרְתִּיךָ, *Under the apple tree I begot you* (*Song of Songs* 8:5; *Rashi* to *Sotah* 11b). Thus, apples are propitious for easy labor and delivery.

• In many communities the father bestows upon his son the blessings: יְשִׂמְךָ אֱלֹהִים כְּאֶפְרַיִם וְכִמְנַשֶּׁה, *May God make you like Ephraim and Menashe* (*Genesis* 48:20). Some add: יְהִי רָצוֹן שֶׁתְּהֵא אָח לְשִׁבְעָה וְגַם לִשְׁמוֹנָה, *May it be His will that you be a brother to seven and also to eight.* This latter blessing is a play on *Ecclesiastes* 11:2, and is an allusion to the princes of Menashe and Ephraim who were the seventh and eighth tribal leaders to bring their offerings at the inauguration of the *Mishkan* [Tabernacle] in the Wilderness (see *Numbers* 7:48, 54). This custom is based upon *Targum Yonasan* to *Genesis* 48:20 who pharaphrases: This blessing will be conferred by a father on the day of his son's circumcision (*R' Yaakov HaGozer*).

• Moroccan Jews place a dish of sand near the *mohel* to signify that the child

should be as fruitful as the grains of sand, as it is written: *And the count of the Children of Israel will be like the sands of the sea, which cannot be measured nor counted (Hosea 2:1).* This sand is also used to cover the excised foreskin.

◄§ Throne of Elijah

◄§ At Syrian circumcisions a special ornate curtain bearing the name of Elijah the Prophet is draped over the chair designated as the Throne of Elijah.

• In Moroccan families, on the night prior to the *brit,* the Throne of Elijah is brought from the synagogue to the home of the infant where it is decorated with many colorful fabrics. During the *brit,* the *sandak* sits on the Throne of Elijah as he holds the infant.

• In Sefrou, Morocco, the Throne of Elijah was placed near a *mezuzah* in the home of the child. This was considered auspicious for long life for the child, as alluded to by the juxtaposition of עַל מְזוּזוֹת בֵּיתֶךָ, *On the doorposts of your house,* with לְמַעַן יִרְבּוּ יְמֵיכֶם, *In order to prolong your days (Deuteronomy* 11:20-21). Unlike other parts of Morocco, in Sefrou the *sandak* did not sit on the Throne of Elijah but on a separate chair next to it.

• Spanish Jews drape the chair set aside for Elijah with purple and gold braided material to give it the appearance of a throne. It is placed next to the *sandak* and a *Chumash* or *Siddur* is placed on it as a reminder that it represents Elijah's presence and is not to be used by anyone else.

◄§ At the Brit

◄§ In many communities an infant is brought to the synagogue where his *brit* is to take place, accompanied by musical instruments. The women ululate in high staccato sounds that sound like "lelelelelelele," a chant of joy in many Middle Eastern countries. (*Zichron Brit LaRishonim,* p. 178).

• It is customary to bring the baby in on a large pillow draped with colorful scarves and shawls of exquisite lace and embroidery.

• Among some Sephardim the family name is included in the naming of the child (e.g., if the family name is Haddad, the child is given the name Moshe ben Gavriel Haddad).

• It is customary to smell fragrant spices following the blessing over the wine. At Moroccan circumcisions dried rose petals are traditionally used for this purpose.
  Some explain the custom for smelling spices as an allusion to the verse in *Genesis* 2:7, regarding the creation of Adam: *And God blew into his nostrils the soul of life and man became a living soul.* Zohar (Shelach) writes that a Jewish male attains his יְסוֹד הַנְּשָׁמָה [lit. basis of the soul] at his *brit.* Therefore the sense of smell, which is reminiscent of the original infusion of the soul into man, is used (see *Ohel David III,* Psalms 44:23).
  Others see the use of fragrances as an allusion to the Midrash (see p. 67) which relates that when Abraham circumcised the members of his household, he piled their foreskins into a heap. The odor of the foreskins rose to heaven and was as appreciated by God as the fragrance of the incense burned on the Altar at the Temple (see *Midrash Shir HaShirim* 4:6 and *Yalkut Shimoni, Lech Lecha* §82).

א{ פזמונים }א

In Sephardic communities, the *brit* ceremony is opened with the recitation of various *pizmonim* [liturgical poems]. Not all communities recite all of the *pizmonim* presented here.

יְהִי שָׁלוֹם בְּחֵילֵנוּ, וְשַׁלְוָה בְּיִשְׂרָאֵל.
בְּסִימָן טוֹב בֵּן בָּא לָנוּ, בְּיָמָיו יָבֹא גוֹאֵל.

הַיֶּלֶד יְהִי רַעֲנָן,   בְּצֵל שַׁדַּי יִתְלוֹנָן,
וּבַתּוֹרָה יִתְבּוֹנָן,   יְאַלֵּף דָּת לְכָל שׁוֹאֵל.
יְהִי שָׁלוֹם בְּחֵילֵנוּ, וְשַׁלְוָה בְּיִשְׂרָאֵל. בְּסִימָן טוֹב בֵּן בָּא לָנוּ, בְּיָמָיו יָבֹא גוֹאֵל.

וּמְקוֹרוֹ יְהִי בָּרוּךְ,   זְמַן חַיָּיו יְהִי אָרוּךְ,
וְשֻׁלְחָנוֹ יְהִי עָרוּךְ,   וְזִבְחוֹ לֹא יִתְגָּאֵל.
יְהִי שָׁלוֹם בְּחֵילֵנוּ, וְשַׁלְוָה בְּיִשְׂרָאֵל. בְּסִימָן טוֹב בֵּן בָּא לָנוּ, בְּיָמָיו יָבֹא גוֹאֵל.

שְׁמוֹ יֵצֵא בְּכָל עֵבֶר,   אֲשֶׁר יִגְדַּל יְהִי גֶּבֶר,
וְלִירֵאָי אֵל יְהִי חָבֵר,   יְהִי בְדוֹרוֹ כִּשְׁמוּאֵל.
יְהִי שָׁלוֹם בְּחֵילֵנוּ, וְשַׁלְוָה בְּיִשְׂרָאֵל. בְּסִימָן טוֹב בֵּן בָּא לָנוּ, בְּיָמָיו יָבֹא גוֹאֵל.

עֲדֵי זִקְנָה וְגַם שֵׂיבָה,   יְהִי דָשֵׁן בְּכָל טוֹבָה,
וְשָׁלוֹם לוֹ וְרֹב אַהֲבָה,   אָמֵן כֵּן יֹאמַר לוֹ הָאֵל.
יְהִי שָׁלוֹם בְּחֵילֵנוּ, וְשַׁלְוָה בְּיִשְׂרָאֵל. בְּסִימָן טוֹב בֵּן בָּא לָנוּ, בְּיָמָיו יָבֹא גוֹאֵל.

חַי זַכַּאי קָדוֹשׁ שְׁמָךְ,   בְּיַד יְמִינָךְ יְהִי מִסְמָךְ,
לְבַקֵּר לַחֲזוֹת בְּנוֹעֲמָךְ,   בְּקֶרֶב עַמּוֹ יִשְׂרָאֵל.
יְהִי שָׁלוֹם בְּחֵילֵנוּ, וְשַׁלְוָה בְּיִשְׂרָאֵל. בְּסִימָן טוֹב בֵּן בָּא לָנוּ, בְּיָמָיו יָבֹא גוֹאֵל.

אֶעֱרוֹךְ מַהֲלָל ניבי,   לִפְנֵי אֱלֹהֵי אָבִי,

לִכְבוֹד חֶמְדַּת לְבָבִי, אֵלִיָּהוּ הַנָּבִיא.

נָטַע הָאֵל בִּישׁוּרוּן,   חֲבַצֶּלֶת הַשָּׁרוֹן,   אִישׁ מִגֶּזַע אַהֲרֹן,
מְשָׁרֵת צוּר מִשְׂגַּבִּי,   לִכְבוֹד חֶמְדַּת לְבָבִי, אֵלִיָּהוּ הַנָּבִיא.

כֹּהֵן לָאֵל עֶלְיוֹן הוּא,   פִּנְחָס זֶה אֵלִיָּהוּ,   הַנָּבִיא יְקָרָאוּהוּ,
הַגִּלְעָדִי הַתִּשְׁבִּי,   לִכְבוֹד חֶמְדַּת לְבָבִי, אֵלִיָּהוּ הַנָּבִיא.

יוֹם קַנֹּא קִנְאַת הָאֵל,   הָרַג בְּכֹחַ וָאֵל,   נְשִׂיא שֵׁבֶט יִשְׂרָאֵל,
וּבַת צוּר שְׁמָהּ כָּזְבִּי,   לִכְבוֹד חֶמְדַּת לְבָבִי, אֵלִיָּהוּ הַנָּבִיא.

דִּין שָׁמַע מִפִּי רַבּוֹ,   אִישׁ אֲרַמִּית מִשְׁכָּבוֹ,   קַנָּאִין פּוֹגְעִים בּוֹ,
וַיֹּאמֶר אָרִיק חַרְבִּי,   לִכְבוֹד חֶמְדַּת לְבָבִי, אֵלִיָּהוּ הַנָּבִיא.

---

§ אֶעֱרוֹךְ מַהֲלָל

The first fifteen stanzas of this prayer depict the life and history of Elijah the Prophet. Based on the Midrash that Elijah and פִּנְחָס, *Phineas*, (the grandson of Aaron) are one and the same person (see *Yalkut Shimoni, Pinchas* §771; *Rashi, Bava Metzia* 114b; *Pirkei d'R'Eliezer* §29), the *piyut* begins with the zealous act of Phineas who killed Zimri, prince of the Tribe of Simeon,

In Sephardic communities, the *brit* ceremony is opened with the recitation of various *pizmonim* [liturgical poems]. Not all communities recite all of the *pizmonim* presented here.

May there by peace in our ranks, and tranquility in Israel.
Auspiciously a son has come to us —
may the Redeemer come in his lifetime.

May this child be vigorous, may he dwell in HASHEM's protection,
May his understanding be in Torah —
And may he teach the Law to every questioner.
May there by peace in our ranks, and tranquility in Israel.
Auspiciously a son has come to us — may the Redeemer come in his lifetime.
May his spring be blessed, may his lifespan be long,
May his table be ever prepared —
May his homage to HASHEM never be disdained.
May there by peace in our ranks, and tranquility in Israel.
Auspiciously a son has come to us — may the Redeemer come in his lifetime.
May his reputation spread everywhere, may he be accomplished in adulthood,
May he be a friend to the God-fearing —
May he be in his generation like Samuel [in his].
May there by peace in our ranks, and tranquility in Israel.
Auspiciously a son has come to us — may the Redeemer come in his lifetime.
With maturity in wisdom and until old age,
May he be saturated with every good, peace to Him and abundant love —
So too, may God say [this] to him.
May there by peace in our ranks, and tranquility in Israel.
Auspiciously a son has come to us — may the Redeemer come in his lifetime.
Living One, Pure One, Holy One, is Your Name.
By Your right hand may he find support
To examine and to gaze upon Your delight — In the midst of His nation Israel.
May there by peace in our ranks, and tranquility in Israel.
Auspiciously a son has come to us — may the Redeemer come in his lifetime.

אֶעֱרוֹךְ מַהֲלַל *I will compose my speech of praise before the God of my father,*
in honor of my heart's beloved, Elijah the Prophet.
ג *God planted in Jeshurun a rose in Sharon,*
a man from Aaron's offspring, the servant of the Rock, my Fortress.
ב *He is the priest to God supreme, Phineas, he is Elijah,*
the Prophet whom they called the Gileadite, the Tishbite.
י *One day he zealously avenged God's honor,*
he killed with strength and power,
a prince of a tribe of Israel, and a daughter of Tzur, her name was Kazbi.
ד *He heard this law from his teacher, 'If a man lays with an Amorite woman,*
the zealous may execute him.' And so he said 'I will unsheathe my sword.'

and the Emorite princess, Kazbi, with whom he had cohabited. For this courageous act of championing the word of God, he was promised the Covenant of Priesthood (see *Numbers* 25:7-15).

The highlights of Elijah's life are depicted with the account of the miracle of the oil and flour (*I Kings* 17:8-16); his revival of the dead child (ibid. verses 17-24); his confrontation with the prophets of the Baal (ibid. 18:19-40); his prophecy that no rain would fall for three years (ibid. 17:1); his appearance

וַיָּקָם מִתּוֹךְ עֵדָה, רוֹמַח בְּיָדוֹ הָדָה, וַיֶּחֱרַד חֲרָדָה,

נִתְגַּבֵּר כְּמוֹ לָבִיא. לִכְבוֹד חֶמְדַּת לְבָבִי, אֵלִיָּהוּ הַנָּבִיא.

דָּקַר בְּחַרְבּוֹ אוֹתָם, כְּדֶרֶךְ שְׁכִיבָתָם, עַל הָאָרֶץ חֲבָטָם,

וּלְמֹשֶׁה אוֹתָם הֵבִיא. לִכְבוֹד חֶמְדַּת לְבָבִי, אֵלִיָּהוּ הַנָּבִיא.

בִּשְׂכַר זֹאת אֵל חַי עוֹלָם, נָתַן לוֹ שָׂכָר מוּשְׁלָם, בְּרִית כְּהֻנַּת עוֹלָם,

וַיְכַפֵּר עֲלֵי חוֹבִי. לִכְבוֹד חֶמְדַּת לְבָבִי, אֵלִיָּהוּ הַנָּבִיא.

נִסִּים עֶשֶׂר וּשְׁתַּיִם, בְּדִבְרֵיהֶם שְׁנוּיִים, עָשָׂה לוֹ דָּר שָׁמַיִם,

צוּרִי גּוֹאֲלִי אָבִי. לִכְבוֹד חֶמְדַּת לְבָבִי, אֵלִיָּהוּ הַנָּבִיא.

אֱמֶת בְּפִיהוּ הָיָה, לְאַלְמָנָה עֲנִיָּה, עֵת אֶת בְּנָהּ הֶחֱיָה,

וּלְנַפְשׁוֹ אָמַר שׁוּבִי. לִכְבוֹד חֶמְדַּת לְבָבִי, אֵלִיָּהוּ הַנָּבִיא.

הַשֶּׁמֶן נֵס בּוֹ שָׂרָתָה, הַבְּרָכָה וְהָיְתָה, כַּד הַקֶּמַח לֹא כָלָתָה,

וַתִּגְדְּלִי וַתִּרְבִּי. לִכְבוֹד חֶמְדַּת לְבָבִי, אֵלִיָּהוּ הַנָּבִיא.

רוֹדְפִים אַחֲרֵי תֹהוּ, הִכָּה בְּשֵׁבֶט פִּיהוּ, וַיֹּאמֶר יהוה הוּא,

וֶאֱמֶת אַתָּה נָבִיא. לִכְבוֹד חֶמְדַּת לְבָבִי, אֵלִיָּהוּ הַנָּבִיא.

וְגָזַר אָמַר עָשֹׁה, מִסְפַּר שָׁנִים שְׁלֹשָׁה, מָטָר לֹא נִתַּךְ אַרְצָה,

הוּא הַמּוֹצִיא הַמֵּבִיא. לִכְבוֹד חֶמְדַּת לְבָבִי, אֵלִיָּהוּ הַנָּבִיא.

נָתַן לוֹ הָאֵל מַהֲלָכִים, בְּעוֹלָם הַמַּלְאָכִים, וּלְעִתּוֹת הַנִּצְרָכִים,

הוּא נִגְלָה בַּעֲרָבִי. לִכְבוֹד חֶמְדַּת לְבָבִי, אֵלִיָּהוּ הַנָּבִיא.

בִּקְדוּשָׁה וּבְטָהֳרָה, עָלָה עָלָה בַּסְּעָרָה, אֵלָיו אֱלִישָׁע קָרָא,

וַיֹּאמַר אָבִי אָבִי. לִכְבוֹד חֶמְדַּת לְבָבִי, אֵלִיָּהוּ הַנָּבִיא.

נַפְשִׁי לַיְלָה אִוִּיתִיהוּ, מִי יִתֵּן אִמְצָאֵהוּ, פְּתַח בֵּיתִי אַרְאֵהוּ,

יַשְׁקִיף בְּעַד אֶשְׁנַבִּי. לִכְבוֹד חֶמְדַּת לְבָבִי, אֵלִיָּהוּ הַנָּבִיא.

חָסִין קָדוֹשׁ אֶקְרָאָה, אִישׁ אֲשֶׁר פָּנָיו רָאָה, זֶה כַּבִּיר יָדוֹ מָצָאָה,

תְּשׁוּרָה אֵלָיו לְהָבִיא. לִכְבוֹד חֶמְדַּת לְבָבִי, אֵלִיָּהוּ הַנָּבִיא.

זָכוּר לַטּוֹב יָאִיר נֵרִי, יְבַשֵּׂר צִיּוֹן עִירִי, וְיֹאמַר הִתְנַעֲרִי,

מֵעָפָר קוּמִי שְׁבִי. לִכְבוֹד חֶמְדַּת לְבָבִי, אֵלִיָּהוּ הַנָּבִיא.

קוֹל זִמְרַת שִׁיר מַהֲלָלִי, יִרְצֶה צוּרִי גּוֹאֲלִי, וְלוֹ דוּמִיָּה לִי,

בְּכָל עוֹד נִשְׁמָתִי בִּי. לִכְבוֹד חֶמְדַּת לְבָבִי, אֵלִיָּהוּ הַנָּבִיא.

אַתָּה אֲהוּבִי, צוּרִי מִשְׂגַּבִּי,

כִּי אַתָּה נָתַתָּ שִׂמְחָה בְּלִבִּי,   בָּךְ אֶשְׁעָן.

בְּיוֹם הַמִּילָה,   עֶבֶד הַלּוּלָה,

בְּשָׂשׂוֹן וּבְשִׂמְחָה, טוֹבָה כְּפוּלָה,   שָׂמָה עַל עַיִן.

רָץ קַל כַּצְּבִי,   אֵלִיָּהוּ הַנָּבִיא,

בֹּא יָבֹא בִּמְהֵרָה, לְכַפֵּר חוֹבִי.   נִצָּב עַל עַיִן.

הַיֶּלֶד בְּנִי,   כְּחוּט הַשָּׁנִי,

בְּסִימָן טוֹב כְּגַן רָטוֹב, לְנִמּוֹל בְּנִי,   מַחְמַד כָּל עַיִן.

ו He arose from among the community, a spear in his hand outstretched.
   A terrible trembling seized him,
                                    but he strengthened himself like a young lion.
ד He pierced them with his sword exactly as they reclined,
   he struck them down to the earth,   and brought them to Moses,
ב In this merit, the God who lives forever gave him a complete reward,
   the covenant of everlasting priesthood. [Phineas said] 'He forgave my sin.'
ג Miracles totaling twelve, as enumerated in the Sages' words,
   were done for him by the One who dwells in Heaven
                                    my Rock, my Redeemer, my Father.
א Truth was in his mouth to the forlorn widow,
   when he resuscitated her son,   saying to his soul, 'Return'
ה Upon the oil rested a miracle, and a blessing that came to be.
   The flour keg never emptied —   it only grew and multiplied.
ד Those who pursued emptiness he struck with the rod of his mouth.
   He proclaimed, 'HASHEM, He is [God] —
                                    and what You prophesy is true.
ו He decreed and it came to be — the number of years was three
   that no rain reached the earth.   It is He who brings out and brings in.
ג He [HASHEM] gave him passageways in the world of angels.
   And at the appropriate times   he appeared as an Arab.
ב With holiness and purity he ascended in a stormwind.
   To him Elisha called out,   saying, 'My Father! My Father!'
ג At night my soul longs for him, if only I could find him,
   the entrance of my home I would show him —
                                    O that he peer through my window.
ח 'O powerful, holy one!' would I exclaim, to one who has seen [Elijah's] face,
   he has found something great —   I would bring a gift to him.
ז May the one remembered for good [Elijah] light my soul's flame,
   may he herald good news to Zion, my city,
   He shall proclaim, 'Awaken!   Get up from the dust! Sit upright!'
ק May the sound of the music of the song of my praise
   find favor with my Rock, my Redeemer.
   To him shall be my hope,   as long as my soul is within me.

אַתָּה אֲהוּבִי You [HASHEM] are my Beloved, my Rock, my Stronghold,
   for You presented joy to my heart   on You, I rely.
ב On the day of circumcision tender a celebration,
   with joy and happiness, and two-fold goodness   placed before the eye.
ר Run swiftly as a deer, O Elijah the Prophet,
   do indeed come quickly to atone for my sinfulness,
                                    May he stand before me.
ה This child, my son is like a scarlet thread,
   auspicious as a flourishing garden. My son will be circumcised,
                                    adored by everyone.

as an Arab before King Ahab (ibid. [See also *Bamidbar Rabbah* 20:25.]
20:38-41); and his ascension to Heaven   The final four stanzas depict the
in a swirling storm (*II Kings* 2:11-12). author's passionate desire to see Elijah.

מַצְרֵף לַכֶּסֶף,   יְהִי מְאַסֵף,

לְזֶרַע אַבְרָהָם, בֶּן פֹּרָת יוֹסֵף,   פֹּרָת עֲלֵי עָיִן.

חַזֵּק אֶרֶץ טוֹבָה,   הָעִיר הָרְחָבָה,

וּבֵית הַבְּחִירָה, מַרְגָּלִית טוֹבָה,   תְּרְאֶינָה עָיִן.

מַה טּוֹב מַה נָּעִים דָּבָר בְּעִתּוֹ,   כָּל אִישׁ יָשָׁר יָשִׂישׂ עַל אִמְרָתוֹ,

כִּי תִגָּלֶה תֵּרָאֶה מַלְכוּתוֹ,   מַלְכוּת עוֹלָם לְכָל בָּאֵי בְרִית.

אֵלִיָּהוּ,   מְבַשֵּׂר הוּא,   נִקְרָאֵהוּ,

בָּעֵת הַהוּא,   לִהְיוֹת עוֹמֵד עַל הַבְּרִית.

יוֹם הַמִּילָה,   נֶצַח סֶלָה,   נְהַלְלָה,

הִיא שְׁקוּלָה,   כְּקַבָּלַת לוּחוֹת בְּרִית.

רֹנּוּ גַּדְּלוּ לַיהוה אִתִּי,   יוֹם הַמִּילָה אֵלָיו פִּי קָרָאתִי,

עֵת בְּחֶסֶד כִּסֵּא הֲכִינוֹתִי,   לְאֵלִיָּהוּ מַלְאַךְ הַבְּרִית.

דּוֹרְשֵׁי אֵל חַי צַדִּיק יְסוֹד עוֹלָם,   יִשְׂמְחוּ קְטַנָּם עִם גְּדוֹלָם,

יַחַד יִשְׂאוּ כַּנְּהָרוֹת קוֹלָם,   בְּהִגָּלוֹת נִגְלוֹת אוֹת הַבְּרִית.

כִּי בָא מוֹעֵד בְּפֵרוֹעַ פְּרָעוֹת,   יַיִן יִתְאַדָּם בְּכוֹס הַיְשׁוּעוֹת,

יִשְׁתּוּ וִיבָרְכוּ אֵל לְמוֹשָׁעוֹת,   עַל הַמִּילָה וְכוֹרֵת הַבְּרִית.

חִזְקוּ אִמְצוּ סַעֲדוּ לִבְּכֶם,   וְלָאֵל דִּרְשׁוּ יָבֹא וְיוֹשִׁיעֲכֶם,

כִּימֵי מָרְדְּכַי מִיַּד צָרֵיכֶם,   כַּאֲשֶׁר כָּרַת אֶת אַבְרָהָם בְּרִית.

עַבְדֵּי הָאֵל תִּזְכּוּ, לְגַן עֶדְנָיו,   וְשָׁם תֹּאכְלוּ מִטּוּב מַעֲדָנָיו,

כִּי תָבוֹאוּ לִרְאוֹת אֶת פָּנָיו,   בִּהְיוֹתְכֶם תָּמִיד, שׁוֹמְרֵי בְרִית.

⁂ סֵדֶר הַבְּרִית ⁂

When the child is brought into the room where the *brit* is to be held,
the assembled guests recite the following *pizmon*.

בְּרוּכִים אַתֶּם קְהַל אֱמוּנַי, וּבָרוּךְ הַבָּא בְּשֵׁם יהוה.

יֶלֶד הַיֶּלֶד יִהְיֶה בְּסִמָּן טוֹב,   יִגְדַּל וְיִהְיֶה כְּמוֹ גַן רָטוֹב,

יַעֲלֶה וְיַצְלִיחַ יִנָּצֵל מִקָּטוֹב,   אָמֵן, כֵּן יַעֲשֶׂה יהוה.

Cong.—בְּרוּכִים אַתֶּם קְהַל אֱמוּנַי, וּבָרוּךְ הַבָּא בְּשֵׁם יהוה.

חֵלֶק יִתֵּן לָנוּ בַּנְּעִימִים,   וּבְיָמָיו נַעֲלֶה לְשָׁלֹשׁ רְגָלִים,

לְבֵית יהוה גְּדוֹלִים וּקְטַנִּים,   וּבָרוּךְ הַבָּא בְּשֵׁם יהוה.

Cong.—בְּרוּכִים אַתֶּם קְהַל אֱמוּנַי, וּבָרוּךְ הַבָּא בְּשֵׁם יהוה.

The author of this prayer is R' David ben Aaron Chassin of the nineteenth century. His name appears as an acrostic: אֲנִכִי דָוִד בֶּן אַהֲרֹן בֶּן חַסִּין חֲזַק, *I am David ben Aaron ben Chassin — be strong.*

I am indebted to his direct descendant, Rabbi Avraham Ben-Chaim, Rabbi of the Sephardic Community in Co-op City, New York, and a leader of Moroccan Jewry, for his assistance in interpreting this prayer.

מ [May he be like] a crucible of silver, may he be a gatherer,
of the offspring of Abraham, May he be like the charming son Joseph,
charming to the eye.
ח Strengthen the good land [Israel] the bountiful city [Jerusalem],
the chosen dwelling [the holy Temple] — that precious Jewel —
May the eye behold it.

מַה טּוֹב How good and how pleasant is a timely event,
Every upright man will rejoice at His word,
When His kingdom will be revealed and seen,
an eternal kingdom for all who enter the covenant.
Elijah, he is the herald, let us invite him, to stand at that time by the milah.
Let us eternally praise the day of the milah, Selah.
It is equivalent to the receiving of the Tablets of the Covenant.
ר Sing and exalt HASHEM with me.
On the day of milah I call out to Him.
The time when, magnanimously, I prepare a chair
for Elijah, angel of the covenant.
ד Seekers of the Living God, the Righteous One, Foundation of the world.
Their young shall rejoice with their elders.
Together they shall raise their voices like rivers,
when the sign of the covenant is revealed.
כ When the time arrives for revealing to be done,
Wine flows red in the cup of salvations!
They will drink and bless the God of Salvations,
'On circumcision' and 'Who establishes the covenant.'
ח Strengthen, fortify, sustain your hearts,
and seek God — may He come and save you,
as in Mordecai's days, from your enemies
just as He established a covenant with Abraham.
O servants of God, may you merit the garden of His pleasures,
There may you eat from the best of His delicacies,
When you come to be seen in His Presence,
for you shall always be guardians of the covenant.

⊰⧼ ORDER OF THE BRIT ⧽⊱

When the child is brought into the room where the *brit* is to be held,
the assembled guests recite the following *pizmon*.

Blessed are you, the community of my faithful,
And blessed is he who comes in the Name of HASHEM.

May this newborn child be an auspicious sign,
May he grow and develop like a flourishing garden,
May he soar, succeed and be spared misfortune.
Amen, may HASHEM make it so.
Cong.—*Blessed are you, the community of my faithful,*
And blessed is he who comes in the Name of HASHEM.
May the lot granted us be pleasant,
And in his days may we ascend for the three pilgrimage festivals.
To the House of HASHEM, old and young
And blessed is he who comes in the Name of HASHEM.
Cong.—*Blessed are you, the community of my faithful,*
And blessed is he who comes in the Name of HASHEM.

זְכֹר רַחֲמֶיךָ וְדַם הַבְּרִית, וּפְקֹד אֶת צֹאנֶךָ צֹאן הַשְּׁאֵרִית,

עַל יַד מְשִׁיחֶךָ אֶת אוֹיְבֵינוּ תַכְרִית, וּשְׁלַח אֶת אֵלִיָּה נְבִיא יהוה.

Cong.—בְּרוּכִים אַתֶּם קְהַל אֱמוּנָי, וּבָרוּךְ הַבָּא בְּשֵׁם יהוה.

הַיֶּלֶד הַזֶּה זָכָה לִבְרִיתוֹ, אָבִיו וְאִמּוֹ יִרְאוּ אֶת חֶפְתּוֹ,

הַמַּלְאָךְ הַגֹּאֵל יְבָרֵךְ אֹתוֹ, יִזְכֶּה לַחֲזוֹת בְּנֹעַם יהוה.

Cong.—בְּרוּכִים אַתֶּם קְהַל אֱמוּנָי, וּבָרוּךְ הַבָּא בְּשֵׁם יהוה.

The entire assemblage greets the infant:

בָּרוּךְ הַבָּא בְּשֵׁם יהוה!

The father takes the child and says aloud:

שָׂשׂ אָנֹכִי עַל אִמְרָתֶךָ. כְּמוֹצֵא שָׁלָל רָב.[1] זִבְחֵי אֱלֹהִים רוּחַ נִשְׁבָּרָה לֵב נִשְׁבָּר וְנִדְכֶּה אֱלֹהִים לֹא תִבְזֶה. הֵטִיבָה בִרְצוֹנְךָ אֶת צִיּוֹן תִּבְנֶה חוֹמוֹת יְרוּשָׁלָיִם. אָז תַּחְפֹּץ זִבְחֵי צֶדֶק, עוֹלָה וְכָלִיל אָז יַעֲלוּ עַל מִזְבַּחֲךָ פָרִים.[2] אַשְׁרֵי תִּבְחַר וּתְקָרֵב יִשְׁכֹּן חֲצֵרֶיךָ.

All present respond:

נִשְׂבְּעָה בְּטוּב בֵּיתֶךָ קְדֹשׁ הֵיכָלֶךָ.[3]

If the *brit* takes place in *Eretz Yisrael* the following verses are recited:

אִם אֶשְׁכָּחֵךְ יְרוּשָׁלָיִם תִּשְׁכַּח יְמִינִי. תִּדְבַּק לְשׁוֹנִי לְחִכִּי אִם לֹא אֶזְכְּרֵכִי, אִם לֹא אַעֲלֶה אֶת יְרוּשָׁלַיִם עַל רֹאשׁ שִׂמְחָתִי.[4]

The following verses are recited responsively by the father and the entire assemblage:

שְׁמַע יִשְׂרָאֵל, יהוה אֱלֹהֵינוּ, יהוה אֶחָד.[5]

יהוה מֶלֶךְ, יהוה מָלָךְ, יהוה יִמְלֹךְ לְעֹלָם וָעֶד.

יהוה מֶלֶךְ, יהוה מָלָךְ, יהוה יִמְלֹךְ לְעֹלָם וָעֶד.

אָנָּא יהוה הוֹשִׁיעָה נָּא. אָנָּא יהוה הוֹשִׁיעָה נָּא.

אָנָּא יהוה הַצְלִיחָה נָא. אָנָּא יהוה הַצְלִיחָה נָא.[6]

Two seats are prepared: one for אֵלִיָּהוּ הַנָּבִיא, *Elijah the Prophet,* and one for the *sandak* as he holds the baby during the circumcision. In some communities only one chair is used, the *sandak* sitting on the כִּסֵּא שֶׁל אֵלִיָּהוּ, *Throne of Eliyahu.* The baby is first placed upon the *Throne of Eliyahu,* by the *mohel* or one of the prominent guests, and the *mohel* says:

זֶה הַכִּסֵּא שֶׁל אֵלִיָּהוּ הַנָּבִיא מַלְאַךְ הַבְּרִית זָכוּר לַטוֹב.

The father then takes the child from the Throne of Eliyahu [or is given the baby by one of the guests] and places him on the *sandak's* lap.

The Ritual / Sephardic Custom [178]

Remember Your mercy and the covenantal blood,
Bear in mind Your sheep, the sheep of the remnant.
Through Your anointed one, may You cut down our enemies,
And send Elijah, the Prophet of HASHEM —
Cong.—*Blessed are you, the community of my faithful,*
And blessed is he who comes in the Name of HASHEM.
This child has merited his milah,
May his father and mother see his wedding canopy;
May the redeeming angel bless him,
May he be worthy to behold the pleasantness of HASHEM.
Cong.—*Blessed are you, the community of my faithful*
And blessed is he who comes in the Name of HASHEM.

The entire assemblage greets the infant:

Blessed is the one who has come in the Name of HASHEM!

The father takes the child and says aloud:

שָׂשׂ I rejoice because of your word like one who finds abundant spoils.[1]
The offerings of God are a broken spirit. A broken and suppressed
heart, God, You will not despise. Do good with Zion, according to Your
will rebuild the walls of Jerusalem. Then you will desire the offerings of
righteousness, burnt offering and whole offering; then they will offer bulls
upon Your Altar.[2] Praiseworthy is the one You choose and draw near to
dwell in Your courts —

All present respond:

may we be satisfied by the goodness of Your House — Your Holy Temple.[3]

> If the *brit* takes place in *Eretz Yisrael* the following verses are recited:
> If I forget you, O Jerusalem, may I forget my right hand.
> Let my tongue adhere to my palate if I fail to recall you,
> if I fail to elevate Jerusalem above my foremost joy.[4]

The following verses are recited responsively by the father and the entire assemblage:
Hear, O Israel: HASHEM is our God, HASHEM, the One and Only.[5]
HASHEM reigns, HASHEM has reigned, HASHEM shall reign for all eternity.
HASHEM reigns, HASHEM has reigned, HASHEM shall reign for all eternity.
O HASHEM, please save [us].   O HASHEM, please save [us].
O HASHEM, please [make us] prosper!   O HASHEM, please [make us] prosper![6]

Two seats are prepared: one for אֵלִיָּהוּ הַנָּבִיא, Elijah the Prophet, and one for the *sandak* as he
holds the baby during the circumcision. In some communities only one chair is used, the
sandak sitting on the כִּסֵא שֶׁל אֵלִיָּהוּ, Throne of Eliyahu. The baby is first placed upon the
Throne of Eliyahu, by the *mohel* or one of the prominent guests, and the *mohel* says:

זֶה This is the Throne of Elijah the Prophet, angel of the covenant, who is
remembered for the good.

The father then takes the child from the Throne of Eliyahu [or is given
the baby by one of the guests] and places him on the *sandak's* lap.

---

(1) *Psalms* 119:116. (2) *Psalms* 51:18-21. (3) *Psalms* 65:5.
(4) *Psalms* 137:5-6. (5) *Deuteronomy* 6:4. (6) *Psalms* 118:25.

In some Syrian communities the father recites this blessing
just before the *mohel* is to perform the circumcision:

בָּרוּךְ אַתָּה יהוה אֱלֹהֵינוּ מֶלֶךְ הָעוֹלָם, אֲשֶׁר קִדְּשָׁנוּ בְּמִצְוֹתָיו, וְצִוָּנוּ
לְהַכְנִיסוֹ בִּבְרִיתוֹ שֶׁל אַבְרָהָם אָבִינוּ. (אָמֵן—All.)

The assembled respond loudly and joyfully:

כְּשֵׁם שֶׁהִכְנַסְתּוֹ לַבְּרִית, כֵּן תַּכְנִיסֵהוּ לַתּוֹרָה וְלַמִּצְוֹת וְלַחֻפָּה וּלְמַעֲשִׂים
טוֹבִים. וְכֵן יְהִי רָצוֹן, וְנֹאמַר אָמֵן.

Just before performing the circumcision, the *mohel* recites:

בָּרוּךְ אַתָּה יהוה אֱלֹהֵינוּ מֶלֶךְ הָעוֹלָם, אֲשֶׁר קִדְּשָׁנוּ בְּמִצְוֹתָיו,
וְצִוָּנוּ עַל הַמִּילָה. (אָמֵן—All.)

As the *mohel* performs the circumcision, the father recites the following two blessings.
[If he has already recited the first blessing earlier, he does not repeat it here.]

בָּרוּךְ אַתָּה יהוה אֱלֹהֵינוּ מֶלֶךְ הָעוֹלָם, אֲשֶׁר קִדְּשָׁנוּ בְּמִצְוֹתָיו,
וְצִוָּנוּ לְהַכְנִיסוֹ בִּבְרִיתוֹ שֶׁל אַבְרָהָם אָבִינוּ. (אָמֵן—All.)

בָּרוּךְ אַתָּה יהוה אֱלֹהֵינוּ מֶלֶךְ הָעוֹלָם, שֶׁהֶחֱיָנוּ וְקִיְּמָנוּ וְהִגִּיעָנוּ
לַזְּמַן הַזֶּה. (אָמֵן—All.)

The assembled respond loudly and joyfully:

כְּשֵׁם שֶׁהִכְנַסְתּוֹ לַבְּרִית, כֵּן תַּכְנִיסֵהוּ לַתּוֹרָה וְלַמִּצְוֹת וְלַחֻפָּה
וּלְמַעֲשִׂים טוֹבִים. וְכֵן יְהִי רָצוֹן, וְנֹאמַר אָמֵן.

Following the *brit* the assembled say:

כְּרֵיחַ נִיחֹחַ אִשֶּׁה לַיהוה.	יְהִי דַם הַנִּמּוֹל בִּקְהַל אֱמוּנָי.
נַקְרִיב זְבָחִים עוֹלוֹת לַיהוה.	וּבִירוּשָׁלַיִם כִּסֵּא יהוה.
לָנוּ וּלְבָנֵינוּ לְעוֹלָם וָעֶד.	חָתַם בִּבְשָׂרֵנוּ לְאוֹת מוֹפֵת וּלְעֵד.
כִּי אֲנַחְנוּ רוֹאֵינוּ וְיֵדְעוּ מוֹנַי.	יַכִּירוּ רוֹאֵינוּ וְיֵדְעוּ מוֹנַי.
כְּרֵיחַ נִיחֹחַ אִשֶּׁה לַיהוה.	יְהִי דַם הַנִּמּוֹל בִּקְהַל אֱמוּנָי.

The following *pizmon* is recited when the *brit* takes place on the Shabbat:

שַׁבָּת וּמִילָה, שָׁם דָּר מְעֹנָה,   חֵלֶק לְשִׁבְעָה, וְגַם לִשְׁמוֹנָה.
אוֹתִיּוֹת שַׁבָּת, מִצְוֹת שְׁלֹשָׁה,   נִכְתַּב בָּהֶם אוֹת, לְאֻמָּה קְדוֹשָׁה.
שַׁבָּת רִאשׁוֹנָה, וּבְרִית חֲדָשָׁה,   וְהָיוּ תְפִלִּין, לְרֹאשׁ אֲמָנָה.
שְׁתֵּי מִצְוֹת הֵם, כְּעַמּוּדִים שְׁנֵיהֶם,   זֹאת הַחַמָּה, וְזֹאת הַלְּבָנָה.
שַׁבָּת וּמִילָה, שָׁם דָּר מְעֹנָה,   חֵלֶק לְשִׁבְעָה, וְגַם לִשְׁמוֹנָה.

The Ritual / Sephardic Custom   [180]

בָּרוּךְ *Blessed are You, HASHEM, our God, King of the universe, Who has
sanctified us with His commandments, and has commanded us to bring
him into the covenant of Abraham, our forefather.*   (All — Amen.)

כְּשֵׁם *Just as you have entered him into the covenant, so may you enter him into
[the study of] Torah, to mitzvos, to marriage and to [the performance of]
good deeds. So may it be the will [of HASHEM], and let us say, Amen.*

בָּרוּךְ *Blessed are You, HASHEM, our God, King of the universe, Who has
sanctified us with His commandments, and has commanded us
regarding circumcision.*   (All — Amen.)

בָּרוּךְ *Blessed are You, HASHEM, our God, King of the universe, Who has
sanctified us with His commandments, and has commanded us to
bring him into the covenant of Abraham, our forefather.*   (All — Amen.)

בָּרוּךְ *Blessed are You, HASHEM, our God, King of the universe, Who has
kept us alive, sustained us, and brought us to this season.*

(All — Amen.)

כְּשֵׁם *Just as you have entered him into the covenant, so may you enter
him into [the study of] Torah, to mitzvos, to marriage and to [the
performance of] good deeds. So may it be the will [of HASHEM], and let us
say, Amen.*

*May the blood of the circumcised one be [considered] in the community of the faithful,
    as a pleasing offering to HASHEM.
And in Jerusalem, Throne of HASHEM,
    may we offer sacrifices and complete burnt offerings to HASHEM.
Sealed in our flesh as a wondrous sign and testimony,
    for us and our children for all eternity.
Those who see us will recognize, and our oppressors will know,
    that we are the children, blessed by HASHEM.
May the blood of the circumcised one be [considered] in the community of the faithful,
    as a pleasing offering to HASHEM.*

*With Sabbath and circumcision, He placed the abode of His habitat,
    A portion for the seventh [day] and also for the eighth.
The letters of Shabbat [ש-ב-ת], represent three mitzvot [שבת, ברית, תפלין],
    It is written regarding each 'A sign' to the holy nation.
Shabbat is first, then the new covenant,
    And tefillin shall be the pinnacle of faith.
Two mitzvot are they, like pillars are they both,
    This is the sun, and that is the moon.
With Shabbat and circumcision, He placed the abode of His habitat,
    A portion for the seventh [day] and also for the eighth.*

After the circumcision, the baby is held by one of the guests, while the following prayers (including giving the name) are recited. The honor of reciting the blessings and of giving the name may be given to one person, or two. Similarly, two people may hold the baby, one during the blessing, one for the naming.

A cup of wine is filled and held in the right hand by the man reciting the blessing.

סַבְרִי מָרָנָן: (All — לְחַיִּים.)

בָּרוּךְ אַתָּה יהוה אֱלֹהֵינוּ מֶלֶךְ הָעוֹלָם, בּוֹרֵא פְּרִי הַגָּפֶן.

(אָמֵן. —All)

Spices or fragrant herbs are held by the man reciting the following blessing, and the applicable word in parentheses is used.

בָּרוּךְ אַתָּה יהוה אֱלֹהֵינוּ מֶלֶךְ הָעוֹלָם, בּוֹרֵא (עֲצֵי/עִשְׂבֵי/מִינֵי)
בְּשָׂמִים:

(אָמֵן. —All)

בָּרוּךְ אַתָּה יהוה אֱלֹהֵינוּ מֶלֶךְ הָעוֹלָם, אֲשֶׁר קִדֵּשׁ יְדִיד מִבֶּטֶן, וְחֹק בִּשְׁאֵרוֹ שָׂם, וְצֶאֱצָאָיו חָתַם בְּאוֹת בְּרִית קֹדֶשׁ. עַל כֵּן בִּשְׂכַר זוֹ, אֵל חַי, חֶלְקֵנוּ צוּרֵנוּ, צַוֵּה לְהַצִּיל יְדִידוּת זֶרַע קֹדֶשׁ שְׁאֵרֵנוּ מִשַּׁחַת. לְמַעַן בְּרִיתוֹ אֲשֶׁר שָׂם בִּבְשָׂרֵנוּ. בָּרוּךְ אַתָּה יהוה, כּוֹרֵת הַבְּרִית.

(אָמֵן. —All)

❊{ קריאת השם }❊

Upon reaching the words in bold type, the reader pauses while all present recite them aloud. The reader then repeats them and continues:

אֱלֹהֵינוּ וֵאלֹהֵי אֲבוֹתֵינוּ, קַיֵּם אֶת הַיֶּלֶד הַזֶּה לְאָבִיו וּלְאִמּוֹ, וְיִקָּרֵא שְׁמוֹ, בְּיִשְׂרָאֵל (baby's name) בֶּן (father's name). יִשְׂמַח הָאִישׁ בְּיוֹצֵא חֲלָצָיו, וְתָגֵל הָאִשָּׁה בִּפְרִי בִטְנָהּ. כָּאָמוּר: יִשְׂמַח אָבִיךָ וְאִמֶּךָ, וְתָגֵל יוֹלַדְתֶּךָ.[1] וְנֶאֱמַר: וָאֶעֱבֹר עָלַיִךְ וָאֶרְאֵךְ מִתְבּוֹסֶסֶת בְּדָמָיִךְ, **וָאֹמַר לָךְ בְּדָמַיִךְ חֲיִי, וָאֹמַר לָךְ בְּדָמַיִךְ חֲיִי.**[2] וְנֶאֱמַר: זָכַר לְעוֹלָם בְּרִיתוֹ, דָּבָר צִוָּה לְאֶלֶף דּוֹר. אֲשֶׁר כָּרַת אֶת אַבְרָהָם, וּשְׁבוּעָתוֹ לְיִשְׂחָק. וַיַּעֲמִידֶהָ לְיַעֲקֹב לְחֹק, לְיִשְׂרָאֵל בְּרִית עוֹלָם.[3] וְנֶאֱמַר: וַיָּמָל אַבְרָהָם אֶת יִצְחָק בְּנוֹ, בֶּן שְׁמֹנַת יָמִים, כַּאֲשֶׁר צִוָּה אֹתוֹ אֱלֹהִים.[4] **הוֹדוּ לַיהוה כִּי טוֹב, כִּי לְעוֹלָם חַסְדּוֹ.**[5] (baby's name) זֶה הַקָּטָן אֱלֹהִים יְגַדְּלֵהוּ. **כְּשֵׁם שֶׁנִּכְנַס לַבְּרִית, כַּךְ יִכָּנֵס לְתוֹרָה וּמִצְוֹת, וּלְחֻפָּה, וּלְמַעֲשִׂים טוֹבִים. וְכֵן יְהִי רָצוֹן, וְנֹאמַר אָמֵן.**

שִׁיר הַמַּעֲלוֹת, אַשְׁרֵי כָּל יְרֵא יהוה, הַהֹלֵךְ בִּדְרָכָיו. יְגִיעַ כַּפֶּיךָ כִּי תֹאכֵל, אַשְׁרֶיךָ וְטוֹב לָךְ. אֶשְׁתְּךָ כְּגֶפֶן פֹּרִיָּה בְּיַרְכְּתֵי בֵיתֶךָ, בָּנֶיךָ כִּשְׁתִלֵי זֵיתִים, סָבִיב לְשֻׁלְחָנֶךָ. הִנֵּה כִי כֵן יְבֹרַךְ גָּבֶר, יְרֵא יהוה. יְבָרֶכְךָ יהוה מִצִּיּוֹן, וּרְאֵה בְּטוּב יְרוּשָׁלָיִם כֹּל יְמֵי חַיֶּיךָ. וּרְאֵה בָנִים לְבָנֶיךָ, שָׁלוֹם עַל יִשְׂרָאֵל.

The Ritual / Sephardic Custom [182]

After the circumcision, the baby is held by one of the guests, while the following prayers (including giving the name) are recited. The honor of reciting the blessings and of giving the name may be given to one person, or two. Similarly, two people may hold the baby, one during the blessing, one for the naming.

A cup of wine is filled and held in the right hand by the man reciting the blessing.

By your leave, my masters. (All — To life!)

בָּרוּךְ *Blessed are You, HASHEM, our God, King of the universe, Who creates the fruit of the vine.* (All—*Amen.*)

Spices or fragrant herbs are held by the man reciting the following blessing and the applicable word in parentheses is used.

בָּרוּךְ *Blessed are You, HASHEM our God, King of the universe, Who creates (trees/grasses/species) of spices.* (All—*Amen.*)

בָּרוּךְ *Blessed are You, HASHEM, our God, King of the universe, Who has sanctified the beloved one from the womb and placed the mark of the decree in his flesh, and sealed his offspring with the sign of the holy covenant. Therefore, as reward for this, O Living God, our Portion, our Rock, may You issue the command to rescue the beloved holy children within our flesh from destruction, for the sake of His covenant that He has placed in our flesh. Blessed are You, HASHEM, Who establishes the covenant.* (All—*Amen.*)

ᣔ⟨ GIVING THE NAME ⟩ᣕ

Upon reaching the words in bold type, the reader pauses while all present recite them aloud. The reader then repeats them and continues:

אֱלֹהֵינוּ *Our God and the God of our forefathers, preserve this child for his father and mother, and may his name be called in Israel* (baby's name) *son of* (father's name). *May the man rejoice in the issue of his loins and may the woman exult in the fruit of her womb, as it says: 'May your father and mother rejoice and may the one who bore you exult.'*[1] *And it is said: "Then I passed by you and saw you downtrodden in your blood,* **and I said to you: 'Because of your blood you shall live!' and I said to you: 'Because of your blood you shall live!' "**[2] *And it is said: 'He remembered His covenant forever; the word of His command for a thousand generations — that He made with Abraham and His vow to Isaac. Then He established it for Jacob as a statute, for Israel as an everlasting statute.'*[3] *And it is said: 'Abraham circumcised his son Isaac at the age of eight days as God had commanded him.'*[4] **Give thanks to HASHEM for He is good; His kindness endures forever!**[5] *May God make this infant* (baby's name) *great.* **Just as he has entered the covenant so may he enter into the [study of] Torah and mitzvos, the marriage canopy, and [the performance of] good deeds. And so may it be the will [of HASHEM]; and let us say, Amen.**

---

(1) *Proverbs* 23:25. (2) *Ezekiel* 16:6. (3) *Psalms* 105:8-10. (4) *Genesis* 21:4. (5) *Psalms* 118:1.

⑆ברכת המזון⑇

אֲבָרְכָה אֶת יהוה בְּכָל עֵת תָּמִיד תְּהִלָּתוֹ בְּפִי. סוֹף דָּבָר הַכֹּל נִשְׁמָע, אֶת
הָאֱלֹהִים יְרָא וְאֶת מִצְוֺתָיו שְׁמוֹר, כִּי זֶה כָּל הָאָדָם. תְּהִלַּת יהוה
יְדַבֶּר פִּי, וִיבָרֵךְ כָּל בָּשָׂר שֵׁם קָדְשׁוֹ לְעוֹלָם וָעֶד. וַאֲנַחְנוּ נְבָרֵךְ יָהּ, מֵעַתָּה וְעַד
עוֹלָם הַלְלוּיָהּ. וַיְדַבֵּר אֵלַי, זֶה הַשֻּׁלְחָן אֲשֶׁר לִפְנֵי יהוה.

Leader — הַב לָן וְנִבְרִיךְ לְמַלְכָּא עִלָּאָה קַדִּישָׁא.
Others — (בִּרְשׁוּת) שָׁמַיִם.
Leader — בִּרְשׁוּת מַלְכָּא עִלָּאָה קַדִּישָׁא

[on Shabbat — וּבִרְשׁוּת שַׁבַּת מַלְכְּתָא]
[on a Festival — וּבִרְשׁוּת יוֹמָא טָבָא אוּשְׁפִּיזָא קַדִּישָׁא]
[on Sukkot — וּבִרְשׁוּת שַׁבְעָה אוּשְׁפִּיזִין עִלָּאִין קַדִּישִׁין]

וּבִרְשׁוּת מוֹרַי וְרַבּוֹתַי וּבִרְשׁוּתְכֶם נְבָרֵךְ אֱלֹהֵינוּ שֶׁאָכַלְנוּ מִשֶּׁלּוֹ.
Others — בָּרוּךְ אֱלֹהֵינוּ שֶׁאָכַלְנוּ מִשֶּׁלּוֹ וּבְטוּבוֹ חָיִינוּ.
Leader — בָּרוּךְ אֱלֹהֵינוּ שֶׁאָכַלְנוּ מִשֶּׁלּוֹ וּבְטוּבוֹ חָיִינוּ.

בָּרוּךְ אַתָּה יהוה אֱלֹהֵינוּ מֶלֶךְ הָעוֹלָם, הָאֵל הַזָּן אוֹתָנוּ וְאֶת הָעוֹלָם כֻּלּוֹ
בְּטוּבוֹ בְּחֵן בְּחֶסֶד בְּרֶיוַח וּבְרַחֲמִים רַבִּים נֹתֵן לֶחֶם לְכָל בָּשָׂר, כִּי
לְעוֹלָם חַסְדּוֹ. וּבְטוּבוֹ הַגָּדוֹל תָּמִיד לֹא חָסַר לָנוּ וְאַל יֶחְסַר לָנוּ מָזוֹן תָּמִיד
לְעוֹלָם וָעֶד. כִּי הוּא אֵל זָן וּמְפַרְנֵס לַכֹּל וְשֻׁלְחָנוֹ עָרוּךְ לַכֹּל וְהִתְקִין מִחְיָה
וּמָזוֹן לְכָל בְּרִיּוֹתָיו אֲשֶׁר בָּרָא בְּרַחֲמָיו וּבְרוֹב חֲסָדָיו. כָּאָמוּר, פּוֹתֵחַ אֶת יָדֶךָ.
וּמַשְׂבִּיעַ לְכָל חַי רָצוֹן. בָּרוּךְ אַתָּה יהוה, הַזָּן אֶת הַכֹּל.

נוֹדֶה לְךָ יהוה אֱלֹהֵינוּ עַל שֶׁהִנְחַלְתָּ לַאֲבוֹתֵינוּ אֶרֶץ חֶמְדָּה טוֹבָה וּרְחָבָה
בְּרִית וְתוֹרָה חַיִּים וּמָזוֹן. עַל שֶׁהוֹצֵאתָנוּ מֵאֶרֶץ מִצְרַיִם, וּפְדִיתָנוּ
מִבֵּית עֲבָדִים, וְעַל בְּרִיתְךָ שֶׁחָתַמְתָּ בִּבְשָׂרֵנוּ, וְעַל תּוֹרָתְךָ שֶׁלִּמַּדְתָּנוּ, וְעַל
חֻקֵּי רְצוֹנָךְ שֶׁהוֹדַעְתָּנוּ. וְעַל חַיִּים וּמָזוֹן שֶׁאַתָּה זָן וּמְפַרְנֵס אוֹתָנוּ.

On Chanukah and Purim:

עַל הַנִּסִּים וְעַל הַפֻּרְקָן, וְעַל הַגְּבוּרוֹת, וְעַל הַתְּשׁוּעוֹת וְעַל הַנִּפְלָאוֹת וְעַל
הַנֶּחָמוֹת שֶׁעָשִׂיתָ לַאֲבוֹתֵינוּ בַּיָּמִים הָהֵם בַּזְּמַן הַזֶּה.

On Chanukah:

בִּימֵי מַתִּתְיָה בֶּן יוֹחָנָן כֹּהֵן גָּדוֹל חַשְׁמוֹנַאי וּבָנָיו כְּשֶׁעָמְדָה מַלְכוּת יָוָן
הָרְשָׁעָה עַל עַמְּךָ יִשְׂרָאֵל לְשַׁכְּחָם תּוֹרָתָךְ וּלְהַעֲבִירָם מֵחֻקֵּי
רְצוֹנָךְ. וְאַתָּה בְּרַחֲמֶיךָ הָרַבִּים עָמַדְתָּ לָהֶם בְּעֵת צָרָתָם, רַבְתָּ אֶת רִיבָם, דַּנְתָּ אֶת
דִּינָם, נָקַמְתָּ אֶת נִקְמָתָם; מָסַרְתָּ גִּבּוֹרִים בְּיַד חַלָּשִׁים, וְרַבִּים בְּיַד מְעַטִּים,
וּרְשָׁעִים בְּיַד צַדִּיקִים, וּטְמֵאִים בְּיַד טְהוֹרִים, וְזֵדִים בְּיַד עוֹסְקֵי תוֹרָתָךְ. לְךָ עָשִׂיתָ
שֵׁם גָּדוֹל וְקָדוֹשׁ בְּעוֹלָמָךְ. וּלְעַמְּךָ יִשְׂרָאֵל עָשִׂיתָ תְּשׁוּעָה גְדוֹלָה וּפוּרְקָן כְּהַיּוֹם
הַזֶּה. וְאַחַר כָּךְ בָּאוּ בָנֶיךָ לִדְבִיר בֵּיתֶךָ וּפִנּוּ אֶת הֵיכָלֶךָ. וְטִהֲרוּ אֶת מִקְדָּשֶׁךָ.
וְהִדְלִיקוּ נֵרוֹת בְּחַצְרוֹת קָדְשֶׁךָ. וְקָבְעוּ שְׁמוֹנַת יְמֵי חֲנֻכָּה אֵלּוּ בְּהַלֵּל וּבְהוֹדָאָה.
וְעָשִׂיתָ עִמָּהֶם נִסִּים וְנִפְלָאוֹת וְנוֹדֶה לְשִׁמְךָ הַגָּדוֹל סֶלָה.

אֲבָרְכָה *I shall bless HASHEM at all times, always shall His praise be in my mouth.*
The sum of the matter, when all has been considered: Fear God and keep His commandments, for that is man's whole duty. May my mouth declare the praise of HASHEM and may all flesh bless His Holy Name forever and ever. We will bless God from this time and forever, Halleluyah. And he spoke to me: 'This is the table before HASHEM.'

Leader—*Give us [the cup] that we may bless the supreme, holy King.*
Others—*(With the permission of) Heaven!*
Leader—*With permission of the supreme, holy King*

[on the Sabbath—*and with permission of the Sabbath queen*]
[on a Festival—*and with permission of the festival day, the holy guest*]
[on Succot—*and with permission of the seven supreme, holy guests*]
and with permission of my rabbis and teachers and with your permission let us bless [our God], of Whose we have eaten.

Others—*Blessed is [our God,] He of Whose we have eaten and through Whose goodness we live.*
Leader—*Blessed is [our God,] He of Whose we have eaten and through Whose goodness we live.*

בָּרוּךְ *Blessed are You, HASHEM, our God, King of the universe, the God Who nourishes us and the entire world, in His goodness — with grace, with kindness, with relief, and with abundant mercy He gives nourishment to all flesh, for His kindness is eternal. And through His great goodness, we have never lacked, and may we never lack, nourishment, constantly for all eternity. Because He is God Who nourishes and sustains all, and His table is prepared for all, and He readied subsistence and nourishment for all of His creatures that He has created with His mercy and His abundant kindness, as is said, 'You open Your hand and satisfy the desire of every living thing. Blessed are You, HASHEM, Who nourishes all.*

נוֹדֶה *We thank You, HASHEM, our God, because You have given to our forefathers as a heritage a desirable, good and spacious land; covenant and Torah, life and nourishment; because You removed us from the land of Egypt and You redeemed us from the house of bondage; for Your covenant which You sealed in our flesh; for Your Torah which You taught us and for the statutes of Your will which You made known to us; for life, grace, and lovingkindness which You granted us; and for life and nourishment with which You nourish and sustain us.*

On Chanukah and Purim:
עַל הַנִּסִּים *For the miracles, and for the salvation, and for the mighty deeds, and for the victories, and for the wonders and for the consolations which You performed for our forefathers in those days, at this time.*

On Chanukah:
בִּימֵי *In the days of Mattisyahu, the son of Yochanan, the High Priest, the Hasmonean, and his sons — when the wicked Greek kingdom rose up against Your people Israel to make them forget Your Torah and compel them to stray from the statutes of Your Will — You in Your great mercy stood up for them in the time of their distress. You took up their grievance, judged their claim, and avenged their wrong. You delivered the strong into the hands of the weak, the many into the hands of the few, the wicked into the hands of the righteous, the impure into the hands of the pure, and the wanton into the hands of the diligent students of Your Torah. For Yourself You made a great and holy Name in Your world, and for Your people Israel You worked a great victory and salvation as this very day. Thereafter, Your children came to the Holy of Holies of Your House, cleansed Your Temple, purified the site of Your Holiness and kindled lights in the Courtyards of Your Sanctuary; and they established these eight days of Chanukah with praise and thanksgiving. You did with them miracles and wonders, so let us give us give praiseful thanks to Your great Name. Selah!*

בִּימֵי מָרְדְּכַי וְאֶסְתֵּר, בְּשׁוּשַׁן הַבִּירָה כְּשֶׁעָמַד עֲלֵיהֶם הָמָן הָרָשָׁע, בִּקֵּשׁ לְהַשְׁמִיד לַהֲרֹג וּלְאַבֵּד אֶת כָּל הַיְּהוּדִים, מִנַּעַר וְעַד זָקֵן, טַף וְנָשִׁים, בְּיוֹם אֶחָד, בִּשְׁלוֹשָׁה עָשָׂר לְחֹדֶשׁ שְׁנֵים עָשָׂר, הוּא חֹדֶשׁ אֲדָר, וּשְׁלָלָם לָבוֹז. וְאַתָּה בְּרַחֲמֶיךָ הָרַבִּים הֵפַרְתָּ אֶת עֲצָתוֹ, וְקִלְקַלְתָּ אֶת מַחֲשַׁבְתּוֹ, וַהֲשֵׁבוֹתָ לּוֹ גְּמוּלוֹ בְּרֹאשׁוֹ, וְתָלוּ אוֹתוֹ וְאֶת בָּנָיו עַל הָעֵץ. וְעָשִׂיתָ עִמָּהֶם נֵס וָפֶלֶא וְנוֹדֶה לְשִׁמְךָ הַגָּדוֹל סֶלָה.

(וּ)**עַל הַכֹּל** יהוה אֱלֹהֵינוּ אֲנַחְנוּ מוֹדִים לָךְ וּמְבָרְכִים אֶת שְׁמָךְ כָּאָמוּר, וְאָכַלְתָּ וְשָׂבָעְתָּ וּבֵרַכְתָּ אֶת יהוה אֱלֹהֶיךָ, עַל הָאָרֶץ הַטֹּבָה אֲשֶׁר נָתַן לָךְ. בָּרוּךְ אַתָּה יהוה, עַל הָאָרֶץ וְעַל הַמָּזוֹן.

רַחֵם יהוה אֱלֹהֵינוּ עָלֵינוּ וְעַל יִשְׂרָאֵל עַמָּךְ, וְעַל יְרוּשָׁלַיִם עִירָךְ, וְעַל הַר צִיּוֹן מִשְׁכַּן כְּבוֹדָךְ, וְעַל הֵיכָלָךְ, וְעַל מְעוֹנָךְ, וְעַל דְּבִירָךְ, וְעַל הַבַּיִת הַגָּדוֹל וְהַקָּדוֹשׁ שֶׁנִּקְרָא שִׁמְךָ עָלָיו. אָבִינוּ רְעֵנוּ זוּנֵנוּ פַּרְנְסֵנוּ כַּלְכְּלֵנוּ, הַרְוִיחֵנוּ, הַרְוַח לָנוּ מְהֵרָה מִכָּל צָרוֹתֵינוּ. וְנָא אַל תַּצְרִיכֵנוּ יהוה אֱלֹהֵינוּ לִידֵי מַתְּנוֹת בָּשָׂר וָדָם, וְלֹא לִידֵי הַלְוָאָתָם, אֶלָּא לְיָדְךָ הַמְּלֵאָה וְהָרְחָבָה, הָעֲשִׁירָה וְהַפְּתוּחָה. יְהִי רָצוֹן שֶׁלֹּא נֵבוֹשׁ בָּעוֹלָם הַזֶּה, וְלֹא נִכָּלֵם לְעוֹלָם הַבָּא, וּמַלְכוּת בֵּית דָּוִד מְשִׁיחָךְ תַּחֲזִירֶנָּה לִמְקוֹמָהּ בִּמְהֵרָה בְיָמֵינוּ.

רְצֵה וְהַחֲלִיצֵנוּ יהוה אֱלֹהֵינוּ בְּמִצְוֹתֶיךָ, וּבְמִצְוַת יוֹם הַשְּׁבִיעִי הַשַּׁבָּת הַגָּדוֹל וְהַקָּדוֹשׁ הַזֶּה. כִּי יוֹם גָּדוֹל וְקָדוֹשׁ הוּא מִלְּפָנֶיךָ, נִשְׁבּוֹת בּוֹ, וְנָנוּחַ בּוֹ, וְנִתְעַנַּג בּוֹ, כְּמִצְוַת חֻקֵּי רְצוֹנָךְ. וְאַל תְּהִי צָרָה וְיָגוֹן בְּיוֹם מְנוּחָתֵנוּ. וְהַרְאֵנוּ בְּנֶחָמַת צִיּוֹן בִּמְהֵרָה בְיָמֵינוּ. כִּי אַתָּה הוּא בַּעַל הַנֶּחָמוֹת. וַהֲגַם שֶׁאָכַלְנוּ וְשָׁתִינוּ חָרְבַּן בֵּיתְךָ הַגָּדוֹל וְהַקָּדוֹשׁ לֹא שָׁכָחְנוּ. אַל תִּשְׁכָּחֵנוּ לָנֶצַח וְאַל תִּזְנָחֵנוּ לָעַד, כִּי אֵל מֶלֶךְ גָּדוֹל וְקָדוֹשׁ אָתָּה.

אֱלֹהֵינוּ וֵאלֹהֵי אֲבוֹתֵינוּ יַעֲלֶה וְיָבֹא וְיַגִּיעַ וְיֵרָאֶה וְיֵרָצֶה וְיִשָּׁמַע וְיִפָּקֵד וְיִזָּכֵר זִכְרוֹנֵנוּ וְזִכְרוֹן אֲבוֹתֵינוּ, זִכְרוֹן יְרוּשָׁלַיִם עִירָךְ, וְזִכְרוֹן מָשִׁיחַ בֶּן דָּוִד עַבְדָּךְ, וְזִכְרוֹן כָּל עַמְּךָ בֵּית יִשְׂרָאֵל, לְפָנֶיךָ לִפְלֵיטָה לְטוֹבָה, לְחֵן וּלְחֶסֶד וּלְרַחֲמִים, לְחַיִּים וּלְשָׁלוֹם, בְּיוֹם

On Rosh Chodesh— רֹאשׁ חֹדֶשׁ הַזֶּה,

On Rosh Hashanah— הַזִּכָּרוֹן הַזֶּה בְּיוֹם טוֹב מִקְרָא קֹדֶשׁ הַזֶּה,

On Succot— חַג הַסֻּכּוֹת הַזֶּה בְּיוֹם (טוֹב) מִקְרָא קֹדֶשׁ הַזֶּה,

On Shemini Atzeret— שְׁמִינִי חַג עֲצֶרֶת הַזֶּה בְּיוֹם טוֹב מִקְרָא קֹדֶשׁ הַזֶּה,

On Pesach— חַג הַמַּצּוֹת הַזֶּה בְּיוֹם (טוֹב) מִקְרָא קֹדֶשׁ הַזֶּה,

On Shavuot— חַג הַשָּׁבוּעוֹת הַזֶּה בְּיוֹם טוֹב מִקְרָא קֹדֶשׁ הַזֶּה,

לְרַחֵם בּוֹ עָלֵינוּ וּלְהוֹשִׁיעֵנוּ. זָכְרֵנוּ יהוה אֱלֹהֵינוּ בּוֹ לְטוֹבָה, וּפָקְדֵנוּ בוֹ לִבְרָכָה, וְהוֹשִׁיעֵנוּ בוֹ לְחַיִּים טוֹבִים. בִּדְבַר יְשׁוּעָה וְרַחֲמִים, חוּס וְחָנֵּנוּ וַחֲמוֹל וְרַחֵם עָלֵינוּ, וְהוֹשִׁיעֵנוּ כִּי אֵלֶיךָ עֵינֵינוּ, כִּי אֵל מֶלֶךְ חַנּוּן וְרַחוּם אָתָּה.

בִּימֵי *In the days of Mordechai and Esther, in Shushan, the capital, when Haman, the wicked, rose up against them and sought to destroy, to slay, and to exterminate all the Jews, young and old, infants and women, on the same day, on the thirteenth of the twelfth month which is the month of Adar, and to plunder their possessions. But You, in Your abundant mercy, nullified his counsel and frustrated his intention and caused his design to return upon his own head and they hanged him and his sons on the gallows. You did wih them a miracle and a wonder, so let us give praiseful thanks to Your great Name. Selah!*

(וְ)עַל הַכֹּל *For everything, HASHEM, our God, we thank You and bless Your Name, as it is written: 'And you shall eat and you shall be satisfied and you shall bless [at this point, the leader should fill his cup] HASHEM, your God, for the good land which He gave you.' Blessed are You, HASHEM, for the land and for the nourishment.*

רַחֵם *Have mercy HASHEM, our God, on us and on Israel Your people; on Jerusalem, Your city, on Mount Zion, the resting place of Your Glory; on Your Temple, on Your Habitation, on Your Holy of Holies, on the monarchy of the House of David, Your anointed; and on the great and holy House upon which Your Name is called. Our Father — tend us, nourish us, sustain us, support us, relieve us; grant us relief speedily from all our troubles. Please, make us not needful — HASHEM, our God — of the gifts of human hands nor of their loans, but only of Your Hand that is full and expansive, that is rich and open. May it be Your will that we not feel inner shame in This World nor be humiliated in the World to Come, and may You return the kingship of the House of David, Your anointed, to its place, speedily in our days.*

On Sabbath:

רְצֵה *May it please You, HASHEM, our God — give us rest through Your commandments, and through the commandment of the seventh day, this great and holy Sabbath. May we rest on it, be content on it, and delight in it according to the commandment of Your will's decrees. Let there be no distress or grief on the day of our contentment. Show us the consolation of Zion, speedily in our days, for You are the Master of consolations. Although we have eaten and drunk, we have not forgotten the destruction of Your great and holy Temple. Do no forget us eternally and do not forsake us forever, for You are God, the great and holy King.*

On Rosh Chodesh and Festivals:

אֱלֹהֵינוּ *Our God and God of our forefathers, may there rise, come, reach, be noted, be favored, be heard, be considered, and be remembered — our remembrance, the remembrance of our forefathers, the remembrance of Jerusalem, Your city; the remembrance of Messiah, son of David, Your servant; the remembrance of Your entire people, the Family of Israel — before You for deliverance, for goodness, for grace, for kindness, and for compassion, for life, and for peace, on this day of*

On Rosh Chodesh— *Rosh Chodesh,*
On Rosh Hashanah— *Remembrance, this holiday, this holy convocation,*
On Succot— *the Succot Festival, this (holy)day, this holy convocation,*
On Shemini Atzeret— *the Shemini Atzeret Festival, this holiday, this holy convocation,*
On Pesach— *the Festival of Matzos, this (holi)day, this holy convocation,*
On Shavuot— *the Shavuot Festival, this holiday, this holy convocation,*

to have mercy upon us on it and to save us. Remember us on it, HASHEM, our God, for goodness; consider us on it for blessing; and help us on it for goodly life in the matter of salvation and compassion. Take pity, be gracious, spare, be compassionate with us and help us, for our eyes are turned to You, because You are God, the gracious, and compassionate King.

וְתִבְנֶה יְרוּשָׁלַיִם עִירְךָ בִּמְהֵרָה בְיָמֵינוּ. בָּרוּךְ אַתָּה יהוה, בּוֹנֵה יְרוּשָׁלָיִם.
(אָמֵן.)

בָּרוּךְ אַתָּה יהוה אֱלֹהֵינוּ מֶלֶךְ הָעוֹלָם, הָאֵל אָבִינוּ מַלְכֵּנוּ אַדִּירֵנוּ בּוֹרְאֵנוּ,
גּוֹאֲלֵנוּ, קְדוֹשֵׁנוּ, קְדוֹשׁ יַעֲקֹב, רוֹעֵנוּ רוֹעֵה יִשְׂרָאֵל, הַמֶּלֶךְ הַטּוֹב
וְהַמֵּטִיב לַכֹּל, שֶׁבְּכָל יוֹם וָיוֹם הוּא הֵטִיב לָנוּ, הוּא מֵטִיב לָנוּ, הוּא יֵיטִיב לָנוּ,
הוּא גְמָלָנוּ, הוּא גוֹמְלֵנוּ, הוּא יִגְמְלֵנוּ לָעַד, חֵן וָחֶסֶד וְרַחֲמִים וְרֵיחַ וְהַצָּלָה
וְכָל טוֹב.

הָרַחֲמָן הוּא יִשְׁתַּבַּח עַל כִּסֵּא כְבוֹדוֹ. הָרַחֲמָן הוּא יִשְׁתַּבַּח בַּשָּׁמַיִם
וּבָאָרֶץ. הָרַחֲמָן הוּא יִשְׁתַּבַּח בָּנוּ לְדוֹר דּוֹרִים. הָרַחֲמָן הוּא
קֶרֶן לְעַמּוֹ יָרִים. הָרַחֲמָן הוּא יִתְפָּאַר בָּנוּ לָנֶצַח נְצָחִים. הָרַחֲמָן הוּא
יְפַרְנְסֵנוּ בְּכָבוֹד וְלֹא בְבִזּוּי, בְּהֶתֵּר וְלֹא בְאִסּוּר, בְּנַחַת וְלֹא בְצַעַר. הָרַחֲמָן
הוּא יִתֵּן שָׁלוֹם בֵּינֵינוּ. הָרַחֲמָן הוּא יִשְׁלַח בְּרָכָה רְוָחָה וְהַצְלָחָה בְּכָל מַעֲשֵׂה
יָדֵינוּ. הָרַחֲמָן הוּא יַצְלִיחַ אֶת דְּרָכֵינוּ. הָרַחֲמָן הוּא יִשְׁבּוֹר עוֹל גָּלוּת מְהֵרָה
מֵעַל צַוָּארֵנוּ. הָרַחֲמָן הוּא יוֹלִיכֵנוּ קוֹמְמִיּוּת לְאַרְצֵנוּ. הָרַחֲמָן הוּא יִרְפָּאֵנוּ
רְפוּאָה שְׁלֵמָה רְפוּאַת הַנֶּפֶשׁ וּרְפוּאַת הַגּוּף. הָרַחֲמָן הוּא יִפְתַּח לָנוּ אֶת יָדוֹ
הָרְחָבָה. הָרַחֲמָן הוּא יְבָרֵךְ כָּל אֶחָד וְאֶחָד מִמֶּנּוּ בִּשְׁמוֹ הַגָּדוֹל, כְּמוֹ
שֶׁנִּתְבָּרְכוּ אֲבוֹתֵינוּ אַבְרָהָם יִצְחָק וְיַעֲקֹב, בַּכֹּל מִכֹּל כֹּל, כֵּן יְבָרֵךְ אוֹתָנוּ יַחַד
בְּרָכָה שְׁלֵמָה. וְכֵן יְהִי רָצוֹן וְנֹאמַר אָמֵן. הָרַחֲמָן הוּא יִפְרוֹשׂ עָלֵינוּ סֻכַּת
שְׁלוֹמוֹ.

On Shabbat:
הָרַחֲמָן הוּא יַנְחִילֵנוּ עוֹלָם שֶׁכֻּלּוֹ שַׁבָּת וּמְנוּחָה לְחַיֵּי הָעוֹלָמִים.

On Rosh Chodesh:
הָרַחֲמָן הוּא יְחַדֵּשׁ עָלֵינוּ הַחֹדֶשׁ הַזֶּה לְטוֹבָה וְלִבְרָכָה.

on Rosh Hashanah
הָרַחֲמָן הוּא יְחַדֵּשׁ עָלֵינוּ אֶת הַשָּׁנָה הַזֹּאת לְטוֹבָה וְלִבְרָכָה.

On Festivals:
הָרַחֲמָן הוּא יַנְחִילֵנוּ יוֹם שֶׁכֻּלּוֹ טוֹב.
הָרַחֲמָן הוּא יַגִּיעֵנוּ לְמוֹעֲדִים אֲחֵרִים הַבָּאִים לִקְרָאתֵנוּ לְשָׁלוֹם.

On Succot:
הָרַחֲמָן הוּא יְזַכֵּנוּ לֵישֵׁב בְּסֻכַּת עוֹרוֹ שֶׁל לִוְיָתָן. הָרַחֲמָן הוּא יַשְׁפִּיעַ עָלֵינוּ שֶׁפַע
קְדֻשָּׁה וְטָהֳרָה מִשִּׁבְעָה אֻשְׁפִּיזִין עִלָּאִין קַדִּישִׁין, זְכוּתָם תְּהֵא מָגֵן וְצִנָּה עָלֵינוּ.
הָרַחֲמָן הוּא יָקִים לָנוּ אֶת סֻכַּת דָּוִד הַנּוֹפָלֶת.

הָרַחֲמָן הוּא יִטַּע תּוֹרָתוֹ וְאַהֲבָתוֹ בְּלִבֵּנוּ, וְתִהְיֶה יִרְאָתוֹ עַל פָּנֵינוּ לְבִלְתִּי
נֶחֱטָא. וְיִהְיוּ כָל מַעֲשֵׂינוּ לְשֵׁם שָׁמַיִם.

וְתִבְנֵה *Rebuild Jerusalem, Your city, soon in our days. Blessed are You, HASHEM, Who rebuilds Jerusalem. [Amen.]*

בָּרוּךְ *Blessed are You, HASHEM, our God, King of the universe, the Almighty, our Father, our King, our Sovereign, our Redeemer, our Maker, our Holy One, Holy One of Jacob, our Shepherd, the Shepherd of Israel, the King Who is good and Who does good for all. For every single day He did good to us, He does good to us, and He will do good to us. He was bountiful with us, He is bountiful with us, and He will forever be bountiful with us — with grace and with kindness and with mercy, with relief and rescue, and all good.*

הָרַחֲמָן *The compassionate One! May He be praised upon the throne of His glory. The compassionate One! May He be praised in heaven and on earth. The compassionate One! May He be praised through us throughout all generations. The compassionate One! May He raise up the pride of His people. The compassionate One! May He be glorified through us to the ultimate ends. The compassionate One! May He sustain us with dignity and not in disgrace; through   permissible and not through forbidden means; in tranquility and not in pain. The compassionate One! May He grant peace among us. The compassionate One! May He send us blessing, relief, and success in all our handiwork. The compassionate One! May He grant success in all our ways. The compassionate One! May He quickly break the yoke of exile from upon our neck. The compassionate One! May He lead us with upright pride to our Land. The compassionate One! May He heal us with a complete recovery, a recovery of the soul and a recovery of the body. The compassionate One! May He open for us His expansive hand. The compassionate One! May He bless every single one of us with His great Name, just as our forefathers Abraham, Isaac, and Jacob were blessed, in everything, from everything, with everything. So may He bless us all together with a perfect blessing. May such be His will, and let us say Amen. The compassionate One! May He spread over us His shelter of His peace.*

On Shabbat:
The compassionate One! May He cause us to inherit the day which will be completely a Sabbath and rest day for eternal life.

On Rosh Chodesh:
The compassionate One! May he inaugurate this month upon us for goodness and for blessing.

On Rosh Hashanah:
The compassionate One! May He inaugurate this year upon us for goodness and for blessing.

On Succot:
The compassionate One! May He privilege us to dwell in the succah of the skin of the Leviathan. The compassionate One! May He cause to flow upon us a flow of holiness and purity from the seven exalted, holy guests. May their merit be a shield and shelter over us.

On Festivals:
The compassionate One! May He bring us to other festivals that come toward us, to peace. The compassionate One! May He cause us to inherit the day which is completely good.

הָרַחֲמָן *The compassionate One! May He implant His Torah and His love in our heart, and may His reverence be upon our face that we not sin; and may all our deeds be for the sake of heaven.*

הָרַחֲמָן הוּא יְבָרֵךְ אֶת הַשֻּׁלְחָן הַזֶּה שֶׁאָכַלְנוּ עָלָיו, וִיסַדֵּר בּוֹ כָּל מַעֲדַנֵּי עוֹלָם, וְיִהְיֶה כְּשֻׁלְחָנוֹ שֶׁל אַבְרָהָם אָבִינוּ, כָּל רָעֵב מִמֶּנּוּ יֹאכַל, וְכָל צָמֵא מִמֶּנּוּ יִשְׁתֶּה. וְאַל יֶחְסַר מִמֶּנּוּ כָּל טוֹב, לָעַד וּלְעוֹלְמֵי עוֹלָמִים, אָמֵן. הָרַחֲמָן הוּא יְבָרֵךְ בַּעַל הַבַּיִת הַזֶּה, וּבַעַל הַסְּעוּדָה הַזֹּאת, הוּא וּבָנָיו וְאִשְׁתּוֹ וְכָל אֲשֶׁר לוֹ, בְּבָנִים שֶׁיִּחְיוּ וּבִנְכָסִים, שֶׁיִּרְבּוּ. בָּרֵךְ יהוה חֵילוֹ וּפֹעַל יָדָיו תִּרְצֶה, וְיִהְיוּ נְכָסָיו וּנְכָסֵינוּ מוּצְלָחִים וּקְרוֹבִים לָעִיר. וְאַל יִזְדַּקֵּק לְפָנָיו וְלֹא לְפָנֵינוּ שׁוּם דְּבַר חֵטְא וְהִרְהוּר עָוֹן. שָׂשׂ וְשָׂמֵחַ כָּל הַיָּמִים בְּעֹשֶׁר וְכָבוֹד, מֵעַתָּה וְעַד עוֹלָם. לֹא יֵבוֹשׁ בָּעוֹלָם הַזֶּה, וְלֹא יִכָּלֵם לָעוֹלָם הַבָּא. אָמֵן, כֵּן יְהִי רָצוֹן.

הָרַחֲמָן הוּא יְבָרֵךְ אֶת בַּעַל הַבַּיִת הַזֶּה, אֲבִי הַבֵּן, הוּא וְאִשְׁתּוֹ הַיּוֹלֶדֶת מֵעַתָּה וְעַד עוֹלָם.

הָרַחֲמָן הוּא יְבָרֵךְ אֶת הַיֶּלֶד הַנּוֹלָד, וּכְשֵׁם שֶׁזִּכָּהוּ הַקָּדוֹשׁ בָּרוּךְ הוּא לַמִּילָה, כָּךְ יְזַכֵּהוּ לְכָנֵס לַתּוֹרָה וְלַחֻפָּה וְלַמִּצְוֹת וּלְמַעֲשִׂים טוֹבִים. וְכֵן יְהִי רָצוֹן, וְנֹאמַר אָמֵן.

הָרַחֲמָן הוּא יְבָרֵךְ אֶת מַעֲלַת הַסַּנְדָּק וְהַמּוֹהֵל, וּשְׁאָר הַמִּשְׁתַּדְּלִים בַּמִּצְוָה, הֵם וְכָל אֲשֶׁר לָהֶם.

הָרַחֲמָן הוּא יְחַיֵּינוּ וִיזַכֵּנוּ וִיקָרְבֵנוּ לִימוֹת הַמָּשִׁיחַ, וּלְבִנְיַן בֵּית הַמִּקְדָּשׁ, וּלְחַיֵּי הָעוֹלָם הַבָּא.

מַגְדִּיל—on weekdays   מִגְדּוֹל—on days when *Mussaf* is said and *Motza'ei Shabbat*

יְשׁוּעוֹת מַלְכּוֹ, וְעֹשֶׂה חֶסֶד לִמְשִׁיחוֹ, לְדָוִד וּלְזַרְעוֹ עַד עוֹלָם. כְּפִירִים רָשׁוּ וְרָעֵבוּ, וְדֹרְשֵׁי יהוה לֹא יַחְסְרוּ כָל טוֹב. נַעַר הָיִיתִי גַּם זָקַנְתִּי, וְלֹא רָאִיתִי צַדִּיק נֶעֱזָב, וְזַרְעוֹ מְבַקֶּשׁ לָחֶם. כָּל הַיּוֹם חוֹנֵן וּמַלְוֶה, וְזַרְעוֹ לִבְרָכָה. מַה שֶּׁאָכַלְנוּ יִהְיֶה לְשָׂבְעָה, וּמַה שֶּׁשָּׁתִינוּ יִהְיֶה לִרְפוּאָה, וּמַה שֶׁהוֹתַרְנוּ יִהְיֶה לִבְרָכָה, כְּדִכְתִיב, וַיִּתֵּן לִפְנֵיהֶם וַיֹּאכְלוּ וַיּוֹתִרוּ כִּדְבַר יהוה. בְּרוּכִים אַתֶּם לַיהוה, עֹשֵׂה שָׁמַיִם וָאָרֶץ. בָּרוּךְ הַגֶּבֶר אֲשֶׁר יִבְטַח בַּיהוה, וְהָיָה יהוה מִבְטַחוֹ. יהוה עֹז לְעַמּוֹ יִתֵּן, יהוה יְבָרֵךְ אֶת עַמּוֹ בַשָּׁלוֹם. עֹשֶׂה שָׁלוֹם בִּמְרוֹמָיו, הוּא בְרַחֲמָיו יַעֲשֶׂה שָׁלוֹם עָלֵינוּ, וְעַל כָּל עַמּוֹ יִשְׂרָאֵל, וְאִמְרוּ אָמֵן.

הָרַחֲמָן *The compassionate One! May He bless this table upon which we have eaten and set out on it all the world's delicacies, and may it be like the table of Abraham, our father, at which all the hungry will eat and all the thirsty will drink. May he lack no good, forever and to all eternity, Amen. The compassionate One! May He bless the master of this house and the master of this meal, him, his children, his wife, and all that is his, with children who will live and possessions that will increase. Bless, O HASHEM, his wealth and find favor in his handiwork. May his possessions and our possessions be successful and convenient to the city. May neither he nor we be forced to contend with any sinful matter or thought of sin, joyful and glad all the days, with wealth and honor, from now to eternity. May he not feel inner shame in This World or humiliation in the World to Come. Amen, may such be Your will.*

הָרַחֲמָן *The compassionate One! May He bless the master of this house, the father of the child, him and his wife who has given birth, from now to eternity.*

הָרַחֲמָן *The compassionate One! May He bless the newborn child. Just as the Holy One, Blessed is He, has privileged him to be circumcised, so may He privilege him to enter into Torah, to the wedding canopy, to commandments, and good deeds. May such be His will and let us say Amen.*

הָרַחֲמָן *The compassionate One! May He bless the eminent sandak, the mohel and the others who participate in the commandment, them and all this is theirs.*

הָרַחֲמָן *The compassionate One! May He give us life, privilege us, and draw us near to the days of the Messiah, the construction of the Holy Temple, and the life of the World to Come.*

On weekdays:	On days when *Mussaf* is recited and *Motza'ei Shabbat*:
He Who makes great	*He Who is a tower*
the salvations of His king	*of salvations to His king*

and does kindness for His anointed, to David and to his descendants forever. Young lions may want and hunger, but those who seek HASHEM will not lack any good. I was a youth and also have aged, and I have not seen a righteous man forsaken, with his children begging for bread. All day he graciously lends, and his children are a blessing. May what we have eaten satiate, what we have drunk bring good health, and what we have left over be a sign of blessing, as it is written: He served them and they ate, and even left over, like the word of HASHEM. You are blessed of HASHEM, Maker of heaven and earth. Blessed is the man who trusts in HASHEM, then HASHEM will be His security. HASHEM will give might to His people; HASHEM will bless His people with peace. He Who makes peace in His heights, May He make peace upon us and upon all Israel. Now respond: Amen!

Additi   MW00761768

Aside from the traditional biblical, talmudic and halachic commentaries and responsa that discuss *bris milah,* the following works contain a wealth of information about this *mitzvah.*

Bris Avos, (also known as *Sharvit HaZahav).* R' Shabsi Lipschitz, 1845-1929.
Bris Avrohom. R' Tzvi Binyamin Auerbach, Frankfurt, published 1880.
Derech Pikudecha. R' Elimelech Shapira, 1785-1841.
Edus L'Yisrael. R' Yaakov Werdiger, published 1964.
Koreis HaBris. Elya Poisek, 1859-1932.
Migdal Oz. R' Yaakov Emden, 1697-1776.
Os Bris. R' Shimon Sidon, 1815-1891
Otzer HaBris. R' Yosef Dovid Weisberg, Jerusalem, 1986.
Os (Chaim Ve) Sholom. R' Chaim Elazar Shapiro of Munkacs, 1872-1937.
S'dei Chemed. R' Chaim Chizkiyahu Medini, 1832-1904.
Sefer HaBris. R' Moshe Bunim Pirutinsky, published 1972.
Zichron Bris LaRishonim. R' Yaakov HaGozer and son R' Gershom HaGozer. 12th century.
Zecher David. R' David Zacuto Modena, printed Leghorn, Italy 1837.
Zocher HaBris. R' Asher Anshil Grunwald, printed 1931.